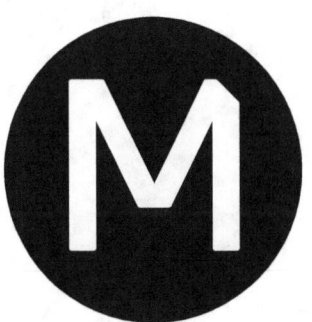

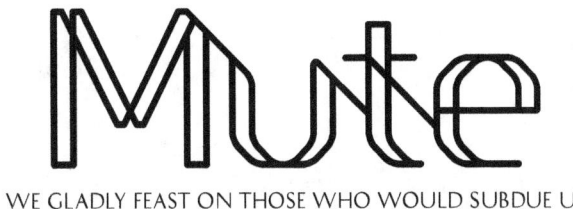

WE GLADLY FEAST ON THOSE WHO WOULD SUBDUE US

VOLUME 3 #4
SLAVE TO THE ALGORITHM
SPRING 2013

Published by Mute Publishing
Print ISBN 978-1-906496-04-3
ISSN 1356-7748-304

Also available as eBook ISBN 978-1-906496-91-3

In collaboration with Post-Media Lab,
Leuphana University

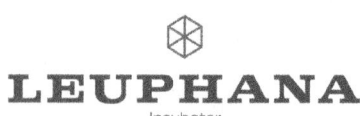

LEUPHANA
Incubator

MUTE VOL 3 #4
SPRING 2013

EDITOR
Josephine Berry Slater
<josie@metamute.org>

ASSISTANT EDITOR
Anthony Iles
<anthony@metamute.org>

EDITORIAL ASSISTANT
Mira Mattar
<miramattar@googlemail.com>

EDITORIAL BOARD
Josephine Berry Slater
Omar El-Khairy
<omarelkhairy@gmail.com>
Matthew Hyland
Anthony Iles
Demetra Kotouza
<demetra@inventati.org>
Hari Kunzru
<hari@metamute.org>
Mira Mattar
Pauline van Mourik Broekman
Benedict Seymour
<ben@metamute.org>
Stefan Szczelkun
<stefan@szczels.plus.com>
Simon Worthington

MUTE PUBLISHING ADVISORY BOARD
Sally Jane Norman
Sukhdev Sandhu
Andrew Seto
Andrew Wilson

PUBLISHERS
Pauline van Mourik Broekman
 <pauline@metamute.org>
Simon Worthington
<simon@metamute.org>

WEBSITE
Metamute.org is run on Drupal FLOSS Software, with additional software services by our very own OpenMute http://metamute.org/services. Graphic design by Atwork, CSS by Roglok <roglok@hyperground.de>, template coding by Effusion http://effusion.co.uk

CHIEF ENGINEER
Darron Broad <darron@kewl.org>

LAYOUT DESIGN
Raquel Perez de Eulate <raquelwebs@googlemail.com>

DESIGN TEMPLATE
Atwork http://www.atworkportfolio.co.uk

OFFICE
Mute, 46 Lexington Street, London, W1F OLP
E: <mute@metamute.org>

GENERAL MANAGER
Caroline Heron <caroline@metamute.org>

ADVERTISING & MARKETING
E: <caroline@metamute.org>

SUBSCRIPTIONS AND DISTRIBUTION
Howard Slater
E: <howard@metamute.org>
W: http://www.metamute.org/subs

CONTRIBUTING
Mute welcomes contributions of all kinds. Email <mute@metamute.org> with your ideas. You can also publish on Mute's website [metamute.org]. Post news, text, events and comments, or upload media. The views expressed in Mute and Metamute are not necessarily those of the publishers or service providers. Mute is published in the UK by Mute Publishing Ltd. and printed by OpenMute [http://metamute.org/services] print on demand [POD] book services.

COVER
John Houck <dashouck@gmail.com>, *Untitled #m007*, 38,415 combinations of a 2×2 grid, 14 colours, 2013, Creased archival pigment print (unique).

SPECIAL THANKS
Peter Cornwell, Sam at Radiance Audio and the Boxing Club, Limehouse Town Hall, Chris Ifold and Hannah Clayden.

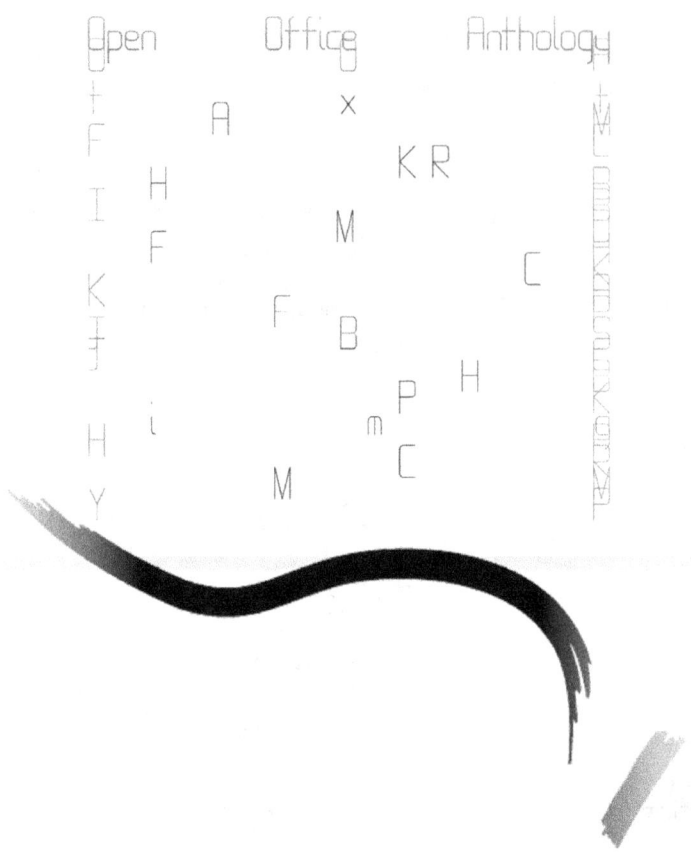

Out Now - **Open Office Anthology**

Arcadia Missa Publications

Digital and Print: **How to Sleep Faster**
journal, and **HTSF E** ejournal.

arcadiamissa.com/index.php/printspublications/

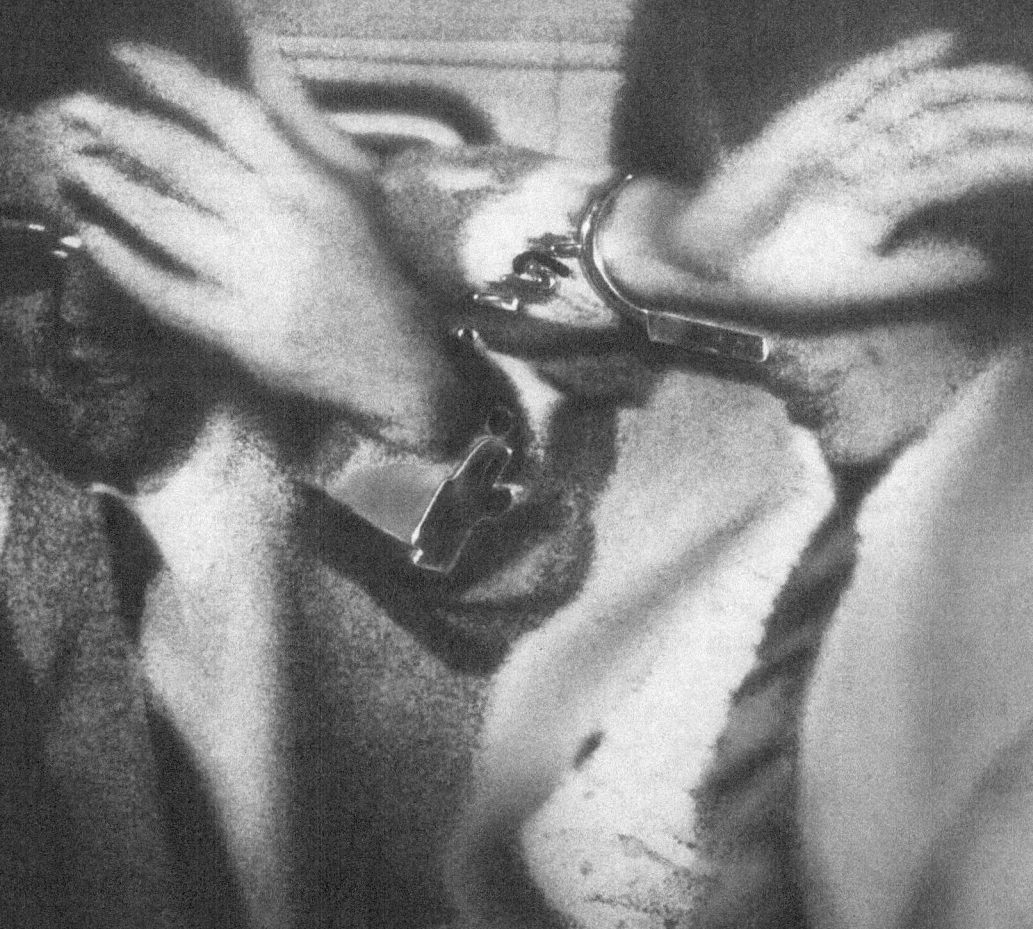

Afterall

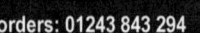
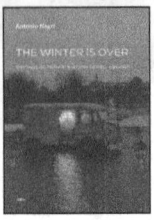
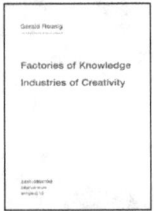
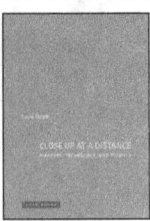
PML BOOKS SERIES

The PML Book series is a collaboration between *Mute* magazine and Post-Media Lab.

During the course of the Lab's activity we will be publishing two large anthologies, the first comprising a reader on the concept of 'post-media', and the second summarising and documenting the activity of the Lab.

The *Post-Media Anthology* collects writings by Adilkno, Clemens Apprich, Felipe Fonseca, Gary Genosko, Michael Goddard, Félix Guattari, Brian Holmes, Cadence Kinsey, Howard Slater, Rasa Smite and Raitis Smits. (Forthcoming, Summer, 2013. ISBN 978-1-906496-94-4)

Alongside these larger publications we will be publishing a series of four short titles by single authors addressing specific themes:

- Digital Networks: Connecting People Apart
- The Subsumption of Sociality
- The Question of Organisation After Networks
- Life vs. Object: Comrade Things and Alien Life

The first books in this short series are:

Felix Stalder, *Digital Solidarity*, (Forthcoming Spring, 2013. ISBN 978-1-906496-92-0)

Claire Fontaine, *Human Strike Has Already Begun & Other Writings*, (Spring, 2013. ISBN 978-1-906496-88-3)

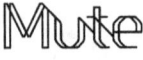 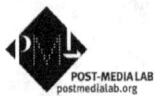 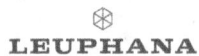 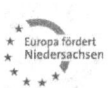

postmedialab.org/publications

MUTE CROWDFUNDING
THANK YOU!

metamute.org/crowdfunding-2012

A very big thank you to everyone who donated to Mute's crowdfunding campaign for its editorial budget. The success of our campaign means that Mute will be able to continue to pay its contributors up until September 2013. We were amazed by how many of you so generously contributed, either through donating artworks, pledging money or circulating information about the campaign. Not only did we hit our target, but we made 10 percent over it. This and the enthusiastic support we received gave us a huge boost and a sense how important it is for us to continue our publishing work for our wide community of readers. A special thank you is extended to all those who helped put the benefit party together, donating their time and skills to helping make it the memorable night that it was. **A huge thank you to the following donors:**

Fanny Aboulker; Absolute Catastrophe; Alcohol Label; All Knees N' Elbows; Jose Alvarado; Brian Ashton; Christopher Bahn; Salem Bajnaid; Rachel Baker; John Barker; Nicholas Beuret; Bryony Beynon; Steffen Boehm; Shumi Bose; Eleanor Vonne Brown; Emile Buges; Jane Burke; Danny Butt; Ted Byfield; Peter Carty; Johnny Coley; Christopher Collier; Peter Conlin; Martin Conrads; Maeve Convery; Sarah Cook; Heather Corcoran; Geoff Cox; Neil Cummings; Deborah H Curtis; Maria Dada; Dérive Sounds; J.K. Dixon; Sean Dockray; Keith Dodds; Felix Dragan; Lettice Drake; John Eden; Benjamin Fallon; Ben Fino-Radin; Fiona Flynn; Jennifer Gabrys; Simon Garnett; Quim Gil; Harry Giles; Marcus Giles; Nicholas Gledhill; Sohrab Golsorkhi; Beth Granter; Greenman; Gary Hall; Sidsel Meineche Hansen; Nick Harlow; A J Harris; Louis Hartnoll; Matt Harwood; Carl Henrik Fredriksson; Yaiza María Hernández Velázquez; Charlie Heron; Jaqueline Hess; Diarmuid Hester; Shaun Hides; Dougald Hine; Julia Hodgson; Phillip Homburg; Martin Howse; Gabriel Humberstone; R.A. Iles; Alan Ingram; David Jacques; Jakob Jakobsen; Damian Jaques; Daniel Jones; Michelle Kasprzak; Jonathan Kemp; Rob Kenn; Robert Kiely; Nicholas Knouf; Hari Kunzru; Kwong Lee (Castlefield Gallery); LimaZulu; Jo Littler; Elyssa Livergant; Shona MacNaughton; Zoe Marden; Ella Margolies; Mira Mattar; Nick Maturo; Melissa McCann; Neil McGuire; Donnchadh McNicholl; Gary McQuiggin; Guy Mercier; Meter Room; John Douglas Millar & Audrey Uhlmann; Tom Moore; Rob Myers; Jacopo Natoli; Hayley Newman; Nico Jabin; Obinna Nwosu; Rachel O'Dwyer; Lois Olmstead; David Panos; Irini Mirena Papadimitriou; Andrea Phillips; Jen Porter; Toni Prug; Josephine Pryde; Paul Purgas; Irene Revell; Kiely Robert; John Roberts; Nuno Rodrigues & Nayia Yiakoumaki; Jane Rolo (Bookworks); John Russell; David Schwertgen; Shawn Selway; Andrew Seto; Jessica Sligter; Helen Sloan; Finn Smith; Cornelia Sollfrank; David Spraggs; Felix Stalder; Bob Stein; Paul Stepan; Dan Stowell; Mike Stubbs; Arthur Swindells; The Centre of Attention; Nick Thoburn; Carolyn Thomas; Maija Timonen; Cara Tolmie; Vamory Traore; Georgina Turner; Magda Tyżlik-Carver; George Vasey; Caleb Waldorf; Neal White; Peter Willis; Camilla Wills; René Wolf; Peter Woodbridge; Richard Wright.

VOLUME 3 #4
SLAVE TO THE ALGORITHM
SPRING 2013

12
EDITORIAL
By JOSEPHINE BERRY SLATER

16
MANIFESTO FOR A THEORY OF THE 'NEW AESTHETIC'
An irreverent guided tour of the 'New Aesthetic' by CURT CLONINGER

28
THE MISSING FACTORY
JOHN ROBERTS considers why work remains absent from film and culture more generally

36
BARBARA SAYS – INDUSTRY DOES IT FASTER
ROMAN VASSEUR reviews the Artist Placement Group's historic brokerage of bureaucracy and art

42
THE GHOSTS OF PARTICIPATION PAST
JOSEPHINE BERRY SLATER reviews Claire Bishop's recent book, *Artificial Hells*

54
LISTENER AS OPERATOR 3
HOWARD SLATER finds in jazz a response to the experience of slavery which preserves and propels a collective being

66
UNTITLED #M001-#M011,
2,325,600 combinations of 16 grays, an artist's project by JOHN HOUCK

74
GAMING THE PLUMBING

ALBERTO TOSCANO inspects the gap between financial fantasies and the
muddy realities of the 'robot phase transition'

86
DESTRUCTIVE DESTRUCTION?

How is high frequency trading's drive to efficiency affecting market
dynamics as a whole? Ask *INIGO WILKINS* and *BOGDAN DRAGOS*

100
FELLOWSHIP OF THE WRONG

A code-splitting tale of lightspeed trading run by *BENEDICT SEYMOUR*,
with illustrations by *RONA TUNNADINE*

114
THE GUEST

A short story by *MIRA MATTAR* exploring the annihilating power
of luxury

118
THE GARDEN OF EARTHLY DELIGHTS

MATTHEW FULLER wades through the Olympic muck to visit
The Crystal World

124
AT THE LIMIT: SELF-ORGANISATION IN GREECE

ANNA O'LORY of Blaumachen identifies some limits to current struggles
in Greece

132
WHOSE REBEL CITY?

NEIL GRAY discusses David Harvey's *Rebel Cities* from the perspective of
the autonomous urban struggles of '70s Italy

EDITORIAL

As the financial crisis fastens its grip ever tighter around the means of human and natural survival, the age of the algorithm has hit full stride. This phase-shift has been a long time coming, of course, and was undoubtedly as much a cause of the crisis as its effect, with self-propelling algorithmic power replacing human labour and judgement and creating event fields far below the threshold of human perception and responsiveness. But as the articles in this issue by Alberto Toscano, Bogdan Dragos & Inigo Wilkins, and Benedict Seymour relate, the adoption of algorithmic tools begun by financial traders in the 1990s has expanded exponentially since 2008 in response to the intensified profits crisis as much as the maturation of tools. Toscano [p. 68] soberingly illustrates the effects of this shift: 'In 1945, US stock was held on average for four years; this dropped to eight months in 2000, two months in 2008, and 22 seconds in 2011.' So algorithms are widely experienced as the replicant horsemen of the apocalypse, swarming through and clogging up markets in their pursuit of tradeable differentials, creating an endless churn of shares which foreclose longer term investment strategies, dangerously automating the assessment of risk and precipitating 'flash crashes', hitting labour markets as supply chain management systems react at light-speed to human or material frictions, sucking up huge financial and energy resources to construct the data infrastructures they require, and even creating tens of thousands of unemployed traders as this elite profession falls victim to its own drive towards efficiency.

But our enslavement to the algorithm has as much to do with our conceptions of it as our replacement by it or, better, the capitalist nature of this replacement. Toscano references a literature of 'materialist micro-sociology' which opens up the black-box of high frequency trading (HFT) to grasp it as a product of 'institutional struggles' over the fixing of legal and technical parameters, and not just the cognitively unmappable computational acceleration and automation of mathematics. In his short story [p.100], Seymour imagines a non-capitalist use of algorithms which are simply given a different aim – to solve mankind's dependency on the value form and hydro-carbons, nix climate change and improve the sum of human happiness – thereby recentering the human and 'enslaving' the algorithm to the needs of mortals. Dragos & Wilkins [p.86] highlight a different finality to HFT than the chaos inducing repetition compulsion of the algorithm itself, namely that of high entropy and noise saturation peaks. As with all isolated systems, they argue, the market is ruled by the second law of thermodynamics which states that entropy will tend towards a maximum. HFT's attempts to eradicate information differentials (e.g. bid-ask spreads) end up offsetting more noise/entropy onto the system as a whole, as it 'browns out' the networks with price requests and the sub-millisecond turnover of trades. If the first two writers stress the algorithm's operation within the logic of capitalism, one which as Marxists they also understand as both an effect and imprisonment of the human development of reason, Dragos & Wilkins widen the focus to think about how HFT is also determined by natural and physical forces; how capitalism precipitates high entropy. While none of these analyses understand algorithmic behaviour as strictly 'out of control', they do nevertheless diverge around the contextual frame in which its autonomising force can be understood. For Toscano and Seymour, algorithms exist within a human driven techno-social development which has unleashed the autonomising power of exchange value. For Dragos & Wilkins, the human evolves as much within the ontological sway of technology – amongst other physical, chemical and biological processes – as vice versa.

The ways in which capital's will to autonomy meets material limits, and the material realm is reciprocally shaped by the forces of abstraction, is naturally as much a problem for city dwellers, farmers, artists, anti-capitalists and philosophers as capitalists themselves. Returning to Marx, Toscano reminds us that the more production is driven by exchange value and hence exchange, the more the physical conditions of circulation become a problem for capital in its bid to 'annihilate' space through time. Similarly, Dragos & Wilkins point out that the (paradoxical, because inimical to profit) pursuit of total efficiency or 'zero information friction' results 'in the non-dialectical destruction of whole swathes of economic actors

largely at the base of steep energy gradients'. This 'resurgence' of the physical sees, for instance, finance capital blasting holes through the Allegheny Mountains to lay fibre optic cables to shave sub-millisecond times off trades between Chicago and New York. It also sees the migration of circulating capital into real estate speculation and rent extraction – discussed by Neil Gray in his extended review of David Harvey's *Rebel Cities* [p.132] – during capitalism's long profits crisis from the early '70s until today. A 'spatial fix' which impacts in the material realm of social reproduction, with more or less insubordinate results across the decades. In both scenarios, automatic intensification causes the resurgence of material frictions: the physical terrain that circulating commodities or trades must cross as much as the social and physical densities of cities.

Artists are likewise provoked by the compulsive effects of automation upon the visual realm. John Houck, who has made this issue's cover and artist's project, has spoken of his desire to pierce virtual objects and their recursiveness. 'I wanted to reclaim them and make them physical', he said in an interview for *Lay Flat* magazine, '[...] To overlay an intuitive system on a combinatorial system was the way out of the dead end of a predictable notational system.' And in his article on the so-called New Aesthetic – a term given to the involuntarily aesthetic effects arising from networked computational and technological assemblages – Curt Cloninger insists on the aesthetic as residing in the affective responsiveness of humans and not within any notional aesthesis of the inorganic.

The escalating circularity between technological intensification and capitalist omnicrisis has become an oppressive and bewilderingly abstract battleground upon which the question of social survival, aims and values is being fought out. To what degree do we see reasoning and technological systems as autonomous from human determination? Can human society challenge its domination by abstract systems (of value) to create new, non-lethal ones? To what degree are we symbiotically integrated with them? How are they extending the limits of humanness or preventing its necessary development? When John Houck folds the print-out of a software driven index graph, re-photographs it and then adds a digital fold, can we still tell the difference between the two folds? Does the manual act of folding do something more than create a delusional sense of the human empowerment to affect our conditions? Or is exerting force against virtual systems, without fantasising our release from them, something we need to learn to do as elegantly as Houck?

JOSEPHINE BERRY SLATER
<josie@metamute.org> is Editor of *Mute*

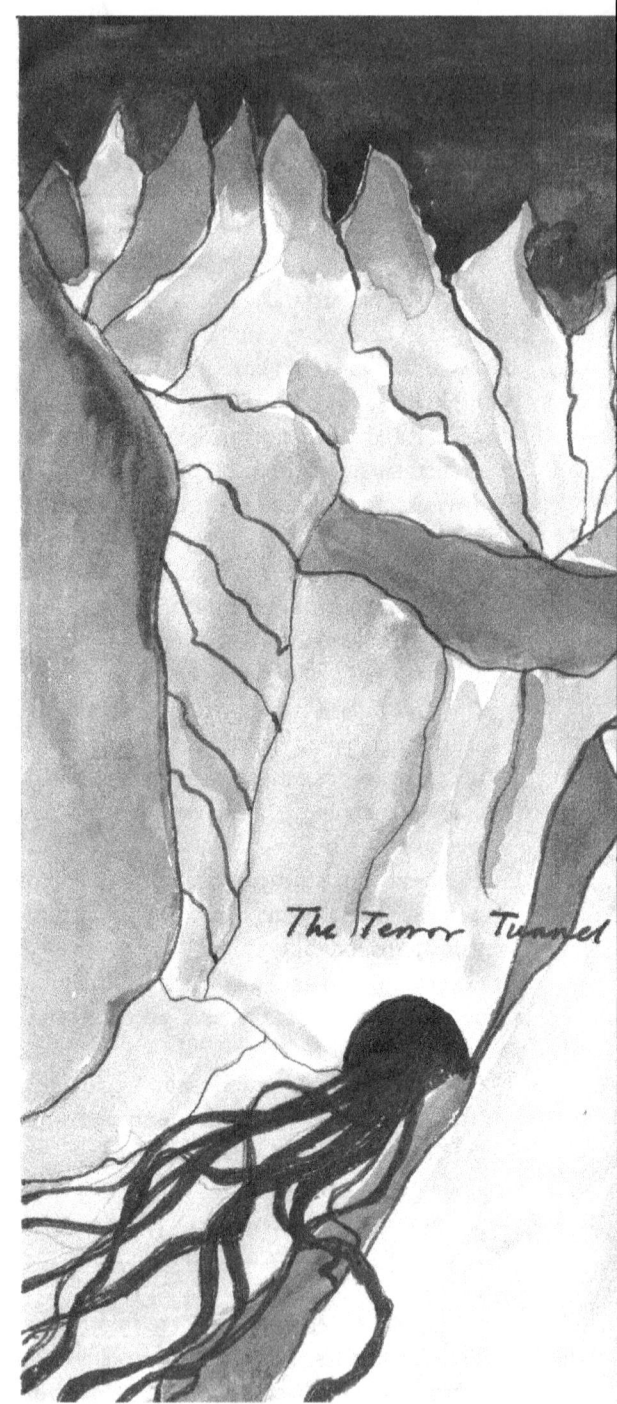

The Terror Tunnel

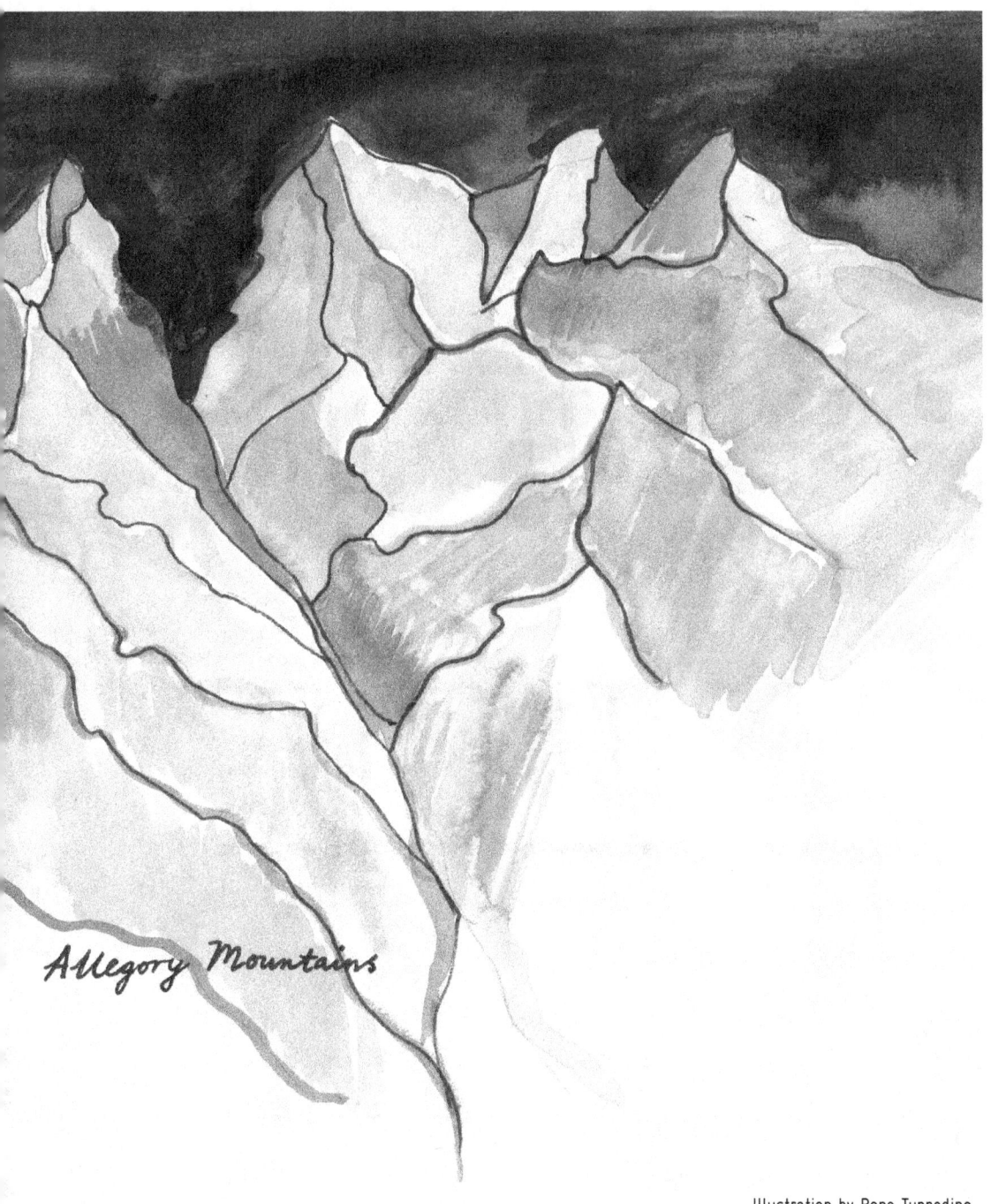

Allegory Mountains

Illustration by Rona Tunnadine

MANIFESTO FOR A THEORY OF THE 'NEW AESTHETIC'

At this high-point of high-tech, machines are producing aesthetic experiences for us as never before. Should we respectfully thank them and consider ourselves their peers? <u>CURT CLONINGER</u> *suggests something more irreverent*

Aesthetic experience is always asymmetrical; it needs to be posed in terms of a subject, as well as an object.
– Steven Shaviro[1]

WHAT IS THE 'NEW AESTHETIC'?

If, according to Debord, 'the spectacle is capital accumulated to such a degree that it becomes an image', then the New Aesthetic is technology accumulated to such a degree that it becomes an image.[2] The New Aesthetic (NA) image is a special kind of image – an image which is bodily, affectively sussable by humans. The NA image is not merely (or even) an image to be intellectually pondered by humans. You 'get it' before you understand it (if you ever even come to understand it).

'Things' don't affectively suss the NA image. Only humans 'get it'.

The New Aesthetic is not new (or it has always already been perpetually new). The fact that the NA has recently hit some sort of pop-meme coagulation tipping point (and acquired an ontological name) is merely evidence that technology has finally accumulated to the point of being easily and widely recognised as a collection of Tumblr *images* without needing to be supported or explained by any underlying *theory* whatsoever. (Indeed, James Bridle's Tumblr launched the New Aesthetic meme, and Bruce Sterling's journalistic blog dispersed it.) The New Aesthetic has been intuited by hands-on coders for decades (perhaps centuries). It has been discussed by media theorists for at least as long. This is why old school media artists like Mez Breeze and old school media theorists like Simon Biggs (on old school listservs like NetBehaviour) are left fairly unimpressed with the current 'gee whiz' enthusiasm about the New Aesthetic. 'The future is already here – it's just not very evenly distributed' (William Gibson, in some places as early as 1993).[3] The future is (always already) in the process of becoming ever more evenly distributed.

When a meme (like 'the New Aesthetic') is initially introduced and received, it is arguably fruitful to leave off theorising about it and avoid trying to codify it. Let speculation and confusion reign and see where things lead. This approach works fine in the beginning; but after a while, it leads to the worst kind of lowest-common-denominator, self-referential, reblogged intellectual sludge.

The 'New Aesthetic movement' exists only in the imaginations of a group of bloggers promoting an agenda for which I have no sympathy whatsoever: actor-network theory spiced with pan-psychist metaphysics and morsels of process philosophy. I don't believe the internet is an appropriate medium for serious artistic debate; nor do I believe it is acceptable to try to concoct an artistic movement online by using blogs to exploit the misguided enthusiasm of impressionable graduate students. I agree with Deleuze's remark that ultimately the most basic task of art is to impede stupidity, so I see little artistic merit in a 'movement' whose most signal achievement thus far is to have generated an online orgy of stupidity.[4]

I have taken the liberty of replacing 'speculative realist' with 'New Aesthetic', 'philosophical' with 'artistic', and 'philosophy' with 'art'.

The New Aesthetic is not a single aesthetic. Drone technology produces its own visual aesthetics. Google Maps produces its own visual aesthetics. Generative Processing code produces its own visual aesthetics. Glitches

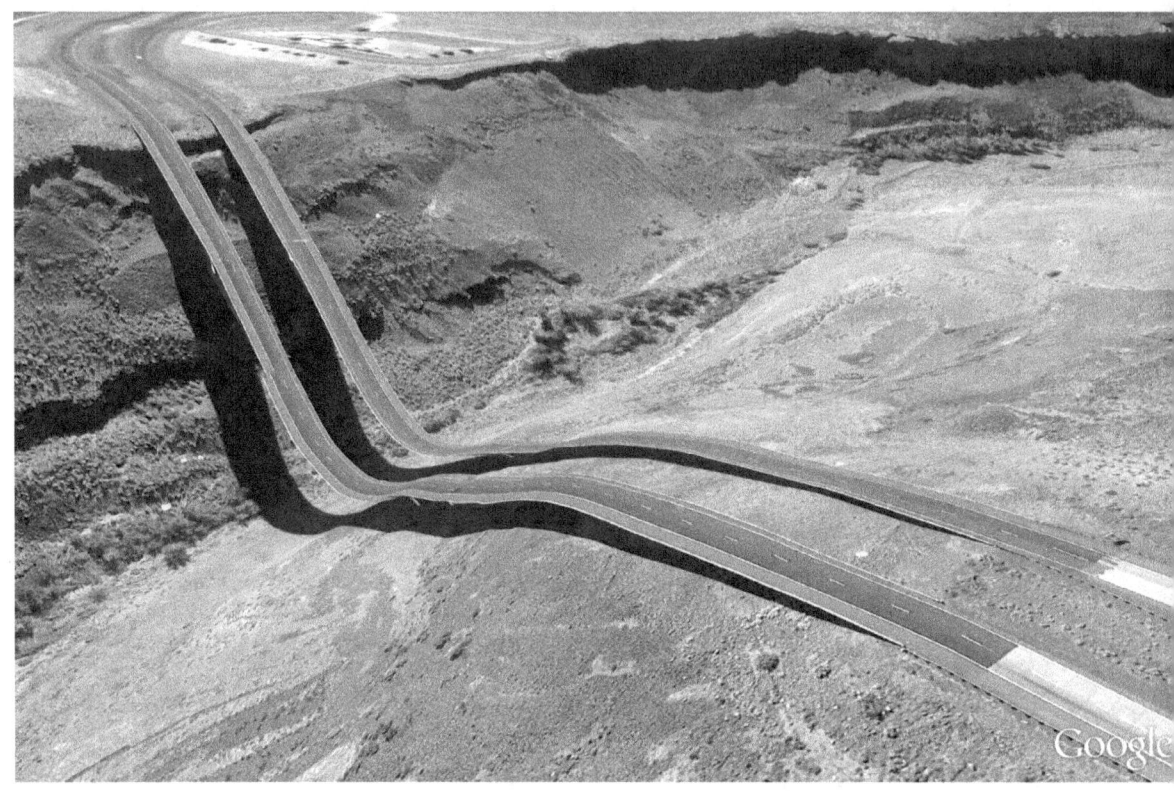

Image enacting the uncanny valley. This image is a New Aesthetic image.
Clement Valla, from *Postcards from Google Earth*, 2011

across various media, compression algorithms, and hardware displays produce their own visual aesthetics. These myriad aesthetics are each as singular and unique as the entangled culture/nature histories which led to the development and deployment of these various technologies and their gradual accumulation into human-sussable images.

The term 'New Aesthetic' is similar to the term 'New Media'. When your descriptive adjective is as vague as 'new' (or 'modern' or 'contemporary'), then all ontological constraints are off. Your movement is open to embrace 'what's happenin' in the [future-]now.

The speculative playing field of the New Aesthetic is even broader than the speculative playing field of New Media; because 'media' are still indebted to the technical, formal, material constraints; whereas aesthetics (even 'old' Kantian aesthetics) have always been philosophically malleable.

Those less theoretically inclined might argue that since the New Aesthetic begins with an affectively intuited image, that's where it should end. Yo Bros, I'm really happy for you. Imma let you finish, but...

The New Aesthetic is not a new flavour of aesthetics. At best, and properly understood, it is a new way of understanding aesthetics altogether, one that renegotiates the relationship between human subject and non-human object. Perhaps we need a less historically-encrusted word for this 'new' relationship than 'aesthetic'. But let's keep 'aesthetic' for now. It forces us to revisit Kant, Schiller, Freud, Heidegger, and Whitehead; and those guys had a lot of Tumblr followers back in the day.

'I'm lost in the dark / Lend me your teeth.' (Devendra Banhart, 2002).[5] Post-Media theorist and curator Domenico Quaranta says the New Aesthetic will never be a critical criterion for

art unless it grows some theoretical teeth.[6] Currently, it is too preoccupied with surface sheen and not concerned enough with cultural analysis. Agreed. So let's try to grow it some teeth and see what happens...

A PROCESS WITHOUT A SINGULAR 'AESTHETIC' INTENTIONALITY

The New Aesthetic image is like outsider art incidentally created by systems.

The New Aesthetic is indifferent to mimesis. The NA image is not the re-presentation of an object. The NA image is the incidental visual residue of the performance or enactment of a process. The process never intentionally alters itself in order to achieve the 'goal' of the NA image. The NA image is a trace, a remnant, a remainder, a residue, a (potential) clue. The 'subject' of the NA image (when sussed, right) is the process itself. In this sense, the New Aesthetic is akin to process art, if we substitute 'world' for 'studio' and 'human/non-human entanglements' for 'artist'.

The New Aesthetic image is a Leibnizian 'texture'. It reveals more about the processes and systems that 'produced' it than it does about itself.

Technology was never *evolving toward* the production of this or that NA image. Beware of teleology! Technology was never *trying* to make this or that NA image. Beware of anthropocentrism! (Especially beware of the kind of anthropocentrism committed in the name of overcoming anthropocentrism.)

The difference between Pollock and Cage: Pollock's process is still *heading toward* the production of an aesthetic art object (as judged by his inherited idea of aesthetics). Cage's process is *heading toward* whatever it winds up being. For Cage, chance operations become a vehicle

New Aesthetic images are produced by entangled nature/culture systems

to escape inherited notions of aesthetics. New Aesthetic images are produced by processes that fall somewhere between Pollock and Cage. NA images are not produced solely by randomness, nor are they produced in order to conform to a pre-conceived human aesthetic. NA images are produced by entangled nature/culture systems. Thus, human will is always partially involved in their production, but it is rarely an aesthetic will *heading toward* the production of NA images. Usually, it is the will to make more money, modulated through complex technological entanglements which have accumulated to such a degree that NA images are incidentally (although not arbitrarily) produced. To fetishise the NA image as a mere 'aesthetic' object is to conveniently ignore the ethical ways in which we are implicit in its production. To fetishistically credit 'machines' as the primary agents behind the production of NA images is to conveniently ignore the ethical ways in which we are implicit in their production.

The New Aesthetic image, in-and-of-itself, *in stasis*, is kind of cool. Cooler yet is the way in which the NA image reveals the historical forces that have come together to 'produce' it *in stasis*. Coolest is the way in which the NA image reveals how things are currently coming together *in process*; and how things may possibly come together in the near future.

New Aesthetic images aren't representative, analogous, archetypal, emblematic, or symbolic of any thing else. They are the actual traces and residues of processes and relationships - traces that have arrived in the visual realm and have entered humans via their eyes. NA images don't symbolise or represent the processes that have led to their creation. Instead, they are incidentally thrown into the world by those processes. The way backwards from the images toward the processes themselves is much more

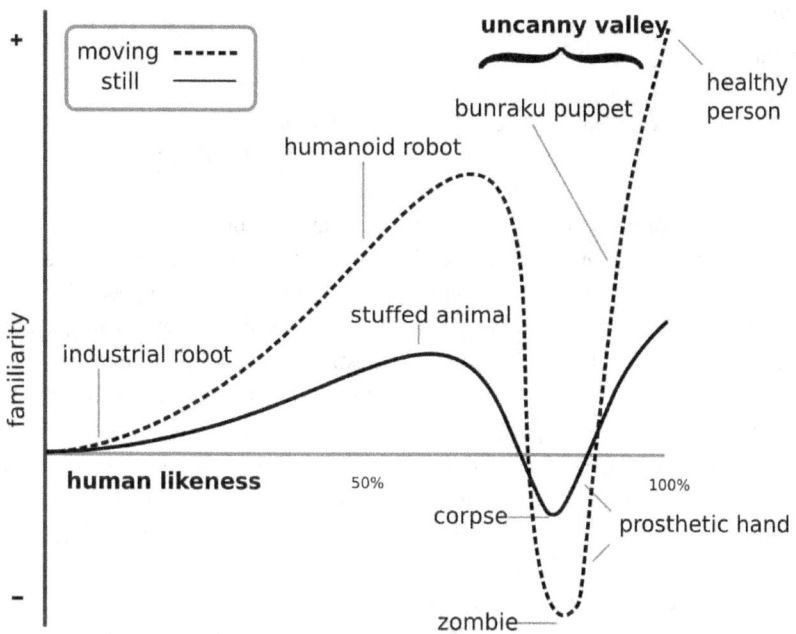

Graph explaining the uncanny valley. This graph is not a New Aesthetic image

complicated that simply intellectually thinking about what these images look 'like'. We initially apperceive NA images bodily and affectively. They are freaky. They trip us out. Only later are we able to reflect on them analytically, letting their own systemic contours and folds guide our theoretical thought.

Because NA images are apperceived and explored along affective lines, submitting these images to pre-existing modes of critical theory (Marxism, feminism, post-humanism, futurist journalism) may not be enough. What escapes may be more fruitful than what is captured.

Which thinkers are most relevant to the development of a New Aesthetic theory? Deleuze starts to become pragmatically (not just speculatively) relevant. (This might turn out to be 'his century' after all.) Bruno Latour becomes increasingly relevant. Benjamin and Debord remain relevant, but less for their

Marxism than their moxie. Baudrillard is a wild goose chase (but then he always was). Graham Harman is a bit of a detour (leading to a dead-end overlooking a noble vista). Alfred North Whitehead is spot on (but then he always was).

We are not merely left to choose between cyber-utopianism and cyber-dystopianism. Because, like modernism/postmodernism, utopia/dystopia are two sides of the same teleological coin. As Bruno Latour rightly asserts, we have never been modern, we just fooled ourselves into thinking we were.[7] When the truly new emerges, if it is indeed properly new, it won't look like utopia, dystopia, modernism, or postmodernism. It will look (and feel) monstrous and uncanny. 'The future can only be anticipated in the form of absolute danger. It is that which breaks absolutely with constituted normality and can only be proclaimed, presented, as a sort of monstrosity.'[8]

NEW AESTHETIC IMAGES ARE AFFECTIVELY SUSSED BY HUMANS, NOT BY THINGS

An overdub has no choice / an image cannot rejoice[9]

It bears repeating: 'Things' don't affectively suss New Aesthetic images. Only humans 'get' NA images. There is no machine 'aesthetic', no robotic 'vision'. Humans invent aesthetic theories regarding the interpretation of machine-generated images. Machines do not invent aesthetic theories regarding the interpretation of circuit-generated images. Likewise, no rock ever invented an ontology. Humans develop ontologies which include rocks. Humans may even philosophically speculate what ontologies rocks might invent. But rocks-themselves do not invent rock-centric ontologies. Nor do rocks-themselves philosophically speculate what ontologies dirt might invent.

If there were a clear dividing line between humans and things, then the 'aesthetics' of the New Aesthetic would lie *mostly* on the side of humans. Between humans and things, there is no clear dividing line.

The New Aesthetic is not just about intellectually 'getting it' when it comes to technology. Heck, Paul Simon 'gets it' as early as 1986:

The bomb in the baby carriage was wired to the radio... The way the camera follows us in slo-mo. The way we look to us all. The way we look to a distant constellation that's dying in a corner of the sky. These are days of miracle and wonder... And the dead sand falling on the children, the mothers, and the fathers, and the automatic earth... Medicine is magical and magical is art... lasers in the jungle somewhere... Staccato signals of constant

information. A loose affiliation of millionaires and billionaires.[10]

Simon's lyric reads like a (much more poetic) version of any number of summative lists recently offered to catalogue the underlying technologies of the New Aesthetic. And that's *Paul Simon* in *1986*. Yes, we all get it. We have gotten it for some time now.

The most intriguing thing about the New Aesthetic is that we all now 'get it' affectively via NA *images*. Our human bodies have a way of 'getting it' before our human intellects do.

New Aesthetic images can teach us humans a New Aesthetic. But as we listen to this New Aesthetic, what we are hearing is neither the *pure* voice of nature nor the *adulterated* voice of machines. We are listening to systems in the world – a world that we are co-creating, a world of which we are always already a part (never apart).

DOWN WITH PAN-PSYCHISM!

Pan-psychism is the idea that all things in the world (rocks, animals, predator drones, weather systems, Hello Kitty lunchboxes) have consciousness. The pipe dream of Artificial Intelligence is related to pan-psychism. Pan-psychism is the played-out rabbit trail of the New Aesthetic. 'It's a trap!' (Admiral Ackbar).[11] Just because we've finally come to recognise that things and systems have their own agency and are not merely passive and inert, this doesn't mean that things and systems have consciousness.

We humans have become so enamoured of honouring 'the other' that we have come to equate self-denigration with ethical behaviour. Not only do we see ourselves as sexist and racist (which we are), we have come to see ourselves as

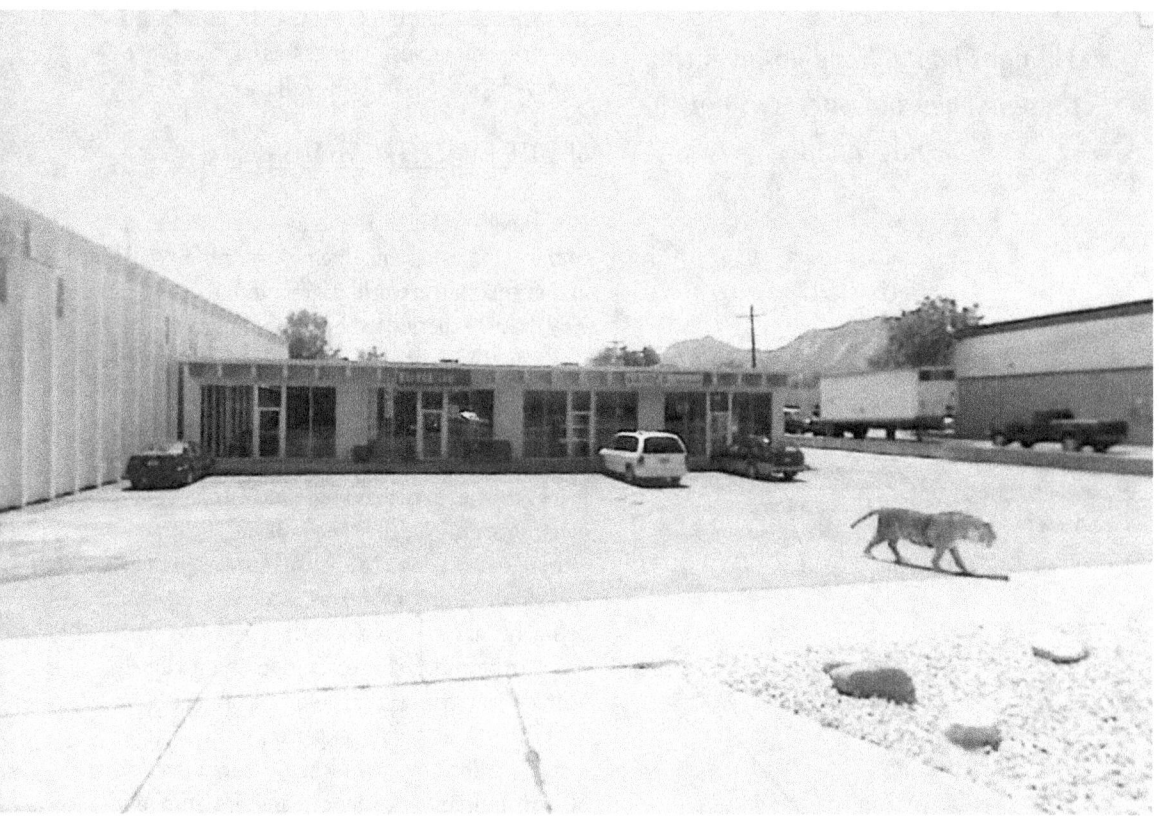

Jon Rafman, from 9-eyes.com, ongoing. Artist/curator/human Jon Rafman 'gets it',
The 9-eyed, vehicle-mounted, Google camera apparatus does not

species-ist (animals are people too) and thing-ist (things are people too). The irony is that, as we seek to honour things-in-themselves (thus nobly overcoming our anthropocentric narcissism), we extend to things the highest honour we can imagine – humanness! To imbue things and systems with a kind of consciousness is actually the epitome of anthropocentrism. The conquering European must first dress the native up in civilised clothes before she can be treated as an equal. And now we extend the same ridiculous, narcissistic 'courtesy' to things.

It is not enough that we seek to elevate things to our level; we feel as if we must lower ourselves to thing level. We humans are now no better than things. We are actually mere things ourselves (or mere systems of micro-things, depending on your scalar preferences). And the rocks bow their heads as we pass by, in deference to our enlightened humility.

As a result, we humans are hubristically tempted to attribute the uncanniness of New Aesthetic images to the pan-psychic agency of AI technology. 'Gee, these systems must be sentient (in a way that we humans are sentient), because we humans sure didn't invent these crazy new images.' This response is half-right and all wrong. We humans had a 'hand' in inventing

Humans had a 'hand' in inventing these images, but ours was not the only 'hand'

these images, but ours was not the only 'hand'. Systems, materials, things, assemblages co-invented these NA images with us.

UP WITH PAN-EXPERIENTIALISM!

Pan-experientialism is the idea that all things in the world experience 'being' over time. Forces and events in the world ingress into things in a way that is experienced by those things.

Few things have the same qualitative types of experience. Rock-being-ness isn't human-being-ness (and human-being-ness isn't what it used to be). Alfred North Whitehead puts it like this: experience is the base of all being; consciousness is the apex of all being. So although rocks don't think like humans (indeed, rocks don't think at all), at some base level of being, humans and rocks both experience.

Furthermore, humans don't consciously 'think' everything that we 'experience'. We affectively and bodily experience all sorts of things we don't ever think at all. Only a fraction of our human experiences ingress into our conscious (or even subconscious) awareness.

Pan-experientialism means that humans are a little more like things than we thought, and that things are a little more like humans than we thought. It doesn't mean that humans are mere rocks, or that rocks have consciousness.

We need to understand things as vector forces enacting within networks, not as anthropomorphised objects. Yes, thing have agency, but their agency is altogether thingy. Emergent systems (AKA things made up of things) exercise all sorts of funky agency: flocking behaviours, attraction to strange attractors, radical modulations at state-change thresholds. Yes, non-inert behaviours; but not sentient behaviours. A painter enters into a kind of pragmatic dialogue with the viscous and luminous behaviours of her paint. She need not speculate about its withdrawn essence.

NEW AESTHETIC IMAGES: THE UNCANNY, THE PRESENT-AT-HAND, THE SUBLIME

Kansas, I've a feeling we're not in Toto any more
– Dorothy (chopped & screwed)

Aesthetics are related to both experience and consciousness. Aesthetics are born in experience and arrive at consciousness. No consciousness at which to arrive, no aesthetics. So when we talk about aesthetics, we're mostly talking about humans. (Unless we want to radically re-define aesthetics, in which case we should probably use a different word.)

Beginning with Freud: New Aesthetic images are uncanny (unheimlich, un-homelike). If NA images were totally familiar, we would read them as family photos. (They are our new family photos.) If they were totally alien, we would read them as so much white noise. Instead, New Aesthetic images are somewhere in-between, in the Uncanny Valley: that disturbing interzone where something 'non-human' is almost human enough to seem 'human', but not quite. We recognise ourselves in NA images, but also something other than ourselves; or rather, still ourselves – but ourselves complicated, enmeshed, othered.

We humans are developing new, more purposefully affective ways of reading these new images.

The only way to read is acrobatically, fast and with lots of background noise (disco music or television), for that encourages more speed and more rapid processing of the information that cannot be processed except as a function of peripheral seeing and distracted absorption [...] To read poetry

carefully and slowly is to miss the point, which is the blur.[12]

On to Heidegger: Graham Harman interprets Heidegger's vorhandenheit (presence-at-hand) as an eruption of the thing out of its normal function in the world (its normal function is zuhandenheit, 'readiness-to-hand'). The thing was there all along; but we never saw it this way until now. This eruption is a useful way of understanding NA images. NA images are visual eruptions of everyday functioning systems in the world, systems humans never saw in this way until now. Like Heidegger's broken hammer – the carpenter only stops to reflect on it once it stops working as expected.

New Aesthetic visuals don't necessarily 'reveal' a hidden 'truth'. It's not as if readiness-to-hand is false and presence-at-hand is true, or vice versa. They are just two simultaneous ways of being in the world. (Heidegger's genius – his 'sleight of hand' – was to draw our attention to readiness-to-hand without turning it into presence-at-hand.)

As per Bruno Latour (and with Heidegger turning in his grave), our current systems have proliferated and hybridised beyond our ken to strange and complex degrees. New Aesthetic images strike at the heart of the modernist myth that man is master and measure of all things. Something much more trippy is actually happening. We are caught up in a proliferation of hybrid hammers ever breaking.

From Heidegger to Kant: New Aesthetic images are more sublime than beautiful. They are sublime because they affectively impact humans in ways which imply the subterranean, ongoing operation of assemblages which have not yet been resolved, and may never resolve; assemblages beyond human mastery, yet in which humans are implicated and entangled. The affective feelings NA images evoke in humans confound Schiller's attempts to reconcile the sensuous and the formal in 'play'. NA images are neither human 'art' nor non-human 'nature'. They were not created to address a static conception of human nature, nor to dialectically overcome preconceived contradictory drives within human nature. Neither were they created by extra-human forces in order to provide human 'subjects' with 'natural' objects for aesthetic contemplation. Instead, NA images are residues that result from current ways of being in the world, entangled ways in which humans are 'always already' implicated. At their best, NA images challenge humans to re-imagine 'humanness', 'being' and 'the world' altogether.

FOUR SUMMARIES, THREE QUOTATIONS AND A CLOSING EXHORTATION

Matter matters. Things (light, networks, economies, rocks, paint, pixels) have their own agency. Things are already in the world, in dialogue with the world, forming and being formed by other things in the world. Indeed, according to Heidegger, things in relationship with other things make up 'the world'. No things; no 'world'. Things don't consciously 'know stuff' about the world, but... things behave in ways derived from their history in the world and from their current entanglements with the world. Things are caught up in the world (of other things), and the world is caught up in things.

'What might things make of the New Aesthetic?' is not a very useful question. 'What might humans make of the New Aesthetic once we realise that we have been entangled with things all along?' is a more useful question. Bruno Latour says that modernism was simply

a time when humans thought we weren't entangled with things, when actually we were. What we made of that time unawares was an even bigger entangled mess (Latour's term is 'a proliferation of hybrids') – atom bombs as inverted guardian angels, global warming debates as orthodox scientific catechisms. At this point, it seems unlikely that we are going to avoid further complex human/thing entanglements, so trying to avoid them is probably something we should try to avoid. On the other hand, we should also avoid passively sitting around, techno-fetishistically dazzled by these 'spectacular new developments', blithely watching a real-time documentary of ourselves watching a real-time documentary of ourselves. Probably, we should spend some time figuring out how these systems flow and function so we can more effectively modulate them (or sabotage them), hopefully for reasons other than making more money.

All of this stuff is cool. Does it mean that objects have souls, psyches, withdrawn essences, or intelligences? No. Does it mean that humans are merely one thing among many things, no more or less endowed with agency? No.

It does mean that humans are recursively entangled with things and forces in increasingly problematic ways (Bruno Latour told us this in 1991).[13] Furthermore, it means that humans affectively experience all sorts of things in the world prior to (and often without ever) cognitively becoming aware of these experiences; it means that things also affectively 'experience' forces in the world; and it means that systems, ideas, networks, entanglements, forces, events, technologies, animals, humans and objects are all 'things' in 'the world'. (Whitehead told us this in 1927.[14] His word for 'things' is 'entities.') The fact that a bunch of people are currently talking about all this stuff online simply means that our technology has accumulated to such a degree that it has become an image – an image we can all (tech geeks, object oriented philosophers, sci-fi journalists, tumblr-ing graphic designers, twenty-something net.artists, rocks) affectively suss.

I have no doubt that in reality the future will be vastly more surprising than anything I can imagine. Now my own suspicion is that the Universe is not only queerer than we suppose, but queerer than we can suppose.
– J. B. S. Haldane, 1927[15]

There is no need to fear or hope, but only to look for new weapons.
– Gilles Deleuze, 1990[16]

Be very very quiet / Clock everything you see / Little things might matter later / At the start of the end of history.
– Steely Dan, 2003[17]

Do carry on funking & wagging, but with rigour. Little things might matter later.

Curt Cloninger ‹curt@ab404.com› is an artist, writer and Assistant Professor of New Media at the University of North Carolina, Asheville, USA. His art undermines language as a system of meaning in order to reveal it as an embodied force in the world. He maintains http://lab404.com, http://playdamage.org and http://deepyoung.org in order to facilitate a more lively remote dialogue with the Sundry Contagions of Wonder

FOOTNOTES

1   Steven Shaviro, 'The Universe of Things', *Theory And Event* 14, No. 3 2011, p.16.

2   Guy Debord, *Society of the Spectacle*, Detroit: Black & Red, 1983, Part 1, Note 34.

3   For more on the gradual historical distribution of this quote, see: http://quoteinvestigator.com/2012/01/24/future-has-arrived/

4   Modified from Ray Brassier, 'I am a nihilist because I still believe in truth', interviewed by Marcin Rychter (Lebanon, February 2011), *Kronos*, 4 March 2011, http://kronos.org.pl/index.php?23151,896

5   Devendra Banhart, lyrics from 'Lend Me Your Teeth', *Oh Me Oh My*, New York: Young God Records, 2002.

6   Domenico Quaranta, 'Una Nuova Estetica?', *Flash Art* 303, June 2012, p.26.

7   See Bruno Latour, *We Have Never Been Modern*, Cambridge, Mass: Harvard University Press, 1993.

8   Jacques Derrida, *Of Grammatology*, Baltimore: Johns Hopkins University Press, 1976, p.5.

9   Carole King, lyrics from 'The Porpoise Song', The Monkees, *Head*, Culver City, California: Colgems Records, 1968.

10 Paul Simon, 'The Boy in the Bubble', from *Graceland*, Burbank, California: Warner Bros. Records, 1986.

11 *Star Wars – Episode VI: Return of the Jedi*, prod. Howard Kazanjian, dir. Richard Marquand, 136 min., Lucasfilm, 1983.

12 Tan Lin, 'Anachronistic Modernism', *Cabinet Magazine* 1, 2000/2001,. http://cabinetmagazine.org/issues/1/anachronistic.php

13 Bruno Latour, op. cit.

14 Alfred North Whitehead, *Process and Reality: An Essay in Cosmology*, New York: Free Press, 1978.

15 J. B. S. Haldane, *Possible Worlds and Other Papers*, New York: Harper & Brothers, 1928, p.286.

16 Gilles Deleuze, 'Postscript on the Societies of Control', *October* 59, Winter 1992, p.3-7. http://www.n5m.org/n5m2/media/texts/deleuze.htm

17 Walter Becker and Donald Fagen, lyrics from 'GodWhacker', Steely Dan, *Everything Must Go*, Burbank, California: Reprise Records, 2003.

THE
MISSING
FACTORY

In the early 1970s, at the meeting point of workplace occupations and critical film-making, 20th century art's attraction to the factory reached a representational impasse. JOHN ROBERTS considers why this hegemonic site of value-production must remain absent from film and bourgeois culture more generally

In an interview Jean-Luc Godard conducted after the release of *Tout Va Bien* (1972), during the time of his participation in the Dziga-Vertov Group, which he co-founded with Jean-Pierre Gorin, he argues, in direct opposition to the reception of the film on the left, that his film was not a film that spoke *for* workers, and neither did he, more generally, as a film-maker. 'Rather than speaking in the "name of" we should speak in our own name.'[1] Thus, at the moment of his self-designation as a political film-maker, he rejects the partisanship of the artist as anything so simplistic as a calling-up to the workers' movement. This distinction is important, and in a sense established the political trajectory of his career: it is the political task of artists – their job as partisans – to speak as artists, not as workers' emissaries. In an interview 35 years later, however, he places a quite different emphasis on the representation of workers' lives: the working class does not want to see images of itself labouring, he says, and therefore any film-maker who inflicts this on their audience is in direct contravention of the spirit of cinema. 'The worker would be bored to tears if he had to watch himself. People don't want to see their lives, only a little bit of their lives.'[2] At one level this seems superficially conservative, and even a betrayal of the earlier comment, but at another level it confirms what Harun Farocki's has called cinema's fundamental resistance to the factory. As Farocki says in the essay accompanying his film, *Workers Leaving the Factory* (1995), a compilation of footage of workers leaving the factory gates culled from feature, documentary,

news and advertising films: 'Most narrative films take place in that part of life where work has been left behind.'[3] That is, film begins when in imagination and actuality, the audience have disconnected from their labours, and the labours of others. Indeed in a brilliant allegorical interpretation of the Lumière brothers' *Workers Leaving the Lumière Factory in Lyon* (1895) – to the best of our knowledge the first projected film – these first flickering images prefigure the very history of cinema as the encapsulation of this leaving, as if the Lumière brothers had invited the workers, on their sprightly emergence into the sunlight, to *become* cinema as opposed to returning to their lives as living labour.

But if cinema, in these terms, is the space that leaves the factory behind, this is not because cinema has not wanted to enter the factory at all and film from the opposite perspective: workers streaming into the factory (as in Karel Reisz's, *Saturday Night, Sunday Morning* (1960)). In fact, in the same 1972 interview, Godard bemoans the fact that 'there's hardly anywhere I can shoot' (and of course he's right). If the cinema is also the imaginary opposite to the factory as a condition of the audience's liberation from waged labour, it is also the place where the production of representation is itself blocked. Firstly, as a consequence of the discipline of the production line, and the pressures of the value-form more generally (the demands of continuity and efficiency). Factory managers do not want documentary film-makers or Hollywood producers disrupting the flow of production, and certainly do not want film-makers asking questions that might reflect badly on worker-management relations. Similarly, in fictive reconstructions of the factory, the noise, intense repetitive labour and, as such, the enforced silence of workers at the point of production, make the social interactions of workers on the shop floor a dramatic dead zone. Moreover, we shouldn't assume that these conditions are any less oppressive today and, therefore, that the facticity of these conditions is any less powerful. These conditions remain as widespread under

---

The factory is the place where representation cannot freely move

---

post-Fordism as they did under Fordism, with the arrival of the mega-Fordist factory in the East and South (China, India and Russia). To present workers' speech in the factory, therefore, is to either denaturalise the conditions of this enunciation – to allow workers to speak when they are unable realistically to speak – or to present speech as moments of respite from the intensity and repetitions of labour (something that narrative cinema, say in the workshop scene in a prison movie such as *The Shawshank Redemption*, is particularly adept at).

So, under these conditions labour can only be *seen* and not represented (in the words of workers themselves), and, as such, filming soon surrenders itself to the inertial drag of repetitive labour – that is, at the risk of abandoning the representation of the intensity of the factory altogether. In short, the factory is the place where representation cannot freely move. And we see this tension in Godard's own reconstruction of the meat products factory in *Tout Va Bien*. Workers speak – as workers –

insofar as they are *not* working, namely striking. That is, the strike at the factory allows Godard to abandon naturalism, inviting the workers (who are played by unemployed actors in the film) to direct their demands and grievances directly to camera, in neo-Brechtian style. If he had staged this at the point of production itself, with workers stopping their labour to speak directly to the camera it would have likely turned the action into the equivalent of a revue, familiar from the comedic anti-naturalistic break in action in a musical, in which the actor switches, with light-hearted and implausible dexterity, from one activity to the next. So, in *Tout Va Bien* the representation of labour – of the capital-labour relation – begins precisely when the labour of the factory has stopped. Consequently, we might say, the representation of the factory begins, or can begin, once we no longer see the factory working, when the production of value is interrupted.

As such this seems to posits a counterweight to that of Farocki's cinema/factory dyad: *labour has to stop before it can be represented*, that is, before workers are able to establish the conditions for their own autonomous speech. No wonder then that the factory is a symbolic dead zone: inside its disciplinary boundaries the labour process and value-form destroys representation and ultimately expels the camera.

This gives us, notionally, a couple of axioms, to work with.

Firstly:

The non-representation of the labour process and workers' speech inside the factory is the obverse of workers' resistance, or indifference outside of the factory, to the representation of their own labour.

And, secondly:

The outcome of this interconnection is that productive labour and the factory cannot be made compatible with the symbolic.

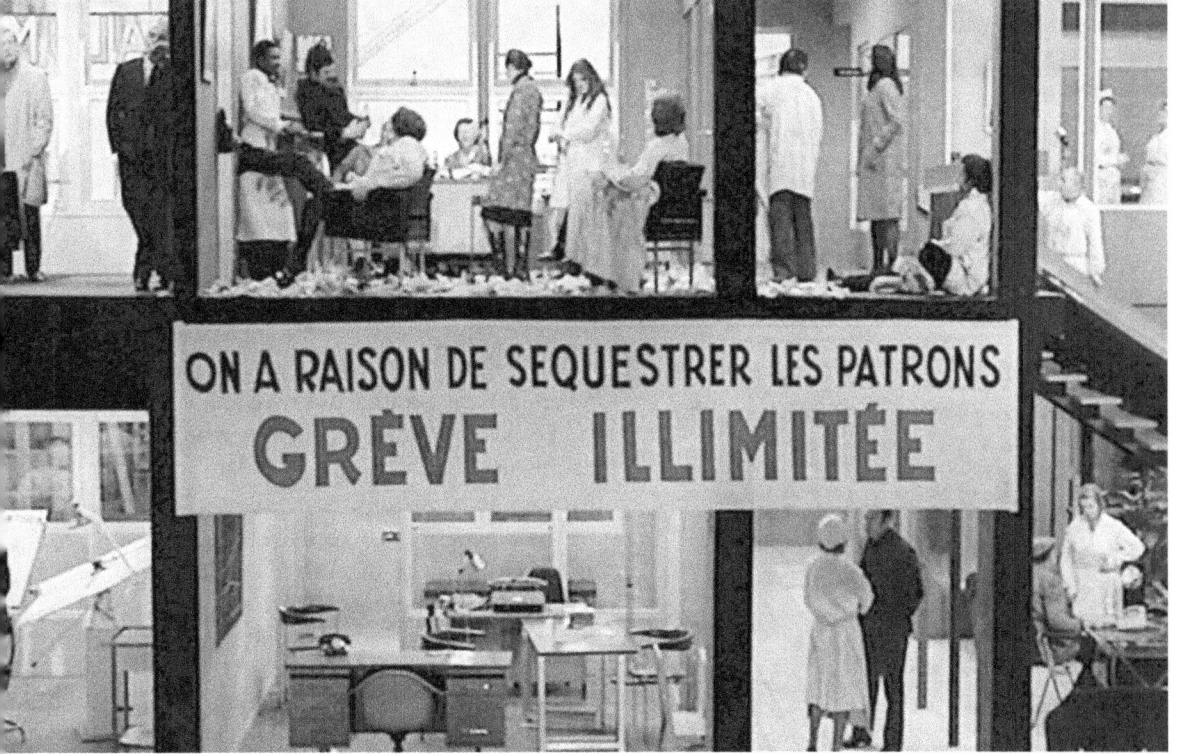

Jean-Luc Godard and Jean-Pierre Gorin, *Tout Va Bien* (1972)

For capital: this is because the entry of representation into the factory destabilises the value process, and therefore has to be excluded and suppressed. For labour: this is because the representation of labour means workers are being encouraged to take pleasure, or pedagogic instruction, from their own alienation, and therefore, the representation of labour, when encountered, has to be 'walked away from'.

This symbolic closure or unavailability of the factory is, of course, part of a broader shift in the labour process that Godard himself touches on in *Tout Va Bien*: the symbolic deposition of the factory from the forefront of the traditional labour imaginary as a consequence of two interrelated forces that were just becoming visible in the early 1970s, i.e. the beginning of post-war capitalism's competitive contraction of its industrial base, or deindustrialisation, as a consequence of the increased productivity of labour (what Karl Marx calls the rising organic composition of capital), and the notion of the 'social factory' made popular in the '70s by autonomists and Italian workerists (the notion that the disciplinary conditions of the factory apply to all places of work, productive and non-

productive alike, and most contentiously to the sites of cultural consumption, such as the museum and the cinema). We see this most obviously at the end of the film in the camera's long, slow tracking shot back and forth behind the checkout tills in the supermarket, in which shopping is shown to be as regulated and disciplined as the labour process in the factory. In these terms, the non-representation of the factory is, from the early 1970s, increasingly underwritten by the symbolic dissolution of the classic Fordist labour process; the discipline of the factory is held to be constitutive, at varying levels of intensity, of all social relations.

So, if the representation of the factory cannot be made compatible with the symbolic, or made so indeterminate as to become symbolically empty, then where *is* the factory today? How is the missing factory *to be* mediated? But if these questions sound necessary and plausible, they are also the wrong questions to ask, for the factory is not waiting for representation to make a breakthrough, or for the emergence of better conditions in the factory for representation. This is because the factory, being the site where cultural relations

Where is the factory today? How is the missing factory to be mediated?

cannot enter fully, represents, in its absent symbolic condition, something far more important: the eventual (and evental) site of bourgeois culture's dissolution. Thus, mourning the missing factory misses why the factory has to *remain* missing under current conditions: that is, it reveals the limits to the bourgeoisie's enculturalisation of the world, and as such moves us beyond the notion that somehow representation of the factory can begin once the exertions of labour power stop.

For the factory to enter the symbolic – as with any other social location and practice – it has to be brought stably under control, as part of the narrative self-representation of capitalist relations. And key to this narrative stabilisation is the generation of a conflictual dynamic, in order to make the interrelations between characters plausible, and their desires believable as part of capitalist relations. The factory, therefore, provides a conflictual dynamic that cannot *be* brought stably under control, insofar as this conflict is fundamental and irreconcilable. This is why historically there is no shortage of glimpses into labour-capital conflict inside the factory in film and photography, but these glimpses cannot be made consistent or persistent, because, for this to happen, these glimpses would have to become definitional of the place of labour *in* the symbolic order and therefore a representative part of it: cinema, the real life of labour and the symbolic would become co-extensive. Consequently, for labour to become a representative part of the symbolic order it would have to dissolve what capitalism disavows: the constitutive split between labour and capital – and this is plainly impossible, indeed, an inversion of the social fact of labour power as a determinate absence. But this is not to deny the distancing and veiling effects of ideology as part of this process: bourgeois

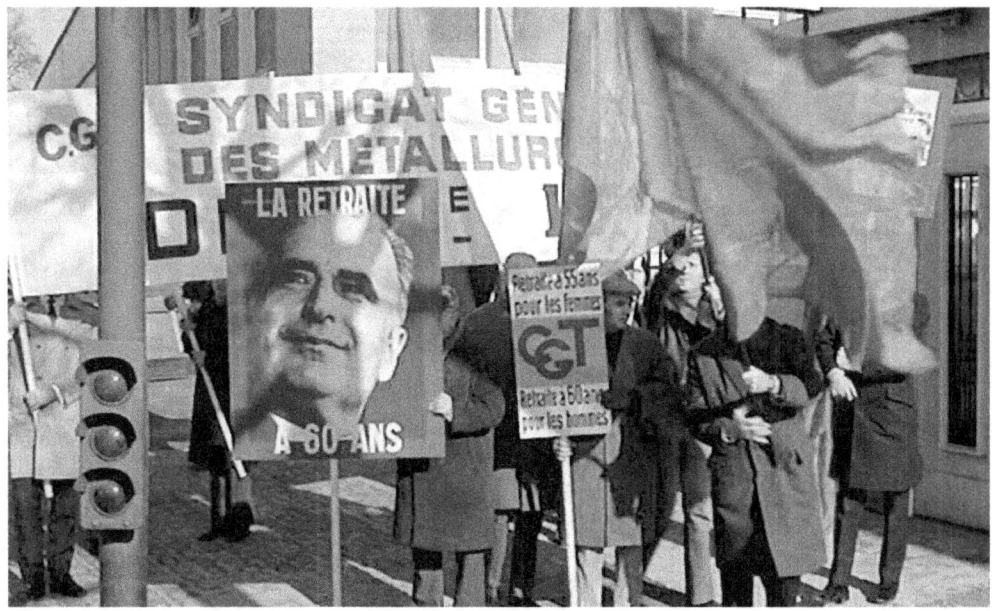

Jean-Luc Godard and Jean-Pierre Gorin, *Tout Va Bien* (1972)

culture cannot incorporate its proletarian critique in its own symbolic reproduction, because to do so is to assume that the symbolic has no material limits and no interested parties. Capital can certainly expose the violence of class relations as part of its symbolic reproduction, but it cannot speak *for* labour. Moreover, if the representation of labour power could break through its own determinate absence under capitalism, and the real life of the factory was able to achieve representativeness, the same short-circuiting of the cinematic experience would still apply: how many films can be made on factory life and struggle when the truth of the factory becomes openly identifiable with the social truth of labour power itself? What possible value might such transparency serve politically and culturally, when its truth has become compatible with empirical appearances and 'common sense'? So, in the first instance the representation of the factory is symbolically

empty because its truth is incompatible with proletarian desire, and in the latter case the factory is symbolically empty because it is superfluous to scientific knowledge.

The problem, therefore, for bourgeois culture is not the outright symbolic repression of the factory, or its transformation into a place of equanimity and harmony, for this is to precisely betray the cinema audience (no worker or even non-worker would find either position acceptable), insofar as it would dissolve the conflictual demands of narrative as such. The 'solution', rather, is to make productive labour, particularly factory labour, the thing that we see (occasionally), but which is not visible - in the sense Lacan articulates in his discussion of the invisible/visible object in the 'Purloined Letter'.[4] In other words, the missing factory is not just about conditions of access, but of *making visible what cannot be seen*. That is, in these terms: what is seen is not visible, and what is

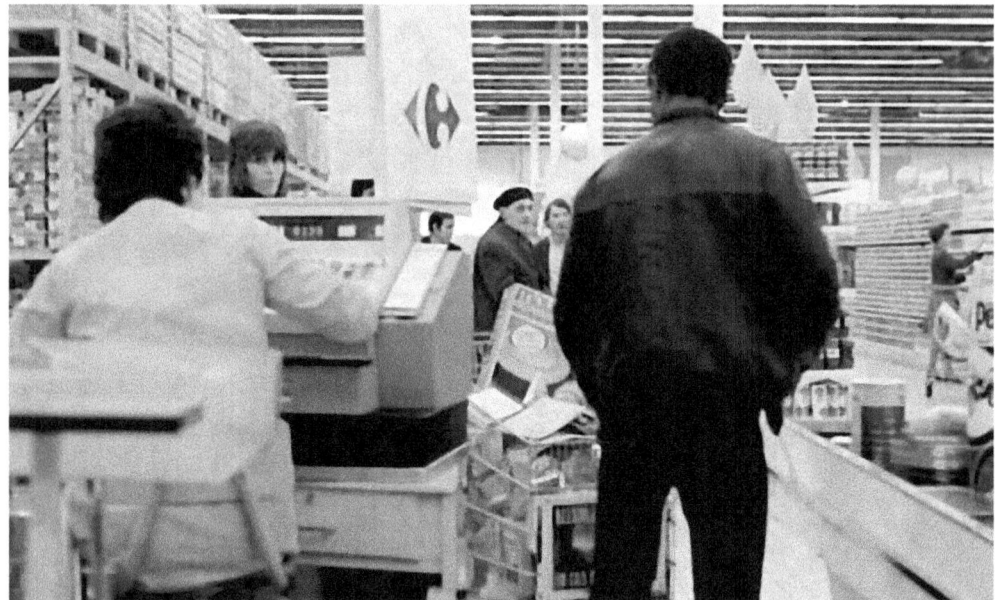

Jean-Luc Godard and Jean-Pierre Gorin, *Tout Va Bien* (1972)

visible is not seen, allowing what is to be seen, when it is seen, to be seen *without consequence*, without full symbolic assimilation. The factory is certainly seen, glimpsed publicly – because the alternative is outright repression or irenic pacification, discordant with the demands of narrative conflict – but not made consistently visible, that is, not actively represented. The factory, then, is not waiting to be *represented* at all (in order to reinstate the worker within the symbolic), but, rather, in a more properly transformative and emancipatory way waiting to be *dismantled*. Hence, the representation of the factory will occur precisely in the process of this dismantling, when its abstract identity as the disciplinary home of the value-form is dissolved.

As such, the factory's relationship to cultural transformation has a far more exacting function than overcoming its blocked entry into the symbolic: it becomes the actual site of emancipatory transformation itself. There is something of this logic in the early years of the Russian revolution, when the factory was briefly at the centre of the imaginative reconstruction of the labour process, or more broadly the Communist Imaginary. For a few years, under the auspices of Constructivism and Productivism, artists entered the factory – or tried to enter the factory – in order to exercise what they hoped to be the beginning of the revolutionary transformation of the relations of production. There were two critical components to this: the possible contribution that artists, engineers and designers might make in improving the production process, and the more radical and oppositional position, the collaboration between artists and workers in the dissolution of the value-form and the eventual dismantling of the factory in its present manifestations. Neither was successful. Rather, the latter was mostly subjected to the former, artists realising that the only transformation of the factory that the labour process would facilitate – certainly under the New Economic Policy (NEP) – was improvement in labour efficiency.[5]

Yet, as the hierarchical site of labour-capital relations and the value-form, the factory remains where 'aesthetic thinking' as the critique of the value-form *must enter eventually*. And it must enter, first and foremost, unencumbered with the notion that the liberation of art from bourgeois relations is compatible with its entry into the labour process – a recurring fantasy of those who would want to ally artistic labour completely with general social technique. The factory, therefore, contra the Soviet productivists of the 1920s, is not the primary site of art's use-values (the place where art will fully emancipate itself through productive labour and its instrumental outcomes), but rather the *destinal* site of art's critique of the value-form. Consequently, the factory is the place where free labour (inscribed in art) must arrive some time in order to confront and challenge the alienations and routinisations of productive and non-productive labour itself – material and immaterial alike. How this will happen and under what terms is unknown, but, whatever forms it will take, the working class will have a direct say in their outcomes.

INFO

A version of this article was presented in discussion with Sam MaCauliffe as part of the film screening series, 'Factory Trouble', at Goldsmiths, organised by Manu Ramos, in 2011, and at the Historical Materialism Conference, No. 8, at SOAS, 2011.

FOOTNOTES

1   Jean-Luc Godard interviewed about *Tout Va Bien*: http://www.youtube.com/watch?v=hnx7mxjm1k0
2   'Interview with Jean-Luc Godard by Emmanuel Burdeau and Charles Tesson', in Jean-Luc Godard, *The Future(s) of Film: Three Interviews, 2001/01*, John O'Toole (trans.), Bern and Berlin: Verlag Gachnang & Springer, 2002.
3   Harun Farocki, 'Workers Leaving the Factory', *Senses of Cinema*, Issue 21, July/August 2002.
4   Jacques Lacan, 'The Purloined Letter', in *The Seminar of Jacques Lacan: Book II, The Ego in Freud's Theory and in the Technique of Psychoanalysis, 1954-1955*, Jacques-Alain Miller (ed.), Sylvana Tomaselli (trans.), with notes by John Forrester, New York and London: W.W. Norton & Company, 1991.
5   See Maria Gough, *The Artist As Producer: Russian Constructivism In Revolution*, Berkeley: University of California Press, 2005, and John Roberts, 'Productivism and Its Contradictions', *Third Text*, No. 100, Vol. 23 No. 5, September 2009, p.536.

John Roberts <jcr3@wlv.ac.uk> is Professor of Art & Aesthetics at the University of Wolverhampton, and is the author of a number of books, including *The Intangibilities of Form: Skill and Deskilling in Art After the Readymade* (Verso, 2007), and *The Necessity of Errors* (Verso, 2011)

BARBARA SAYS – INDUSTRY DOES IT FASTER

A meticulously curated survey show of the Artist Placement Group at Raven Row gallery provides scope for a nuanced understanding of the unusual relationship they brokered between bureaucracy and art; one that rejects glib notions of collaboration in both fields. Review by ROMAN VASSEUR

In the luxuriously long cabinet gracing the wall of Raven Row Gallery that features the eight inserts completed for *Studio International* by Artist Placement Group (APG) in May 1970, a picture of Barbara Steveni in glamorous profile is captioned 'Barbara Says – Industry does it quicker'. Between visits I'd remembered the caption as 'faster' not 'quicker'. Further into the show a recording of Steveni's breathless Dictaphone notes for APG unnerves through its lack of irony and urgent embodiment of management speak. That APG's over-identification with industry and government's management rituals should stand out at Raven Row suggests the possibilities for current practices that this considered and carefully curated show offers up. In so doing it manages to narrowly avoid what might have ended in a lament both for the audacity of APG's approach and the politics of the period in which they formed. Reading the organisation's time-line in the accompanying publication it becomes clear that the pairing of APG's blood lines with its aristocratic host's in the form of Raven Row gallery throws into relief the performative roots of APG's inception and its private political life. A survey show at a public museum concerned with the measurable social impact of its work might have obscured the questions raised in this exhibition as to how art pictures itself 'doing power' through performative and quasi-situationist approaches. The *Studio International* caption acts as a piece of détournement, framing APG's relationship to the passions of production as post-Fordist – underscoring its desire and its contradiction to be accepted by industry and government whilst retaining its autonomy as art.

Both past and present critiques of APG have produced a gap between the symbolic and ethical outcomes of the project, from which tragedy has arisen as the dominant ground for discussing the effect and/or affect of their work. The question remains over whether they effected real social change or figured as dandies too naive to understand the politics and economics of the hosts they courted? This exhibition's narrative partially denies casting the APG project as a tragic struggle against power that would have inscribed their legacy into the tablet of history as an act of heroic alterity. Instead it suggests how – and particularly in the case of John Latham's approach – theirs was an audacious demand for an extended, even cosmological time-frame within which to imagine the artwork's unfolding, thereby altering an understanding of the technocratic forms of governance APG appeared to ape, hollow out and occupy. Much of APG's work can be summarised in a catalogue, or a lecture or online, but it was the fragments of language displayed in the documents and ephemera that countered the expectation of an informational exposition that would have presented theirs as a purely dialogical set of practices. What begins to appear is both absurdist and metaphysical in its relationship to power.

In *Art Power* Boris Groys speaks of the way in which business, due to its increased aestheticisation, has moved towards art and therefore into a space that can be critiqued as art. If our present is a time where 'the meeting' has become *the* site and image of collaboration and productivity, then APG's fetishisation of the meeting place as 'The Sculpture' for its residency at the Städtische Kunsthalle, Düsseldorf in

1971, was a premonition of a current reality where management's claims of utility exist in excess of utility itself. The contemporary image of the meeting serves to display and construct connectivity as value and as a means of obscuring capital's losses and speculative work. In contrast, for APG the meeting remains excess but also a form of explicit role-playing

---

Latham was very clear that the term 'collaboration' would not define APG's activities

---

that explores executive decision making in opposition to the collaborative act. Latham was very clear that the term 'collaboration' would not define APG's activities. This leads to both a sense of discomfort and nostalgia that arises from looking at the material and timelines in the show – a desire to see a time when centres of power were more clearly identifiable and less consultative.

Steveni and Latham in their 2003 interview with *Mute* suggested that the opaqueness of their own terminology was what made it possible to maintain the uniqueness of APG's mission – that the project was in effect a turn of language tied to an idea of 'event structure' that ignored technocratic and political time-frames. In addition to the term 'incidental person' was that of the 'disappearing artist', a term only partially developed by Stuart Brisley and John Latham for the 1968 Industrial Negative Symposium. The term returned fleetingly in the panel discussion held at Raven Row, UK Industry in Transition 1966–79; APG from the Corporation's Perspective, in connection with artist Roger Coward's assignment to

Birmingham City Council on the council's urban renewal programme. Coward's embeddedness in the processes he developed suggested a hypothetical conclusion to the project in which he finds himself many years later holding down a permanent post with Birmingham City Council. He has become an active resident and member of the community that was originally the subject of his placement and has forgotten he was sent there as an artist. Ideally, this future scenario would extend to a time when Coward, the 'disappeared artist', becomes the focus of an artist led consultancy in the burgeoning culture of art and regeneration schemes of the late '90s and early '00s. The ending of this fiction sees the embedded artist design counter-consultancy strategies at which point his memory is restored and he returns to London seeking his former life and an identity that has been destroyed.

That the placements threatened disappearance – and for some artists caused a crisis in their studio production, gallery and museum careers – demonstrates how the time-frame Latham proposed would uncouple artists from their own subjective rituals. The 'open brief' (APG's manifesto for working with institutions) produced a subtext to many of the placements' overtly stated objectives. This included encounters that were often unrecorded, informal, private, clandestine and absurdist. There were clearly quantifiable effects both within and outside contractual arrangements, including Ian Breakwell's work with Broadmoor and Rampton high security psychiatric hospitals where Breakwell managed to find a means of making public otherwise embargoed observations through his own artworks, which later fed into a two part TV documentary on high security hospitals. That Breakwell found other ways of disseminating his work outside the period of the placement

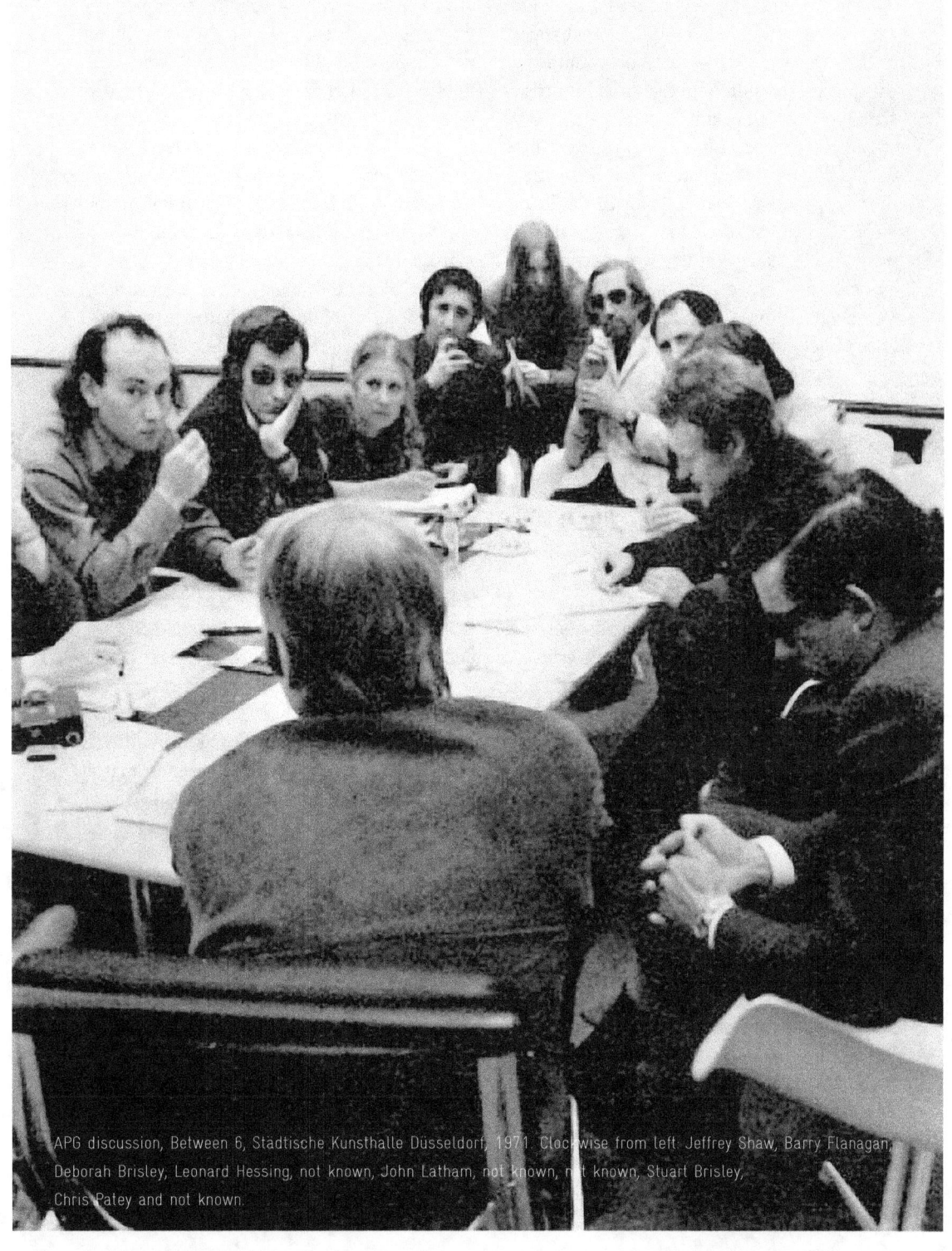

APG discussion, Between 6, Städtische Kunsthalle Düsseldorf, 1971. Clockwise from left: Jeffrey Shaw, Barry Flanagan, Deborah Brisley, Leonard Hessing, not known, John Latham, not known, not known, Stuart Brisley, Chris Patey and not known.

points to a commonly experienced problem for many public art projects, even those that appear to have a clear objective but then atomise as the process of fulfilling the brief unfurls a series of parasitic interests, organisational structures and procedures. As an artist, how do you capture the collateral that arises from the nervous breakdown of a project? Or do you let this collateral of reactions and narratives work atavistically without your continued authorship or expectation of a return on your energies? In these circumstances questions arise of how to define, if at all, what the work

---

How do you capture the collateral that arises from the nervous breakdown of a project?

---

is and where meaning emerges? Questions of how to locate 'the work' are endlessly prompted by documents in the Raven Row exhibition and the accompanying discussions. For example, the letters stemming from the placement of artist George Levantis with Ocean Fleets Ltd. between 1974-75 takes on a tragicomic turn that could be called 'the work'. Levantis attempted to act as a listening ear to members of the crew on the cargo ship's voyages to Africa and Asia. In the process he designed and made for himself a mock naval uniform in order to be accepted as a member of the crew. He caused grievances amongst some passengers and crew who were expecting art classes on one journey and subsequently suffered the indignity of having his temporary art constructions thrown overboard. These letters and the poster work by Latham advertising the sale of the Hayward Gallery combine situationist tactics with a form

of power brokering – acting in the capacity of what Stuart Brisley called 'a tightly knit, highly autocratic family business'. APG conducted its own curating in line with point three of its manifesto: 'That the proper contribution of art to society is art'. Even when that art was business. That Steveni's voice should have been so dominant at the sessions held at Raven Row is partly due to this fact – that the organisation's management was also its curation.

APG continually re-digested its organisational framework, carefully considering its media representation. For example, by filming camera crews filming their meetings during their residency at the Städtische Kunsthalle Düsseldorf in 1971. A feedback loop was created between the language of its management and the placements; one that denied any space for a conventional commissioning agency to occupy, or a moderating role for the Arts Council to inhabit. That APG worked on behalf of the artist *and* the host organisation is significant in relation to recent historical public art commissioning that can artificially separate the interests of the artist and the host organisation. That APG was its own commissioning agency able to problematise its representation by mixing its chosen format of the corporate annual report with, as Steveni has said, the language of the Pirelli calendar and advertising, suggests that the group owes some debt to the work of the Independent Group and the curating of Lawrence Alloway. I am particularly thinking of the 1956 exhibition This is Tomorrow at the ICA. Where This is Tomorrow celebrated popular mass culture, technology and the display strategies of the trade fair, The Individual and the Organisation mined APG's concern with the technologies of management. Peter Fuller's historical criticism of APG's political and economic naivety, along with other voices at Raven Row events concerned with APG's rush towards the boardroom door and not the shop floor, demonstrate discomfort with APG's conjoining of executive power with art as opposed to a communal power that we assume to be the privilege and remit of critical art practices.

APG's performative experiments in executive power act as a rebuttal to the apotheosis of collaboration in art and business, taking a severe modernist stance in self-appointing a select band of individuals to instigate, manage and carry out specialist roles. Steveni and Latham primarily made the decision that in order to have effect they would need to become an institution but be sovereign and so able to suspend and rewrite its laws whenever they and a close group of colleagues deemed it necessary for the maintenance of their objectives.[1] It seems that this act of will was the only means by which to move away from an abstract set of principles and into a life situation. For this reason a large part of the project remains within a plane of formalism, which is modernity. Its approach suggests that forms of publicness and power are formed in small collectives, sometimes as art and sometimes as an opaque even occulted activity. The group's imaginative occupation of bureaucratic procedures aided by close personal, political and intellectual interactions enabled it to instigate projects that leeched out psychic debris over many years, and continues to talk through its own excess to the excesses of our current utility.

Roman Vasseur <roman@romanvasseur.com> is an artist living and working in London. He has exhibited at the ICA, Jeffrey Charles Gallery, Project Dublin, in Berlin and the USA. He acted as Lead Artist for Harlow New Town between 2008-2011, where he was asked to consider the art and architecture principles of the town's original masterplan during a period of reassessment and regeneration. His recent solo show for Cubitt Gallery, London, ran from 17 January to 17 February 2013. Vasseur lectures in the UK and abroad, including at the School of Fine Arts, Kingston University, London

INFO

The Individual and the Organisation: *Artist Placement Group 1966-79* was at Raven Row from 27 September to 16 December 2012, http://www.ravenrow.org/exhibitions/artist-placement-group/

FOOTNOTES

1 This reading of APG is derived from 'Carl Schmitt in the Age of Post Politics' by Slavoj Zizek in *The Challenge of Carl Schmitt,* Chantal Mouffe (ed.), London and New York: Verso, 1999, p.18.

THE GHOSTS
OF
PARTICIPATION
PAST

Claire Bishop's recent book, **Artificial Hells**, considers the history of participation as an organising principle of avant-garde art, but also of liberal democracy. Review by
JOSEPHINE BERRY SLATER

Nearly 400 pages long, bearing an arresting title and featuring a cover image of a mounted policeman directing a crowd inside the Tate Modern, Claire Bishop's latest book seems to demand our full attention. With participation as its key subject, this impressive survey of its developmental role within art practice is set to be a key reference text for some time to come. But what does this buzzword 'participation' really mean after all? Is it a euphemism that sells the obligation to cooperate, to play along? Is it a moral imperative, a condition of the social? Is it just a way of emphasising the necessarily plural nature of activity in general? Can it describe the active contemplation of something without any expressive extension, or does it demand the extension of thought outwards, the connection of thought to action? This loose concept, used as a thread to connect some of the most uncompromising art of the 20th and early 21st century in Bishop's *Artificial Hells: Participatory Art and the Politics of Spectatorship*, remains all too elusive. As does the implication of its title, for Bishop is in no simple sense condemning what has by now become a default virtue of 'progressive art', as one might infer. Instead, *Artificial Hells*, which takes its name from an essay by André Breton dissecting a disappointing Dada action in a Paris churchyard in 1921, opens up the aesthetic politics of art works that depend upon more or less active audiences to a wide, but sometimes vague, horizon of consideration.

If the term 'participation' might seem to lock work from distant eras into the concerns of contemporary aesthetics, then it is nevertheless a great achievement of Bishop's book that the application of this term opens channels into aesthetic and political conundrums as old as antiquity. Bishop isn't interested in dealing with the limited scope presented by Nicolas Bourriaud in his epoch flattening concept 'relational aesthetics', used to define art that takes social relations as its medium albeit within the limits of the art world's pain tolerance. Instead, she largely departs from the heavily rotated hits of western art history to uncover what artists' desires to activate spectators might have meant in the different moments and political geographies of modernity. In her exhaustive trawl, which she has been undertaking since 2004 – funded by a series of research grants and residencies which glimmer like sinking treasure in the straits of 2012 – she focalises three historical moments in which social upheaval fuelled the desire to bring art and life into catalytic proximity.

The first is the fascist and communist convulsions of Europe c.1917, the second is the build up to May '68 in Europe but significantly also South America, and the last is the resurgence of participatory art before and after the fall of the Wall in '89, as artists from the former East came into contact with the West. Despite this historical and geographical breadth, the main connective work she performs between aesthetic and economic relations centres on Britain's transition into neoliberalism. Here she uses a close reading of the Artist Placement Group and its pioneering of industrial placements from the late 1960s, as well as the journey of community arts from self-instituting power to state-complicit extension of social work, as switch-points for the subsumption of radical aesthetic agendas into the creative economy which would become a fig leaf for post-Fordist restructuring.

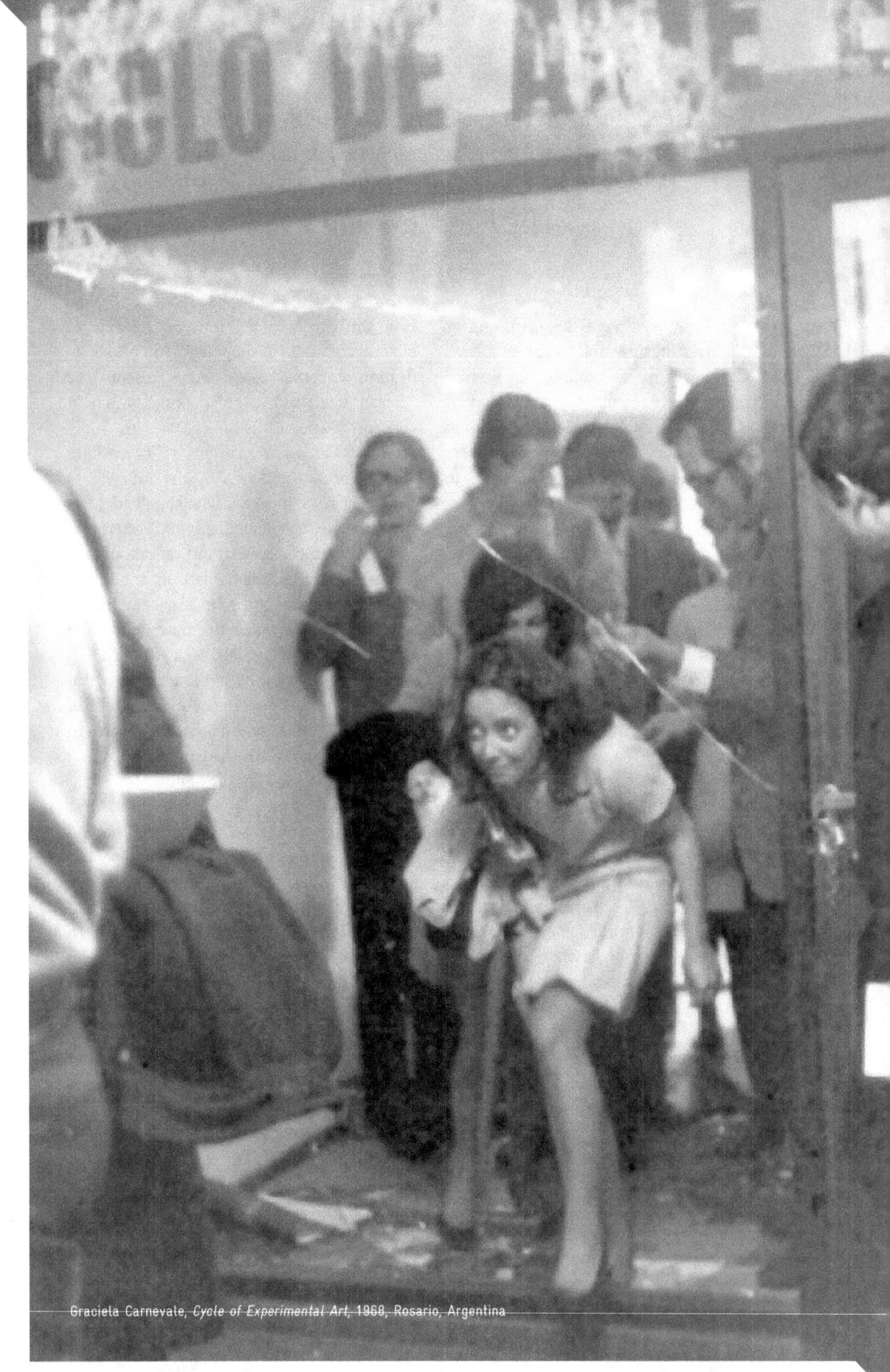

Graciela Carnevale, *Cycle of Experimental Art*, 1968, Rosario, Argentina

'Participatory art', in Bishop's account, can therefore be used to bracket together a dizzyingly diverse set of experiments. Her conceptual web binds together such multi-scalar events as: the 1920 reenactment of the storming of the Winter Palace, directed by Nikolai Evreinov, and involving 8,000 participants and 100,000 spectators; Czech artist Milan Knížák's 1971 piece *Stone Ceremony* in which a handful of participants stood silently inside circles made of stones in a remote landscape; or Marina Abramovic's untitled piece for MoCa Los Angeles' annual gala in 2011, in which performers kneeling under tables graced by glitterati poked their heads through holes to create living table ornaments. It might come as no surprise, given this categorical elasticity, that Bishop fails to generate either a compelling definition of participatory art, or a coherent optic through which to read the desire to fuse art with the living in the fascinating material she assembles.

But what could such a connective reading entail? A key ground to this discussion which cries out for exploration is the scale of the reversal from older aesthetic orders to this one, and what broader shifts this reversal expresses. Reading Hannah Arendt's *The Human Condition* directly after putting down *Artificial Hells*, I began to understand the degree to which the earliest aesthetic philosophy took a diametrically opposed position. In a nutshell, the serene contemplation required for the production and enjoyment of 'the beautiful' demanded *in*activity, and relegated activity to the realm of bodily necessity and the labour of sustaining life (the *oikos*) which was performed by slaves and women, of course.[1] The cultivation of beauty and the quest for immortality through great works and deeds were arrived at through non-coerced activity and placed on the side

of freedom, whereas the productive activities relating to the necessities of the body, the economy and later even politics, were placed on the side of heteronomy or unfreedom. This freedom, however, was predicated on slavery. The aesthetic elevation of inactivity continued through the mid-18th century, culminating in Denis Diderot's pre-revolutionary advocacy of 'absorption'. France's foremost art and theatre critic found in this attribute the defining characteristic of the arts, both in the subjects depicted and in the experience of the spectator who should be drawn away from the circumstances of spectating into a '*repos delicieux*'.[2] Diderot even advised that theatre should be produced and acted as if a wall had been erected between the stage and the audience. The means of appearance should on no account be allowed to appear for fear the spell of the *repos* may be shattered. And indeed the spell was shattered by the French Revolution, through which the art work began to open up to the contingent dynamics and uncertainties of action – be that of the subjects represented, the means of representation themselves or ultimately the art object's dematerialisation into a field of action. This brief sketch starts to give 'participation' some stronger historical coordinates, and could be interestingly pursued into the contemporary paradox of participation as agent of normativity. One begins to see that participation for-itself implies the outward *dramatisation* of activity, or the staging of action and its consumption, since contemplation without externalisation can't be counted as an active enough engagement. It seems important, therefore, that we connect 'participative art' to a broader fetishisation of action within modernity's generalisation of labour.

Everywhere throughout modernity, as Bishop's book amply demonstrates, the values of classical aesthetics have been overthrown. Filippo Marinetti wanted audiences to end their passivity and develop 'commitment to a cause' through violent participation, delivering themselves up to the art work 'heart and soul'. The sensationalism of the Futurist *serate*, staged at music halls, was designed to antagonise and exhilarate the audience, whose seats were sometimes covered in glue, tickets' oversold, and who were treated to spectacles of monstrosity, slapstick and gymnastics. They duly responded, with one audience member handing Marinetti a pistol and inviting him to kill himself on stage, while others blew car horns or threw rotten eggs and vegetables. A ritualised slanging match which would have made Diderot rotate in his grave. Platon Kerzhentsev, Proletkult's theoretician of theatre, didn't want people to say 'I am going to see something' but 'I am going to participate in something'; generally didactic retellings of the triumphant progress of the class struggle.[3] Groupe Recherche d'Art Visuel, the Paris-based '6os art collective, wrote a manifesto declaring that audiences should be 'made' to participate, and then solicited passers-by to balance on 'permutational sculptures' reminiscent of soft-play centres. The Argentinian collective who mounted the Cycle of Experimental Art in Rosario in 1968, the year of General Ongania's military coup, made work which 'obliged' audiences 'violently to participate'. In a famous work by Graciela Carnevale, gallery visitors were locked into a room with a shop-front window, and only escaped when a passer-by smashed the glass. The Brazilian director Augusto Boal, acting against the notion that catharsis in classical theatre was merely a means to maintain the status quo, declared, 'I don't want the people to use the theatre as a way of not doing in real life'. These are just some of the more striking of

many calls to action which crowd the pages of *Artificial Hells* – the list is potentially endless, and Bishop certainly brings it up to the present.

So how then does she explain this reversal by which contemplation, and indeed beauty, are relegated and the activation of the spectator turned into an article of faith? Rather than creating any synthetic or developmental analysis, she chooses to concentrate instead on the radical ambivalence of artists' desire to provoke participation in works scattered across the 20th century. Participation metastasises across contexts, always differently inflected and drawing with it a number of contradictions. Be that as it may, the book nevertheless registers a general shift in audience participation from crucial ingredient and aim of revolutionary and radical cultures to state-endorsed language of post-Fordist conformity. Bishop clearly articulates New Labour's 'social inclusion' policies (which she understands, properly, as the rhetorical elision of class and class tensions, used to deflect attention away from the roll-back of the welfare state and the introduction of privatised risk) as a capitalist appropriation of radical culture's fostering of participative self-actualisation. 'To be included and participate in society means to conform to full employment, have a disposable income, and be self-sufficient', she says.[4] What is perplexing though, is that despite fully grasping the political use of participation as euphemism for work, Bishop holds this understanding separate from her reading of the aesthetics of late and postmodernity. The general apotheosis of labour and productivity embodied in modernity, be that capitalist or socialist, isn't sufficiently connected to a reading of the aesthetic apotheosis of participation.

Bishop is also fiercely critical of the parallel appropriation of a once subversive tendency by

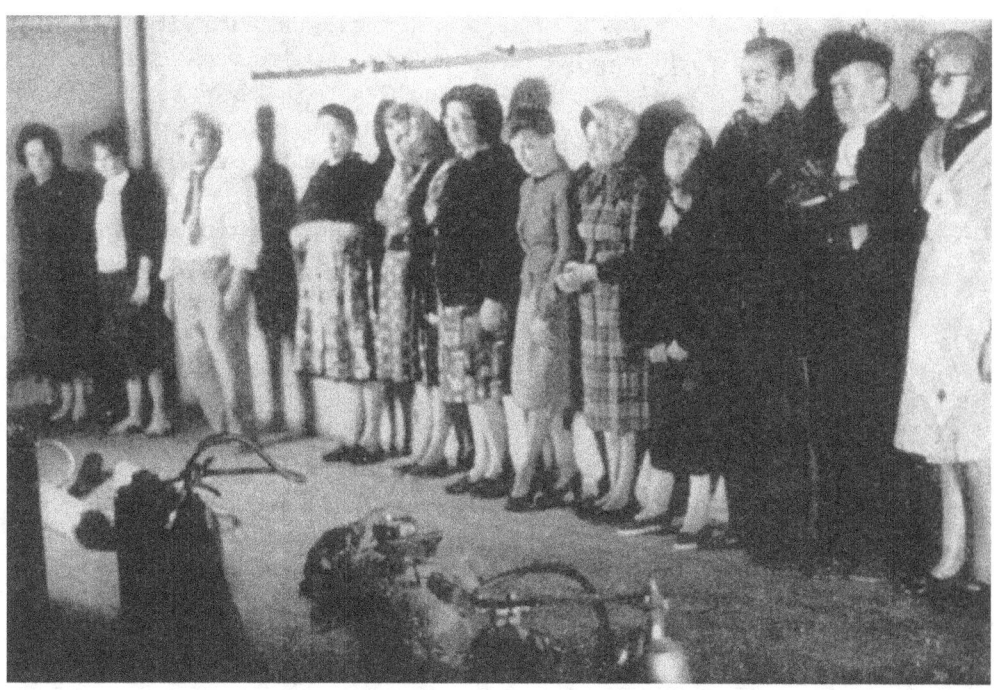

Oscar Massotta, *To Induce the Spirit of the Image*, 1966

a liberal art world which fetishises utilitarian art that operates 'directly' upon social life, producing a manifold of 'modest gestures'. This liberal regime, she claims, tends to a suspicion of aesthetics and aesthetic judgements (something that Bishop repeatedly champions without really explaining what happens to aesthetics when the art work dematerialises into situations nor how judgement might work in post-Duchampian art) and promotes, instead, the 'ethical work'. But this liberal regime doesn't actually go so far as to compare art works with non-art works on a 'scale of effectiveness'. As Bishop observes, art works are only compared with other art works. In this way, it would seem, autonomy is snuck back in through the back door; art continues to coast on its old privileges but can't admit to them. However, she doesn't say this. Instead, Bishop leans heavily on Jacques

Rancière's argument made in his *Malaise dans l'esthetique*. The exemplary ethical gesture in art, she explains via Rancière, works to blur the political and the aesthetic (in ways that seem to repeat the gesture of neoliberalism's call for social inclusion). This is achieved,

> by replacing matters of class conflict with matters of inclusion and exclusion, [contemporary art] puts worries about the 'loss of the social bond', concerns with 'bare humanity' or tasks of empowering threatened identities in the place of political concerns. Art is summoned thus to put its political potentials at work in reframing a sense of community, mending the social bond, etc. Once more, politics and aesthetics vanish together.[5]

Although she says that Rancière's account leans too heavily on Bourriaud's relational

Participation metastasises across contexts, always differently inflected and drawing with it a number of contradictions

aesthetics, and is unfair to much contemporary work, she nevertheless seems satisfied with his account of the depoliticised yet ethical art work.

This easy acceptance could offer another clue to what could uncharitably be described as the missing spine of *Artificial Hells*. By counterposing class conflict as properly political against the toothless ethics of 'bare humanity', it seems that Rancière, and Bishop with him, are missing a key ground of struggle and hence politics – namely 'bare life' and the sphere of necessity itself. Bishop often uses the term 'social justice' when wishing to invoke politics – a term that refers us to a liberal political imaginary of human rights guaranteed, ultimately, by citizenship and the rule of law. A position which is unable to grasp the role of the modern nation state in producing structural exclusions from the sphere of the 'community', let alone that of politics, based on the inherently jingoistic horizon of popular sovereignty; something Foucault calls simply 'state racism'. When sovereignty is distributed to the People who become its referent, the fact of their birth in the territory of the state becomes all important (*nascere*, meaning 'to be born', is also the root of 'nation'). A clue that Giorgio Agamben seizes upon in his exploration of the *biopolitical* nature of modern democracies. While life, now reconfigured as the basis of sovereignty, is in this respect liberated and endowed with rights, it is also brought into the calculus of politics and economics as never before. As Agamben explains, '[modern democracy] wants to put the freedom and happiness of men into play in the very place – "bare life" – that marked their subjection.' Thus for Agamben, the fatal 'aporia' of modern democracy – which cannot endow all life with rights, but wants to decide on *which* life is worthy – gives rise to totalitarian and liberal regimes

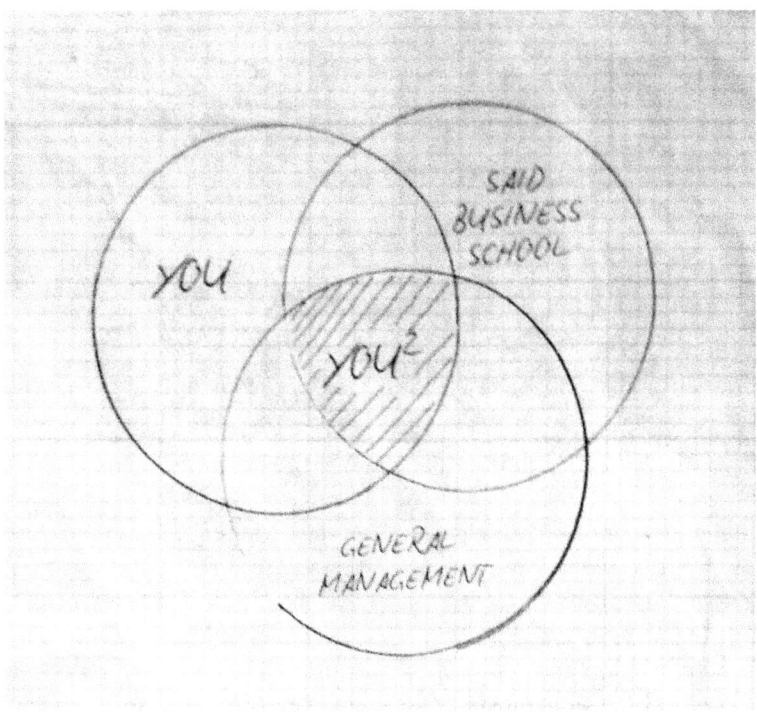

Said Business School advertisement, *Financial Times*, September, 2012

simultaneously. In a related development, the gesture of distributing authorial control into the popular body of the audience could be said to exert a more invasive control over the site of its former subjection – namely the privacy and muteness of contemplation and the spectator's free disposition over their own activity. The elevation of participation, then, seems deeply linked to this redistribution of sovereignty, both in the ubiquity of state-capitalist decisions over deserving and undeserving forms of life, and through the aesthetic conscription of parts of our deserving interiority in the co-production of expression. A sorting activity between subjects, their forms of activity and their internal states which, in the worst cases, is unthinkingly extended by the ethical utilitarianism of relational aesthetics or

repeated, if hopefully with a knowing nod, by the lugubrious integration of living ornaments into the scaffold of ruling class enjoyment.

The participative art discussed in Bishop's book can be found on either side of this border between totalitarianism and liberalism, and much of it likewise contests life's exploitation or valorisation and looks to free it. It is often the work that emerges in the countries where people are apparently less free that, for me at least, proved the most incisive in revealing the increasing state and/or capitalist extension of control over life. The heart of the book, and the way in which it helps to remake the contemporary art map, entails Bishop's surveys of South American art of the late '60s and that of Eastern Europe in the '60s-'80s. In both territories, and in totally different ways, artists

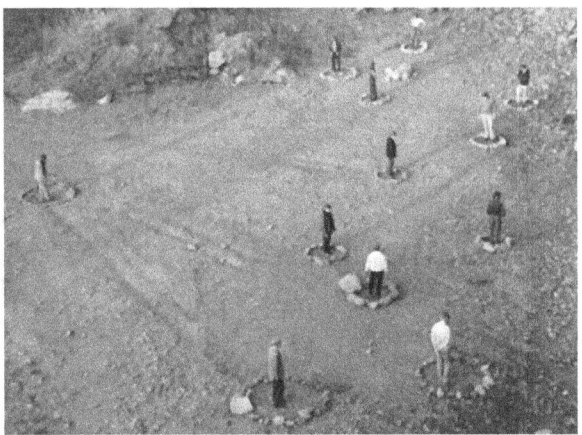

Milan Knížák, *Stone Ceremony*, 1971

opened up the ambivalence of participation, often making today's relational art look naive and unhistorical by comparison.

Targeting the media construction of 'immediacy' and especially the celebration of bohemian happeners, the Argentinian artist Oscar Masotta, running on a heavy dose of post-structuralist theory, formed El Grupo de los Artes de los Medioa Masivos in 1966. Their first decidedly 'cool' work, *Total Participation*, was a spoof event relayed to the media through a series of photographs of revelling hipsters. The pictures were duly printed by the Argentinian press and sensationalised as a *bone fide* event. But if this exposé of the artifice of vitality was both edifying and amusing, the piece *To Induce the Spirit of the Image*, made by Masotta later in the year in the lead up to General Ongania's military coup, stands as one of the most affecting works discussed in this book. The construction of vitality gives way to the exploration of 'living currency', the weighing of life as value. In this piece, 20 elderly people were paid to stand in a storage room in front of an audience, and subjected to fire-extinguishers, a high-pitched noise and blinding white light.

At the beginning of the event, Masotta lectured the audience on control and reminded them that they'd paid 200 pesos to watch, while the performers had been paid 600. In a later text entitled 'I Committed a Happening' Masotta commented: 'I felt as though something had slipped loose without my consent, a mechanism had gone into motion.'[6]

Amongst other things, this motion describes the automatism of exchange value which convinces us that simply everything, even suffering, can be bought and sold. Accepting the spectacle of others' suffering is made to seem reasonable through this logic which has been massaged into our psyches from birth. The commodity form extends n-dimensionally and it hasn't stopped at the human being, whose labour power has long ceased to be the limit of capital's interests. And if everything is coloured by exchange value, then our self-relation is no exception. A truth revealed with its usual brute elegance by the advertising industry in a recent ad for the Said Business School. A Venn diagram of the part of 'you' that also overlaps with the set of 'general manager' is overlaid onto another set which is the business school – an overlap of resources which gives rise to a 'you²'. The regime of human capital and self-appreciation is one in which activity is reversed from the despised lot of slaves to become the aspiration of every self-respecting soul and ethical artist. The problem, both for art and politics, is that

---

'Criteria of success' sounds more like a policy impact assessment exercise than an aesthetic judgement

---

activity both secretes value as well as making art or politics possible at all through the human capacity to begin something, to appear, or to trigger 'social action'. Of course the art world has become the smelting pot of appearance and action, efficiently forging resistant activity into creative capital. Today, it comes as no surprise to see photos of Santiago Sierra's (heavily Masotta inspired) act of 'social sadism' – the tattooing of a single line across a row of paid human backs – in a Barclays Bank sponsored exhibition at Autograph's Rivington Place gallery this summer.[7] Masotta's strategy of making 'social sadism explicit' by redistributing it from the field of state control and capitalist social relations to that of art seems to have become disturbingly ineffectual. Perhaps this is because we regard ourselves as human capital as never before, due in no small part to the appreciation of creativity as an *individual* capacity of the highest worth. Today, social sadism and individualistic creativity have become two sides of the same biopolitical coin.

If the creative economy represents the high water mark of a self-appreciative elevation of activity, then the USSR could be said to have

forked the apotheosis of labour into a distinct but related development. State socialism's religiose celebrations of heroic proletarian productivity were directed towards a non-personal, (inter)national form of appreciation. Undoubtedly these concussive paeans to glorious labour triggered a more reclusive and tentative kind of participative art which took place in apartments, involved surreptitious acts of nomination, hacks of the parcel service, or walks in the countryside. Strangely, given Bishop's critiques of the utilitarianism of the 'ethical' art work that aims to effect 'social change', it is her reading of these more reclusive works that falls furthest of her own mark. Of the Czech artist Milan Knížák, whose work developed from a fluxus-inspired ludic street improvising, through absurdist instructional works to increasingly introspective pieces such as *Stone Ceremony*, she remarks:

> One should resist the temptation to make leftist political claims for this non-conformity: the work sprang from an existential impulse, seeking to generate a territory of free expression, a celebration of idiosyncrasy rather than social equality.[8]

Her counterposing of free expression and social equality reveals the extent to which she seems not to have conceived a politics of the subject, a crucial point of intersection for her parallel exploration of the 'commodification of human bodies in a service economy' and the conscription of participation into politics and art. She compounds this problem by disparaging Knížák's public *Letter to the Population* as 'nonsensical', from which it is hard not to infer that she finds this project too absurd to be 'socially useful'. His instructions such as 'Do not drink at all for 3 days' or 'Commit suicide!' are not allowed the interpretive generosity of perhaps parodying *reasonable* social commands such as those crystallised in the Said Business School ad, or the too beatific instructional works of US fluxus artists like Yoko Ono. Or, more tendentiously, this work could be read as proposing a politics of the 'human strike' *avant la lettre;* something being worked on by artists and political theorists thinking routes out of total reification today. With Knížák's piece *An Event for the Post Office, the Police, and the Occupants of no. 26 Vaclavkova Street, Prague 6, and all Their Neighbours, Relatives and Friends* (1966), she asks: 'What were his criteria of success for such a piece? Since none of the participants actually went to the cinema, did he consider his work to be a failure?'[9] 'Criteria of success' sounds more like a policy impact assessment exercise than an aesthetic judgement.

In *Ten Appearances* (1981), another Soviet piece explored by Bishop, by the Collective Actions Group, a small handful of participants gathered in a field outside Moscow, each holding a string of 2-300 metres attached to a board. They were instructed to walk outwards while unwinding it in different directions towards the forest at the edge of the field. At the end of the thread was a piece of paper bearing a 'factographic' text: the name of the organisers, time, date and place of the action. From here the participants needed to decide for themselves what to do next: some continued walking and got on a train back to Moscow, others rejoined the group. Those who returned were given photographs of themselves appearing from a forest, taken a few weeks earlier, but indistinguishable from this forest. This piece doesn't give rise to 'unified collective experience' writes Bishop, but 'difference, dissensus and debate: a space of privatised experience, liberal democratic indecision, and a plurality of hermeneutical speculation'.[10] She then quotes the group's key theorist, Andrei Monastrysky, explaining how the work's engagement of the participant differs from the 'tunnel vision' of Stalin or Brezhnev era aesthetic contemplation:

> When one comes to a field – when one comes there, moreover, with no sense of obligation but for private reasons of one's own – a vast flexible space is created, in which one can look at whatever one likes. One's under no obligation to look at what's being presented – that freedom, in fact, is the whole idea.[11]

This near concurrence, but ultimate clash, of interpretations reveals both the potentials and shortcomings of *Artificial Hells*. Where the British art theorist apparently wants the same thing as the Russian, namely dissensus as a means to deflect the conscription of art and experience to social programmes, she nevertheless closes down the space of its appearance into liberal-democratic contours in which 'private' is read as 'privatised' and 'whatever one likes' becomes political 'indecision'. In this seemingly slight mutation we can find evidence of a too dualistic reading of interiority as individual, and exteriority as social. If this logic is ramified, it leads to the conclusion that what (not who) we are is the property of ourselves (on which we'd be mad not to speculate), and what can be considered social is that which is divisibly external to the self. At another point Bishop calls this era of Soviet apartment-art 'metapolitical' in Rancière's sense of creating a 'redistribution of the sensible' rather than assuming an 'identifiable (and activist) political position'. What she misses here too is that activist politics has also been working with a 'metapolitical' multiplication of 'private' experience during the same historical time-span, showing not only how 'the personal is political', but also how new publics can be built through the appearance of private experience. In this sense appearance and action as well as self and other become inextricably entwined. And if appearance is in part conditional on the inactivity of private thought as well as an externalisation incited by the web of social relations, then this may also be a route out of the fetishism of a participation for its own sake, that causes nothing but its own being active to appear.

Josephine Berry Slater is editor of *Mute* and co-author with Anthony Iles of *No Room to Move: Radical Art and the Regenerate City*, 2010

INFO

Claire Bishop, *Artificial Hells: Participatory Art and the Politics of Spectatorship*, London and New York: Verso, 2012

FOOTNOTES

1   In classical Greece activity itself was actually considered antithetical to the experience of thought and beauty to which aesthetics belongs. For Aristotle, what distinguishes us humans from our animal counterparts are the ways we are able to live which are free of the work and labour induced by necessity. Unlike the slave, artisan or merchant who had 'lost the free disposition of their movements', the three *bioi* – forms of life enjoyed only by the citizens – were concerned with the beautiful (the life of enjoying bodily pleasures in which the beautiful is consumed, the life devoted to matters of the *polis*, in which excellence produces beautiful deeds and the life of the philosopher devoted to the inquiry into and contemplation of things eternal.) Increasingly in late antiquity, contemplation was isolated and identified as a higher form of (nevertheless bodily) existence distinguished from the *vita activa*; the philosopher, as advocated by Plato, lived in

'complete quiet' and, somewhat enigmatically, it was 'only his body which inhabits the city'. See Hannah Arendt, *The Human Condition*, (1958), Chicago: University of Chicago Press, 1998, p.12 and p.16.

2   See Michael Fried, *Absorption and Theatricality: Painting and Beholder in the Age of Diderot*, Chicago: University of Chicago Press, 1988.

3   Proletkult was a revolutionary arts institution established in Soviet Russia to develop new, revolutionary working class aesthetics worthy of the revolution.

4   Claire Bishop, *Artificial Hells: Participatory Art and The Politics of Spectatorship*, London and New York: Verso, 2012, p.14

5   Rancière, cited in ibid., p.28.

6   Masotta cited in ibid., p.109.

7   Autograph ABP's Roma-Sinti-Kale-Manush, was at Rivington Place, London 25 May - 28 July, 2012.

8   Bishop, op. cit., p.134.

9   The event targeted an apartment building in Prague at random. The residents were subjected to three types of intervention: being sent packages in the post containing oddities such as lumps of bread; being confronted with a strange assortment of objects in the communal parts such as goldfish or unmade beds; and finally being sent free cinema tickets to a movie, where they would ideally sit together due to the seat reservations. Ibid., p.136.

10   Ibid., p.160.

11   Monastyrsky, cited in Bishop, p.160.

LISTENER
AS
OPERATOR (3)

In its encouragement of a group expression that supports musicians to 'play beyond themselves' and to evolve singularities within a shared 'reservoir of artistic richness', HOWARD SLATER finds in jazz a response to the experience of slavery; one that evolved outside channels of sanctioned expression, and which preserves and propels a collective being. This is his third music column for Mute

We are still black
And we have come back

Nous sommes revenus

We have come back
Brought back
to our land Africa
the music of Africa

Jazz is A black power
Jazz is A black power
Jazz is An African power
Jazz is An African music
Jazz is An African music

We Have Come Back

TELLINGLY INARTICULATE (3)

Rough and beautiful in the nobility of coarseness
– Frank London Brown

The above dedication is a verbatim transcript of words spoken as the Archie Shepp set kicks into action at the 1969 Pan-African Festival in Algiers. The music that follows contains a mélange of Shepp's jazz outfit accompanied by Tuareg percussionists and Algerian musicians and singers. At first the speaker of the above dedication continues on with his words listing figures from jazz history, but this verbal honouring of the general intellect of jazz is soon drowned out by a practical rendition of a culture's social wealth. Not an ostentatious display, not a string of solos, but a confluence of intensities backed by an incantatory drumming and the sharp sound of reed flutes. As the rock and pop scenes go global, there is here, at the Pan-African festival, an almost subterranean internationalism. The excitement of 'being back' whilst being welcomed by Algerian musicians is palpable; a meeting point for something more or less inarticulate from the perspective of the prevailing rock scenes of the time. For instance the 12 tone system is rendered inexistent; non-standard pitching thrives and the outlines of the instrumentation, the perspective of background and foreground (especially in the massed percussion), are blurred to the point of amorphous joy.

Collective culture, then, sounds a little like this. It dispenses with the sad articulation of the negative in favour of its being harnessed as a 'drive'. It doesn't seek the con of the quest for perfection. It seeks its motivating succour in a group-process that cannot but re-articulate the negative as the pleasure of disalienation. From Bennie Moten to Duke Ellington to Sun Ra to Shepp's ensemble in 1969, an unquestioned togetherness informs the sound as it merges together singularities in a tone-palate that, as Cedric Robinson has said in reference to the radical black tradition, 'preserves the collective being'.[1] Preserves? Yes, because that tradition has had, in the main, to maintain itself 'outside' those very organisations (such as the Labour Movement) that one would have thought were pre-disposed to it; and, being 'outlandish', its wavering non-admittance could be misrepresented as an impulse towards transcendence rather than a material effect of racism. So, Shepp and Co. sound inarticulate because such a collective culture (here celebrated as a jam session of black consciousnesses across continents) cannot delineate itself as a single bounded institutional entity. They form an assemblage of enunciation that could be said to resist reification by being 'out', by not having to speak articulately. They ignore the discipline enforced by the tenets of 'music', by musically claiming, as Aimé Césaire said in his resignation from the French Communist Party (PCF), the 'right to initiative, the right to personality'.[2]

The right to free jazz. The right to singularity. Claiming these rights and claiming them via the wordless illicity of colliding continents and the partial egocide of a heavy hearing of the other, is to claim that the alienating line between the individual and the collective, is here and in countless other ensemble jazz moments, not so much surpassed but corroborated as non-existent in the first place and preserved in the music of jazz from a moment prior to bourgeois enlightenment. This 'prior moment' (disqualified from 'history') that goes back further than a memory of the land, has been celebrated in the form of musical praxis by such as Duke Ellington who called-out the collective black tradition in such tracks as 'Rhythm Pum Te Dum', and albums like *Liberian Suite* and *Black, Brown and Beige*. Such a musical praxis, from the crafting of the very instruments (the 'banza' or 'strum strum' which eventually becomes the banjo) through 'derisive singing' and the prohibition of slave dances to Ellington's symphonic history writing, makes jazz an ongoing moment of politicised disalienation. It is an implied politics, a praxis that, making its own form as it moves, is often unintelligible. It is tellingly inarticulate because, caught up as

many of us are in the unavoidable pathology of individuality (its inferiority-fears and interior walls), we cannot hear the liberation-from-self as a politicising practice that singularises itself by means of an assemblage (be that, in this case, the jazz ensemble or the black radical tradition), because this would be to similarly face the trauma of psychical placelessness across time; a kind of dispersal to points of inarticulacy where the boundary between self and other dissolves but, and aptly, the 'new' begins.

MUSIC AND AGONY (3)

I am sick of these weeping half-days
– Henry Dumas

In *Black Skin, White Masks* Frantz Fanon offered 'before it can adopt a positive voice, freedom requires an effort at disalienation'.[3] It is an agony to kind of know that 'freedom', like 'love', can take on mythic proportions. These very proportions garner an idealistic hue that further traps us within the painful limits of a bourgeois self. A heavily signposted way out gets blocked. So, the interpellation of aims and ambitions take the form of ego-ideals and the concomitant activation of a de-communalising narcissism not only builds internal walls against a recognition of our interior world as a social-psyche, they ward-off the dangerous outbreak of singularities. Is Fanon's advice to make an effort at disalienation partly connected to arriving at an awareness of our social psyche? To become, as strange as it may sound, disalienated from an individualism that, deep rooted, disbars the notion of a self as already a collective? Free Jazz, without having to articulate a 'politics', seems to effortlessly concur with such propositions.

Such a disalienation is agony enough. One is placeless, no longer the centre of anything.

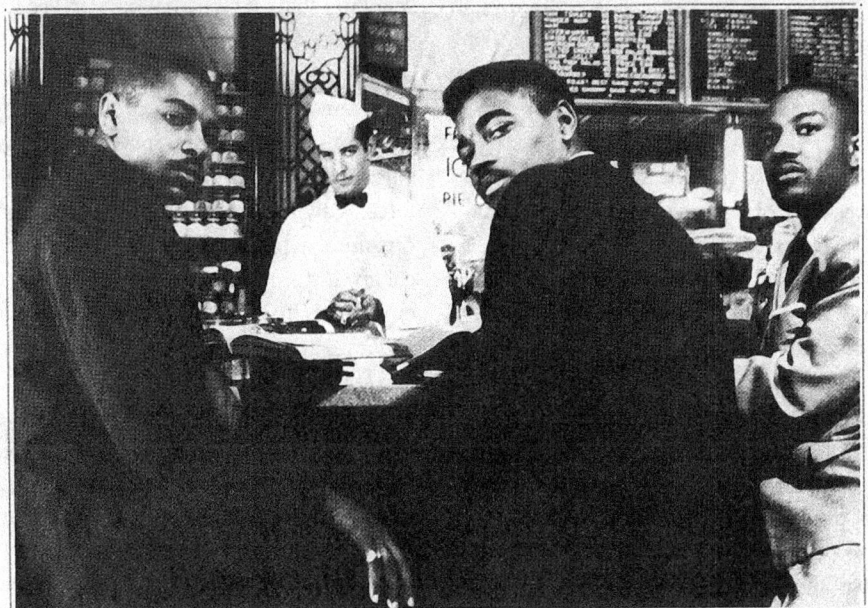

Max Roach, *We Insist! Max Roach's Freedom Now Suite*, 1960

One is interchangeable. One can only labour abstractly. But isn't there in the sound of jazz some supreme overcoming of the temptation to an alienating negativity? Listening to many jazz players it is possible to be enlivened by the very lack of shame of the singularities that are set free by means of the music. Singularities are maybe embraced in the assemblage of jazz not simply as a harnessing of a mythic Dionysian creativity, but as a result of the urge-inducing agony of genocide that Black Codes and then Jim Crow Laws set going in the American South:

> Anyway, when we got there in the woods,
> everyone started crying and turning their heads
> away in horror. I looked up at the man. I knew
> him, yet he was so messed up I could not tell who
> he was. He was naked and they'd put tar on him
> and burnt him.[4]

As hard as it is to write that out it's maybe necessary to have this as backing to our appreciation not just of the spleenage-at-the-reed of players like Ayler and Sanders, but also to honour the supreme effort of jazz musicians to maintain their propellant positivity. More than that, is it not the experience of Jim Crow barbarism that binds these jazz musicians to a collective notion of their self as black from which basis singularising becomes an easier next step to take? A step unfraught by the guilt of standing out and standing up and one that is no longer afraid to express. A hundred years after the 'Emancipation Proclamation' trumpeter and ensemblist Philip Cohran could say: 'We're all denied the privilege of expressing what is in us'.

The knotted agony of not being able to speak up or protest (an inculcated 'terror of the self' as Calvin Hernton refers to it) comes undone and the dam is burst by the mid '60s.

The 'liquid lyric moans', as poet and communist activist Claude McKay describes '20s jazz, are transformed into the guided rage of having so much to say that words are bypassed by the dense emotional simultaneity of free jazz propulsion. That Calvin Hernton, writing of his childhood in the American South, speaks of taking a beating from his grandmother for regularly chatting with a white girl (a danger he could not perceive at the time), and that he talks also of a social life that has to be closely self-monitored down to a control of glances, is just one element of racism's psychic damage that surely must inform free jazz as a disalienating force. Calvin Hernton: 'I am not absolutely certain at what age I became conscious of my colour as a limitation on where I could go, sit, or with whom I could associate.'[5] Such constant vigilance may train the mind in an acuity of perception and contextual sensitivity that, as agonising as it is, could well inform the later ease of a non-fanfared collective awareness and free space for singularities that marks those early '60s assemblages such as Charles Mingus' Jazz Workshop, Sun Ra's Arkestra, Horace Tapscott's Pan Afrikan Peoples Arkestra, the Association for the Advancement of Creative Musicians (AACM) and Philip Cohran's Artistic Heritage Enemble.

JAZZ AND ORGANISATION (1)

Where no one is more alone than any other
– Joseph Jarman

There can be no agonising terror of the self (a block to singularising) when the shared trauma of racist genocide comes to bind you tightly to a collective notion. The same could well be said of exploited classes in general, upon whom is meted out an ongoing psychic damage that ends up in self-loathing, affective insecurity and the internalisation of inferiority (its 'epidermalisation' in the words of Frantz Fanon). These latter can amount to a terror of the self, a terror of subterranean force that can be a serious

---

'Consider a system of politics and art that is fluent, as functional, and as expansive as black music'

---

hindrance to the consistency in any coming together. Whether this supra-personal fragility be dealt with as an isolating retreat or as an appeasement of the terror of the self by recourse to the ideological mediations of a joining up of ego-ideals, the terror can be both repressed through the ongoing act of an 'abstract' belonging as well as projected (as repressed) into forming the wayward unconscious forces of the group. The organisational form that results can come, after Didier Anzieu, to be one that could be described as bearing a 'group illusion': 'There was a desire in the group for a superficial unity to plaster over the contradiction between declared principles and actual behaviour'.[6]

The problem for groups may well lie, then, in these 'declared principles' that become a disconnective abstraction, that determine the meaning of group membership and that give rise, not to singular expressions, but to a guilty vigilance that comes from conformity. Throughout the history of jazz, save for the sizeable Pan-African and Black Nationalist political hue of the '60s, there has been scant recognition of its ensemble practice as providing methods and means of organisation for political movements. Larry Neal, viewed as a co-founder of the Black Arts Movement,

still had cause, in the 1980s, to bemoan this and urged his readers to 'consider [...] a system of politics and art that is fluent, as functional, and as expansive as black music'.[7] Perhaps a factor in this lack of fluency is the blockage created by the subterranean persistence of, as Fanon said, self-evaluatory comparison and the quest to fulfil the ego-ideal. In other words the persistence within organisations of forms of bourgeois individualism (personal merit and self-fulfillment) mediated by organisational forms that militate against what Aimé Césaire called for as he resigned from the PCF: 'the deepening and co-existence of all particulars'.

From swing to the be-bop era, the space to solo, to singularise within the assemblage, was given to all musicians in the combo. Extemporisation around a theme (or in other parlance, playing with particles of the general intellect of the 'standard') enables these particulars to be co-extensive with other particulars. In the world of free jazz one could say that the mélange of particulars (simultaneous soloing) forms the universal itself! So, what to many ears, say in the Archie Shepp track mentioned above, is a mess, is not only an un-recouperable mess (deliberately inarticulate), it is the sound of the overcoming of a terror of the self by means of creating together the incomparable through which the question of merit does not arise. Neither does it seem that the contradiction between declared principles and actual behaviour arises: the principles aren't 'declared' but outline a problem of action. So, in the 1969 track we are not listening to a 'group illusion' that stems from the fear of 'wrongness' and ambivalence, but to an almost definite disalienation that, being a group effort, does not have to 'watch itself'. Here improvisation adds to rather than detracts from the ad-hoc organisational form as the 'indefiniteness of not knowing how the music is going to sound' is a non-declaration of principles, but yet is a declaration of co-existent singularities attempting disalienation by means of the jazz ensemble and its historical perserverance.[8]

By the late '60s it could be perhaps remarked upon that the era of combo, the steady line-up group (i.e. Coltrane's classic quartet, Coleman's too) were being replaced by looser, ad-hoc, almost nomadic, groupings of musicians and a temporary assembling when studio time was being paid for. The form of organisation of the swing era, the big band with its large personnel and long-term performance engagements, was maybe, after the 1944 Cabaret Tax, becoming less viable. The be-bop combo could be said, as Will Menter mentions, to replace the band leader/arranger with a lead soloist and an 'equal opportunity' to solo (rather than maintain the backing riff so elegantly scored as tone-parallels by Duke Ellington). This form of the combo was adopted by the likes of Ornette Coleman and John Coltrane, but they began to break up this form of organisation by adding to their combos and, as with their large ensemble pieces ('Free Jazz' and 'Ascension' respectively), there was a step, as with Mingus, Max Roach and Sun Ra, into re-articulating the backing-riff of the big band, but this time atonally: an 'inarticulate' and confident move that, at the threshold of the civil rights movement, tells of an organising rise in black political consciousness. So, it is not like there is some supercession of organisational forms as we are wont to believe by a system that would rather have us forget, but an infusement of a collective tradition in which the general intellect figures as, after Cedric Robinson, an 'ontological totality'.

However, if we focus on the late '60s and this sense of the ad-hoc session we are maybe in the realm of the meeting of singularities that bring with them an instilled and moveable collective awareness: an 'ontological totality' of belonging to a history that is shareable and shared-in. At his first 'audition' for the AACM in Chicago, Wadada Leo Smith reports that he was playing together in an ensemble with other musicians and then one by one his fellow players stepped down and began talking in a huddle, leaving Wadada to play alone. One could say that in this moment Wadada was left with the terror of the self as well as being made aware that, as far as the AACM was concerned, there was no 'group illusion' in the AACM; that 'declared principles' and 'actual behaviour' would be resolved by a singular praxis within a collective assemblage (that 'Together Alone' is the title of an LP by AACM members Joseph Jarman and Anthony Braxton is perhaps testament that they had a similar experience to Wadada Leo Smith). Such an experience seems to suggest that as an individual player you are nothing special, but as an individual player you have to have the confidence in your instrument and its place in the tradition: you have to be able to singularise without becoming an individualist (be prepared to improvise-amidst) and to be a member of the AACM without losing your particularity (play to enhance another's score). Such an incomplete musing may be an example of the functional fluency that Larry Neal was calling to be more widely applied as a politics.

JAZZ AND ORGANISATION (2)

How do individuals enter into composition with one another?
– Gilles Deleuze

Ongoing debates about spontaneity and organisation, about structure and structurelessness, can maybe be tempered by the example of such

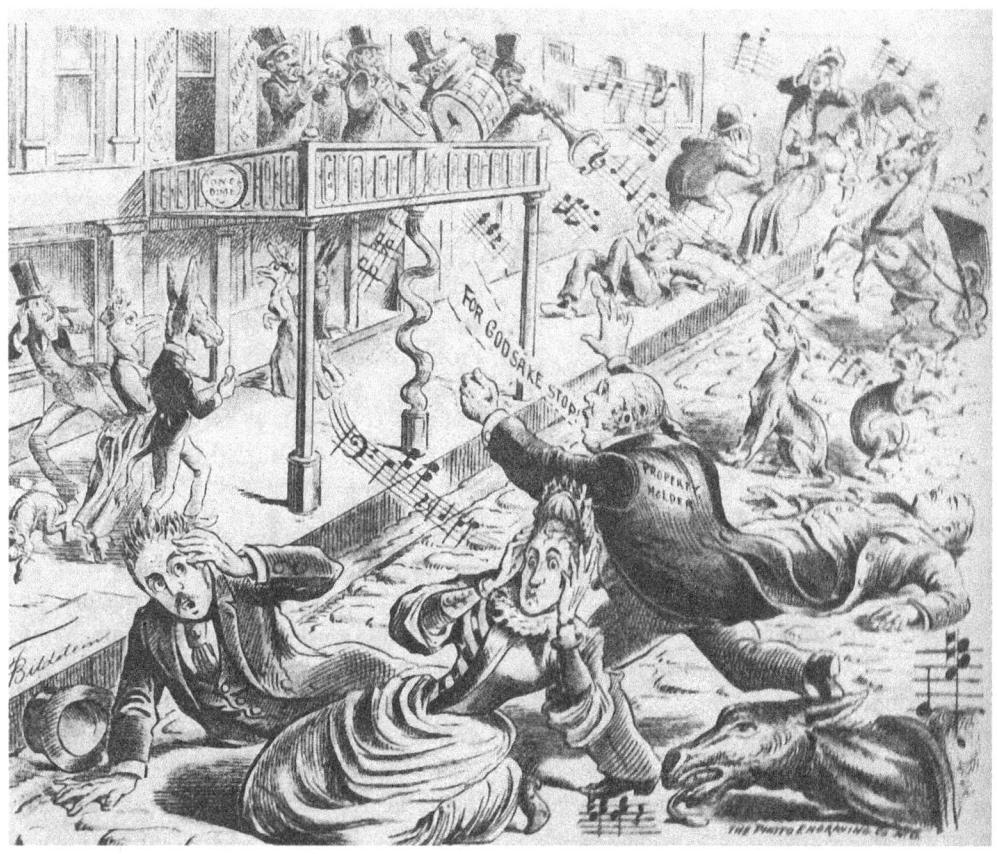

Earliest known image of a jazz band. The cover of New Orleans newspaper *The Mascot*, 15 November, 1890.
'Robinson's Band Plays Anything'

organisations as the AACM. The AACM has been noted for the special place it allots to both composition and improvisation. One seems not to be valued over the other and it's maybe that there is a synthesis in AACM practice that leads us in the direction that Larry Neal urged. That said, any synthesis is not visible as a 'declared principle', but as a singular praxis that differs from Roscoe Mitchell to Muhal Richard Abrams to Anthony Braxton to Wadada Leo Smith; all of whom, Will Menter informs us, have developed their own notation systems and ways of using notation within improvisation (composing themselves). This goes against the grain of hearing in free jazz a pure visceral spontaneity as some level of organised sound is sought-after by those who learned through the AACM. However, it seems to be that the improvisatory element is that which brings through the 'emotional counterpoint' that, in a sense, brings in the 'non-accordant sounds' of the tellingly inarticulate that is at the roots of the black jazz tradition. When Wadada Leo Smith spoke recently of his work with an orchestra on his *Ten Freedom Summers*, he reported that in order to bring flexibility to the orchestral players he

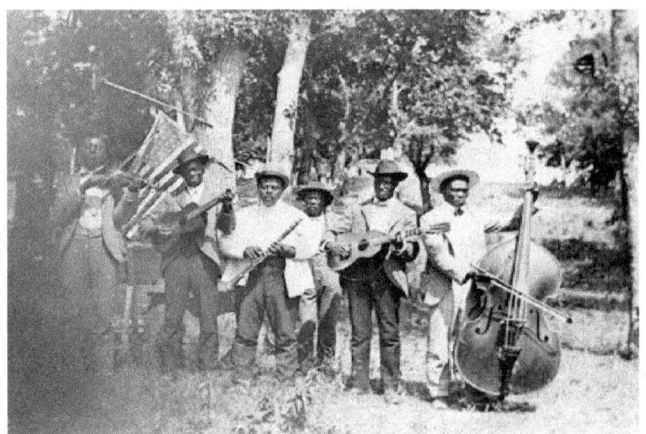

Oldest known photograph of a Juneteenth celebration, Austin, Texas, 1900

wrote music that was impossible to play: 'My instruction to them was while you're playing this and you cannot completely play it correctly, keep going forward. At some point it's going to breakdown completely – at that point you're improvising'.[9]

In terms of organisation it is the emotional counterpoint, an attention given to the terror of the self, that gets lost amidst the declared principles of the group; the struggle to express articulately enough that, without recourse to the 'tellingly inarticulate' (the breakdown of the playing) makes us give up trying to speak (or more aptly, give up trying to 'play') beyond ourselves. In his discussion of Roscoe Mitchell's 'Little Suite', Will Menter offers that what marks out this piece (and it applies to other pieces by AACM members) is that 'it sounds spontaneous overall, even though one is aware that it must have been substantially pre-structured.'[10] He goes on to suggest that this is achieved through 'ensuring musicians oriented their playing towards the *growing music* as opposed to individual expression' (my emphasis). Perhaps one cannot discount that both are in operation as 'individual expression' is not placed in the

service of a bravura performance (the sections of this piece are too small and collage-like), but in service of the partially structured score that is information as the piece progresses through time. However, the organisational advantage that can be gleaned, and which Menter mentions in relation to Mitchell, is that 'a method of distancing has been developed which meant that no longer must every sound that was made be taken at face value as a serious personal or collective expression'. These latter two, the 'face value' of individualism and its competition for recognition and the pathology of its illusory 'supercession' through group membership alone, are the bane of organisations as they can still be experienced.

WE DARE TO SING (2)

What we could not say openly we expressed in music
– Duke Ellington

This modulation of improvisation and composition, of what was formally instinctual and impulsive being acted upon and informing a grounding structure, does not so much mean that either one is replaced by the other, but that when both are taken together there is an expansion of the 'ontological totality'. There is, as Cedric Robinson puts it, a 'breaking of the evolutionist chain'.[11] Instead of succession and development that pampers the bourgeois logic of hierarchies and linearity, instead of a carpetbagging there is a contributing-to, in this case, the black radical tradition that is jazz. Muhal Richard Abrams urged his collaborants in the AACM to 'add copiously to an already vast reservoir of artistic richness handed down through the ages.'[12] Such 'adding-to' resonates with the distancing necessary to elude bourgeois individualism whilst at the same time liberating expressive and 'impersonal' singularities. A fine example of this can be heard on Arthur Doyle's solo sax and vocal rendition of the '40s tune 'Nature Boy'. Whilst much of what's being said here is far better expressed by Arthur Doyle is it not by such means, a 'preserving the collective being', that the guilt of self-expression is appeased? Is it the 'ontological totality', the belonging to something multi-personal and meta-categorical, that can dare us to sing?

Richard Wright wrote of jazz as the 'rhythmic flaunting of guilt feelings' and Calvin Hernton wrote that 'each in our idiom hold the nightmare of our singularity'.[13] Both Wright and Hernton (as members of a radical intelligentsia) seem to me to be expressing something that a replenishing jazz tradition helped them to overcome. For Wright in the '40s and '50s it may well be that the voiceless and inferiorised have no 'right' to express themselves and those that 'dare to sing' do so, but yet feel guilty to transgress both the taboo on their expression from a racist society and from being misconstrued as trying to escape from their own communities (c.f. Charlie Parker and heroin). For Calvin Hernton, on the other hand, the '60s seem to throw up the sense that the terror of the self (its traumatic disalienation) is what both inspires and holds back self-expression as a process of singularisation. There is a massive risk, Hernton seems to be saying, in expressing yourself within a bourgeois context that tempts one to lose oneself through what Aimé Césaire refers to as 'walled segregation in the particular or dilution in the universal.'[14]

But this singularity is no nightmare when it takes as its ground the multiplicities that have formed it and with which it communicates. That the jazz ensemble figures as a collective assemblage of enunciation from which some dare guiltlessly to sing is a testament to the preservation of a collective being that contains within it the attempt to disalienate. This attempt is made almost unavoidable because of the abreactive proviso to much jazz playing. Nat Hentoff says of Charlie Mingus that 'he expected his men to learn their parts through what their own feelings tell them about the music'. This isn't a technique of playing the right notes but, as an abreaction of feeling, it's maybe more a matter of playing between notes and, as a player, bringing to the 'part' the unwritten states of feeling that cannot yet be named. This shared abreactive premise to the music, audible as plaintive anger and rough sonority on Mingus' 'Faubus Fables', may make it possible to say that 'individual expression' as such is annulled in favour of processes of singularisation that can be expressed as simply as in these words of AACM member Fred Anderson: 'All music is basically the same, but what makes it different is different cats have different ways of speaking and communicating'[15] These different ways could be the source of guilt, the 'nightmare of our singularity', in that without the abreaction of feeling they can become aids to separation, but they are also the challenge of performing and enacting a complex communication (a modulation of feeling) whereby neither is dominated nor subsumed by the other, but complemented and encouraged to make a composition of the assemblage, to be disappearing in the elasticity of a form. If we dare to sing we may find that the structure no longer expresses us, but that we, instead, come to form an assemblage, a reiterative structure that is expressive of us: the anonymous singularising solo of the general intellect.

Howard Slater <howard.slater@gmail.com> is a volunteer play therapist and writer. His book, *Anomie/ Bonhomie & Other Writings*, was published by Mute Books in January 2012.

APPENDIX ONE

Tellingly Inarticulate

In his sleeve notes to Max Roach's *We Insist! Freedom Now!* Nat Hentoff records that there was an impromptu squawk from Coleman Hawkins' tenor sax on the track 'Driva Man'. Hawkins is reported as saying: 'No don't splice it… when it's all perfect, especially in a piece like this, there's something very wrong'. This track sung by Abbey Lincoln with lyrics from Oscar Brown Jr. is still seen as one of the more forthright political jazz records of any day:

> Git to work and root that stump,
> driva man will make you jump.
> Better make your hammer ring
> Driva man'll start to swing
> Ain't but two things on my mind
> Driva man and quittin' time.
>
> When his cat-o-nine tails flies
> You'll be happy just to die

This record was out around the time of the Greensboro student sit-in in 1960 and was released on Candid, an independent record label. Another strong statement was made by Charles Mingus on his 'Faubus Fables'

track. This latter features an ongoing call and response between Mingus and drummer Danny Richmond:

> CM: Name me a handful that's ridiculous, Dannie Richmond.
> DR: Faubus, Rockefeller, Motherfucking Eisenhower.
> CM: Why are they so sick and ridiculous?
> DR: Two, four, six, eight: they brainwash and teach you hate.

Yet again Hentoff writes up in his sleeve notes for this album a comment made by Eric Dolphy: 'I play the notes that would not ordinarily be said to be in a given key, but I hear them as proper'. The squawk, the non-key, the emotional counterpoint, proper.

APPENDIX 2

We Dare to Sing

A great song arose, the liveliest thing born this side of the seas. It was a new song. It did not come from Africa, though the dark throb and beat of that Ancient of Days was in it and through it. It did not come from white America – never from so pale and hard and thin a thing, however deep those vulgar and surrounding tones had driven. Not the Indies nor the hot South, the cold East or the heavy West made that music. It was a new song and its deep and plaintive beauty, its great cadences and wild appeal wailed, throbbed and thundered on the world's ears with a message seldom voiced by man. It swelled and blossomed like incense, improvised and born anew out of an age old past, and weaving into its texture the old and new melodies in word and in thought.
– W.E.B. Du Bois

APPENDIX 3

Jazz and Organisation

> each man-string
> doing his own thing
> vibrating at the
> each-to-each volume
> sounding at the
> each-to-each pitch
> all being heard
> at the same time

no one pushing
no one behind
each knowing each's
rhythm and sign
– Henry Dumas, except from 'Greatness'

APPENDIX 4

Music and Agony

Hair – braided chestnut,
    coiled like a lyncher's rope,
Eyes – faggots,
Lips – old scars, or the first red blisters,
Breath – the last sweet scent of cane,
And her slim body, white as the ash
    of black flesh after flame
– Jean Toomer, 'Portrait in Georgia'

DISCOGRAPHY

Didier Anzieu, *The Group and the Unconscious*, London: Routledge & Keegan Paul, 1984.
Anthony Braxton & Joseph Jarman, *Together Alone*, Delmark 1974/2008.
Aimé Césaire, 'Letter to Maurice Thorez' in Salah M. Hassan, *Documenta (13)*, 2012.
John Coxon in conversation with the Author.
Gilles Deleuze, *Spinoza: Practical Philosophy*, San Francisco: City Lights, 2001
Arthur Doyle, 'Nature Boy' at http://www.youtube.com/watch?v=z6l6rAyZeN8
W.E.B. Du Bois, *Black Reconstruction in America 1860-1880*, New England: Free Press 1998
Henry Dumas, *Knees of a Natural Man*, New York: Thunder's Mouth Press, 1989.
Frantz Fanon, *Black Skin, White Masks*, London: Paladin 1973.
Calvin C. Hernton, *Sex and Racism*, London: Paladin 1969.
Calvin C. Hernton, *Medicine Man*, New York: Reed Canon and Johnston, 1976.
Claude McKay, *Selected Poems*, Mineola: Dover, 1999.
Will Menter: *The Making of Jazz and Improvised Music: Four Musicians' Collectives in England and the USA*, PhD Thesis, University of Bristol, 1981.
Charles Mingus, *Mingus Presents Mingus*, New York: Candid, 1960/1989.
Ken Rattenbury, *Duke Ellington: Jazz Composer*, Boston: Yale University Press, 1990.

Max Roach, *We Insist! Freedom Now Suite*, New York: Candid, 1960/1989.
Cedric J. Robinson, *Black Marxism: The Making of the Black Radical Tradition*, Chapel Hill, NC.: University of North Carolina Press, 2000.
Franklin Rosemont & Robin D.G. Kelley, *Black, Brown and Beige – Surrealist Writings from Africa and the Diaspora*, Austin: University of Texas, 2009.
Jean Toomer, *Collected Poems*, University of North Carolina Press, 1988.
Archie Shepp, *Live at the Pan-African Festival*, Get Back, 1969/2002.

FOOTNOTES

1 Cedric J. Robinson, *Black Marxism: The Making of the Black Radical Tradition*, Chapel Hill, NC.: University of North Carolina Press, 2000, p.171.
2 Aimé Césaire, 'Letter to Maurice Thorez' in Salah M. Hassan, Documenta (13), 2012, p.36.
3 Frantz Fanon, *Black Skin, White Masks*, London: Paladin 1973, p.165.
4 Calvin C. Hernton, *Sex and Racism*, London: Paladin 1969, p.99.
5 Calvin C. Hernton, ibid., p.55.
6 Didier Anzieu, *The Group and the Unconscious*, London: Routledge & Keegan Paul, 1984, p.149.
7 Franklin Rosemont & Robin D.G. Kelley, *Black, Brown and Beige – Surrealist Writings from Africa and the Diaspora*, Austin: University of Texas, 2009, p.240.
8 Ornette Coleman in Franklin Rosemont & Robin D.G. Kelley, ibid., p.128.
9 Ben Beaumont-Thomas, 'Ishmael Wadada Leo Smith: "The black experience is American experience"', *The Guardian*, 23 September 2012, http://www.guardian.co.uk/music/2012/sep/23/ishmael-wadada-leo-smith-int...
10 Will Menter: *The Making of Jazz and Improvised Music: Four Musicians' Collectives in England and the USA*, PhD Thesis, University of Bristol, 1981, p.138.
11 Cedric J. Robinson, op. cit., p.276.
12 Will Menter, op. cit., p.100.
13 Cedric J. Robinson, op. cit., p.302; and Calvin Hernton, *Medicine Man*, New York: Reed Canon and Johnston 1976 p.51.
14 Aimé Césaire, op. cit., p.38.
15 Will Menter, op. cit., p. 21.

John Houck, *Untitled #m001 - #m011*,
2,325,600 combinations of 16 grays, 2013

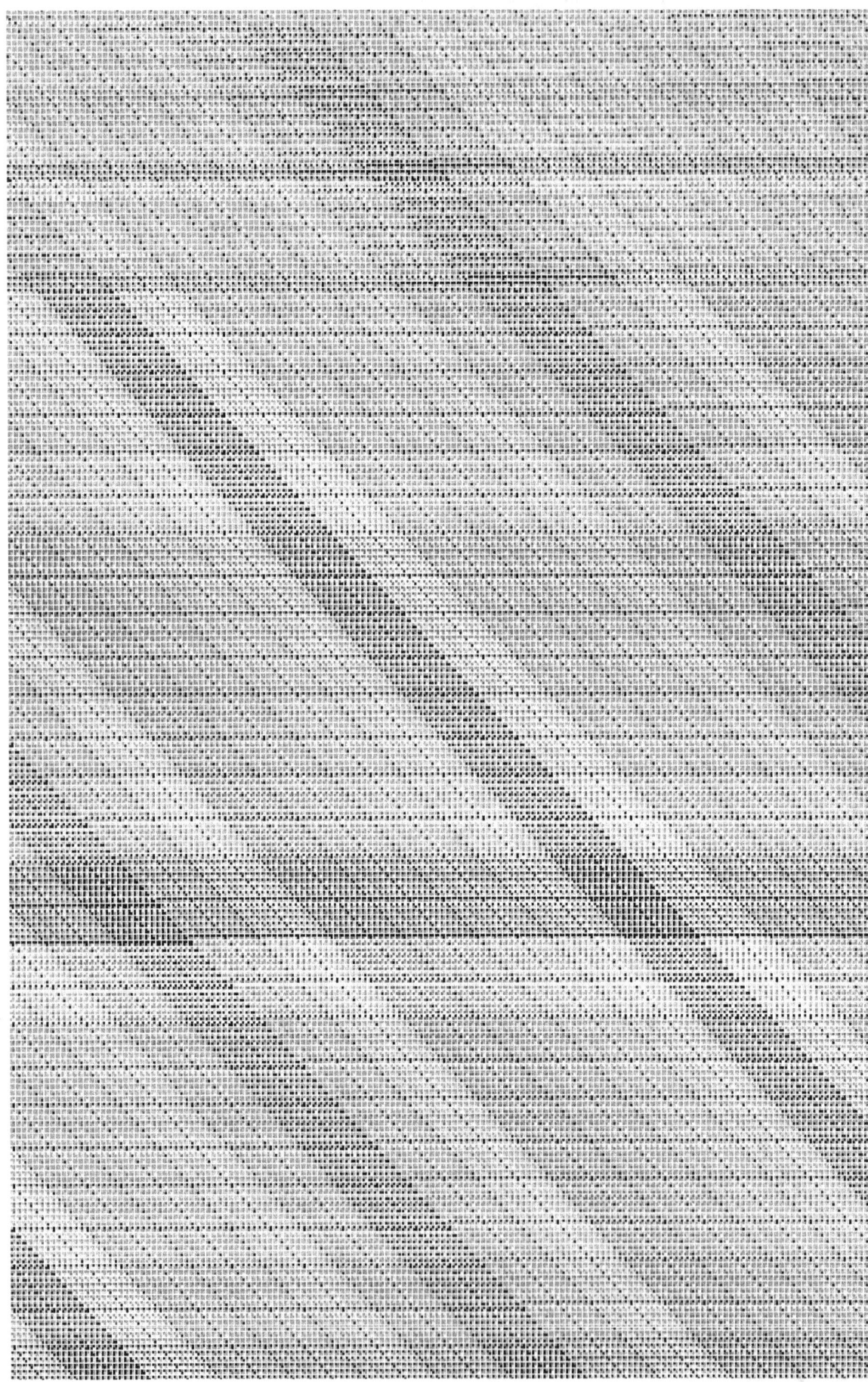

GAMING THE PLUMBING: HIGH-FREQUENCY TRADING AND THE SPACES OF CAPITAL

While high frequency trading is often mystified as capitalism's immaterial transcendence, an all-out war is raging to overcome spatial and material frictions in the pursuit of sub-millisecond advantages. <u>ALBERTO TOSCANO</u> *inspects the gap between the financial fantasies and muddy realities of the 'robot phase transition'*

THE DEATH AND REBIRTH OF REPRESENTATION OUT OF THE SPIRIT OF FINANCE

The inscrutable, abstract subsumption of life by finance seems to have become a matter of everyday experience, the anxious perception of causalities and constraints beyond our understanding and response. This state of affairs can only be intensified by hyped and hectic news of the 'algorithmic revolution' which has made it possible for automated high-frequency trading (HFT) to rapidly corner 77 percent of the volume of transactions on the UK market and 73 percent of the US market, by some estimates.[1] Mathematical instruments of formidable complexity and mutability, exchange velocities that demand the application of relativity theory to financial markets, catastrophic events (the 'flash crash' of 6 May 2010) that stymie explanation – for many, automated algorithmic trading has turned into the very paradigm of speculation as dystopia. Inevitably, the dystopia has also inspired its fascinated coterie of anti-humanist boosters, celebrating the coming singularity, the rise of the machines, information as substance become subject. For a phenomenon whose material and mathematical dynamics so resist figuration, it is perhaps symptomatic that it periodically calls forth representations which principally serve to reiterate its black-boxed menace and aura.[2]

Discussions of HFT are often accompanied by graphic presentations of the operations of particular algorithms, with their geometric periodicities, or of jagged trends in the overall volume of algorithmically controlled buy and sell orders.[3] The effort to diagram and envision capital has a long genealogy, and it has been plausibly argued that different representational orders have successively shaped dominant conceptions of the economy, beginning with the 'zigzag' of Quesnay's *tableau économique* which,

> if properly understood, cuts out a whole number of details, and brings before your eyes certain closely interwoven ideas which the intellect alone would have a great deal of difficulty in grasping, unravelling and reconciling by the method of discourse.[4]

The *tableau* thus allowed for a kind of synchronic totalisation of temporal and material movements, which a sequential, *narrative* account of production would be incapable of figuring. From the *tableau* to the physical models of the economy, representation has arguably been at the core of the making of the economy.[5]

But these activities of modeling, diagramming and envisioning are representational in what is perhaps a counter-intuitive sense, since they break with a model of representation as mirror, photograph, correlation. They are, *pace* Donald MacKenzie, engines *and* cameras, or camera-engines.[6] As representations of practically abstract processes and relations, they are also representations of invisibilities. What is it that we see in fact, when we 'see' the economy? In Buck-Morss' account of Adam Smith's vision

This elision of the social is nigh-on total in the case of HFT

of the market in *The Wealth of Nations*, only the results ('invisible except in its commodity effects'); from them, by induction, we are to posit the underlying, generative process: the division of labour. In Buck-Morss' gloss: 'We see only the material evidence of the fertile process of the division of labor: the astounding multiplication of objects produced for sale. Commodities pile up [...]'.[7]

The shift between different regimes of economic practice can also be traced in terms of styles of envisioning, which is also to say of forms of abstracting – in the sense of selecting, extracting, and shaping material for cognition and action. Indeed, Buck-Morss traces an increasing formalisation and stylisation in the movement from classical political economy to neoclassical economics, which is both inscribed in and impelled by an alternative representational regime. We can then in a sense 'read off' the politics of neoclassical economics from its relation to visual display:

> Neoclassical economics is microeconomics. Minimalism is characteristic of its visual display. In the crossing of the supply-demand curve, none of the substantive problems of political economy are resolved, while the social whole simply disappears from sight. Once this happens, critical reflection on the exogenous conditions of a 'given' market situation becomes impossible, and the philosophy of political economy becomes so theoretically impoverished that it can be said to come to an end.[8]

This elision of the social is nigh-on total in the case of HFT. The algorithm as a representation that is itself productive – in other words, a *rule*, and an evolving one at that – can of course be frozen, but in ways that tell the layperson nothing. The jagged geometry of Michael Najjar's digital correction of Argentinian mountains into the peaks and troughs of the markets in his *High Altitude*, that 'subprime sublime', or the dead screens of high-frequency trading photographed and re-installed by Beate Geissler and Oliver Sann, are ciphers of our incomprehension more than visual articulations of relations open to cognition and intervention.[9]

If HFT appears as a terminal case of the impossibility of cognitive mapping from one angle, it can also be seen, in its self-generated utopia of algorithms that would react at the speed-of-light to global events (which, needless to say, have to be measured and formatted as instantaneous, itself a momentous conceit), as the fantasy of a world innervated by information, ceaselessly mapping and remapping itself. Scott Patterson's pacy tale of the rise of AI finance, *Dark Pools*, tells of Kinetic Global Markets, a start-up hedge fund in NY's attempt to integrate Big Data into light-speed finance:

As computers spread across the world, more and more information was available about... well, *everything.* Shipping trends in the Persian Gulf. The amount of wheat grown in Kazakhstan. Rainfall in British Columbia. Birth rates in Latin America. Oil shipments in the Strait of Hormuz. The list was endless. One fact was clear: The human mind could never process the Big Data. But a computer, perhaps? And perhaps, a Big Data trading machine could troll the Web and other data systems and discover patterns, *untold patterns.* Those patterns, if all worked as planned, could provide signals that a machine could use to buy and sell stocks for a massive profit'.[10]

Or consider the proposal by MIT academics Alex Wissner-Gross and Cameron Freer to scatter the planet with 'optimal intermediate locations between trading centers', leading to

this science-fictional scenario of a terraforming, inhuman distributed finance:

unmanned pods of densely packed microprocessors overseen by next-generation AI Bots processing billions of orders streaming out of unmanned AI pods positioned optimally around the world, the silent beams of high-frequency orders shifting trillions across the earth's oceans at light speeds, all automated, beyond the scope of humans to remotely grasp the nature of the transactions'.[11]

Curiously for Wissner-Gross himself the financial terraforming turns out to be an instrument for making 'our planet smarter', financing integrated knowledge systems capable of modeling and coping with climate change, for example. What from one angle appears as a catastrophe of representation, emerges from another as its plethoric utopia.

THE SOCIAL LIFE OF ALGORITHMS

Among the virtues of the contemporary sociology of finance, with its roots in actor-network theory (ANT) and science and technology studies (STS), has been to counter the visions of homogeneity and dematerialisation that drive many of the technophilic and technophobic, utopian and dystopian visions of phenomena like HFT. Recently, Donald MacKenzie and his collaborators have been particularly thorough in refuting the superficial perception of the algorithmic revolution in finance as the demise of agency, history and matter. To the contrary, an investigation of the genesis of financial automation, sensitive to the multiple conflicts and contingencies that governed the emergence of the particular material, political and economic arrangement of HFT out of specific institutions like the

Chicago Mercantile Exchange shows the traces of those power-struggles and the ineliminable differences and specificities that continue to command what to the outsider might appear as the inevitable outcome of a linear technological development.[12] The bodily space of the pit leaves its marks even in the most impersonal of rules. A market algorithm isn't simply an automated rule, it is also a 'social space', a device that is both conditioned and conditioning. Mechanisation is not a uniform process, but the outcome of a contest of knowledges and strategies. I will turn in a moment to what this foregrounding of the contingent history of finance elides, but I wish first to dwell on the manner in which MacKenzie and his co-authors home in on HFT as an object-lesson in the materiality and spatiality of finance.

As processing power and speed gain paramount significance, the customs, networks and hierarchies that governed market-making on the trading pit are increasingly shifted to the search for competitive advantage at the level of the fixed capital of finance: the data centres that provide co-location for companies wishing to reduce to zero their distance from the matching engines linking buy and sell orders, the fibre-optic cables laid through the Allegheny mountains to shave 3 milliseconds off the speed of a transaction between New York and Chicago, at a cost of a 100 million per millisecond. In a financial domain whose operations are difficult to qualify as anything but 'unproductive' we nevertheless encounter, in hypertrophic guise, the lineaments of a Marxian general intellect in which the social brain of science turns human labour into an appendage tasked with oversight (in the case of the 'flash crash', to those responsible for pushing the button or pulling the plug). The 'algorithmic revolution' could thus also be seen as a phase-shift in the organic

composition of finance, curiously a domain that had fiercely resisted the depersonalisation and deskilling of labour like few others.[13] This devaluation of the embodied knowledge of the pits is the obverse of the valuation of bleeding-edge knowledge in physics, mathematics and the 'plumbing' of markets – confirming after a fashion Georg Simmel's link between the dominion of money and the hegemony of the 'intellect'.[14] Similarly, the annihilation of space by time – of which HFT seems a paragon – is the other side of a reassertion of the significance of the spatial infrastructures of capitalism, and of the monopolies that 'naturally' accrue to them.

MacKenzie et al. approach these transformations through the notion, drawn from Carruthers and Stinchcombe's economic sociology, of the 'social structure of liquidity': market liquidity being conceived here as requiring continuous competitive auction, market-makers willing to price and transfer large quantities of stocks for a small margin, and the legal-technical formatting of homogeneous commodities. One of the tasks of the sociology of markets would thus be to excavate the conditions of possibility of such liquidity, its character as a complex and contested achievement. HFT provides the occasion for MacKenzie et al. to stress, with respect to what appears at first glance as the most mathematically abstract and immaterial of financial innovations, the material nature of markets:

> A price is not an abstraction: to be conveyed from one human being to another, or from one automated system to another, a price must take a material form, whether that be the sound waves created by speech, the electrical signals of the telegraph or telephone, or the optical signals that now flow through high-speed networks.[15]

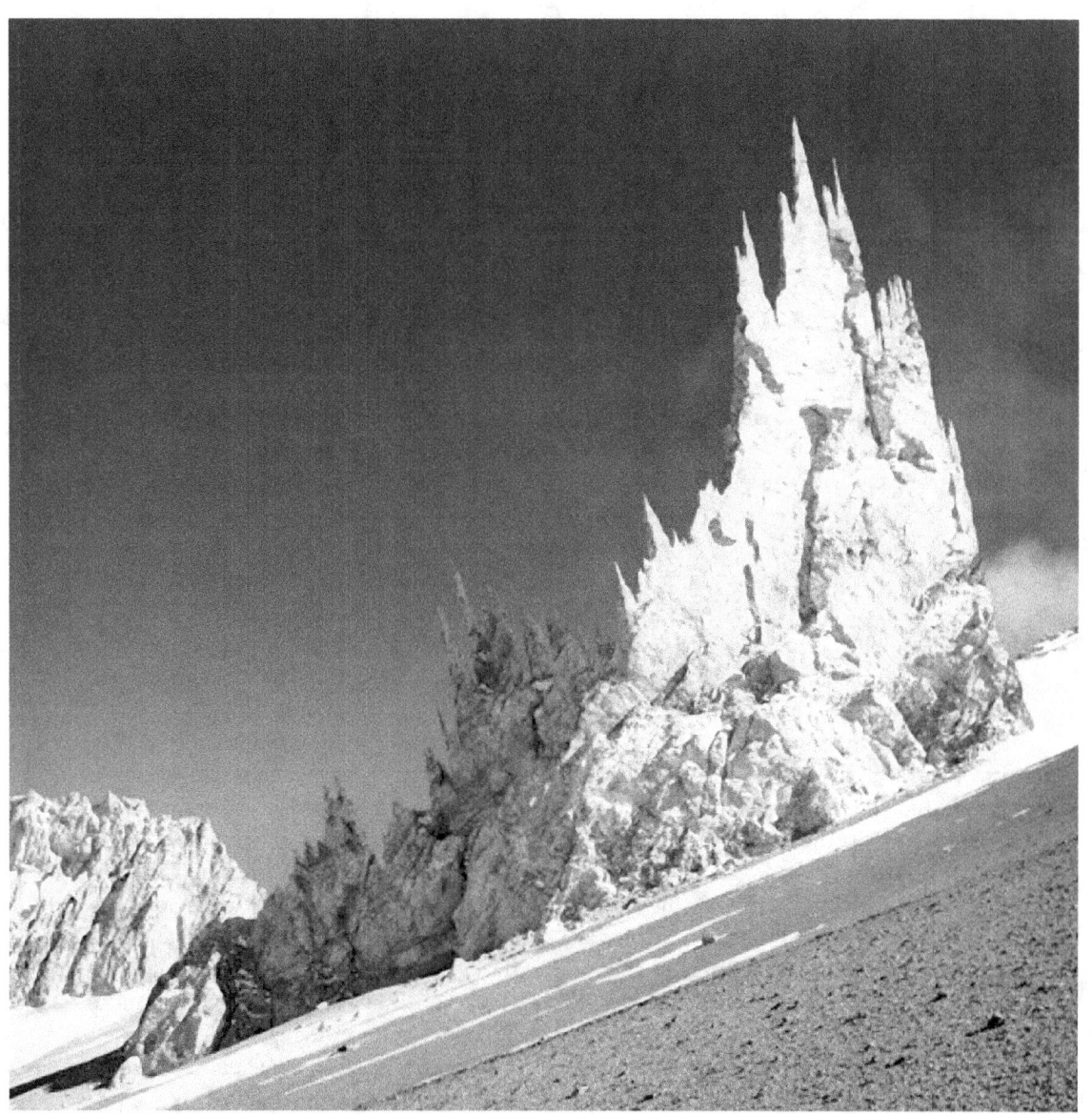

Michael Najjar, *Lehman Brothers 92-08,* from the series High Altitude, 2008-2010

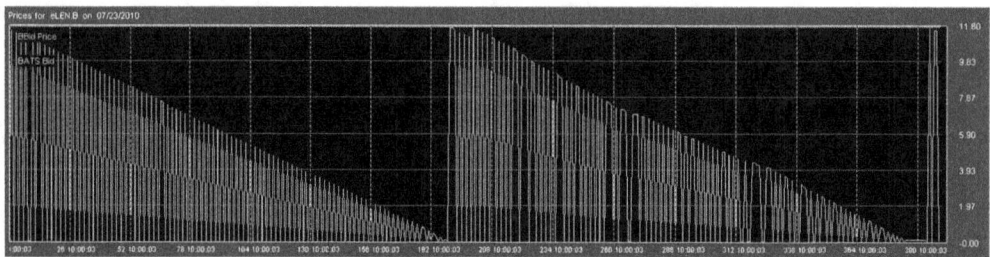

'Stubby triangles' chart showing high quotes being made and then immediately followed by a stub order of $0.01 (basically cancelled in most contexts). The quote is then remade at a lower price and followed with another stub quote. This cycle happened at the rate of 380 quotes a second

With HFT, the social structure of liquidity takes on an Einsteinian cast: 'high-frequency trading gives the obdurate physical reality of space a renewed prominence, and a physical constraint – the speed of light – is of growing importance'; as some industry commentators note that the state of the market will appear differently in different geographical locations, others remark that the speed of transactions means that one needs to 'abandon the idea that there is a universal truth for the best currently available price'.[16] We thus confront a compression of market-making transactions to speeds far below the threshold of individual human cognition, and an asymptotic acceleration of market turnover. The fastest trading chip executes a transaction in 740 nanoseconds (or 0.00074 milliseconds) while human reaction time to a visual stimulus is around 190 milliseconds.[17] In 1945, US stock was held on average for four years; this dropped to 8 months in 2000, 2 months in 2008, and 22 seconds in 2011.[18] In his *Intellectual and Manual Labour*, Alfred Sohn-Rethel had hypothesised that in commodity exchange, the real abstraction of value was the unconscious determinant underlying an ultimately false consciousness of use and quality. Here the situation is in a sense reversed: the algorithms that enact

these exchanges are the product of immensely sophisticated, conscious design, while the acts of exchange are beneath the experienceable threshold of human consciousness, as the exchange-abstraction materially approximates its formal characteristic, again according to Sohn-Rethel, as both timeless and spaceless.[19]

The 'obdurate physical reality' brought into relief by HFT takes many forms: the hollowing out of high-rises from Manhattan to Frankfurt to make room for co-location servers, the building of vast data centres at strategic geo-economic locations, the costs and ecological repercussions of the industrial cooling systems needed to run these data centres, and the laying of fibre-optic cable through mountains and across oceans to minimise 'latency'.[20] Armed with the intuitions of the kind of materialism proffered by ANT and STS, MacKenzie et al. inquire into the intricate negotiations – involving political regulators, legal frameworks, market agents, and material devices – required to wrest 'fairness' out of this spatio-temporal shift in the social structure of liquidity. Emblematic for them in this respect is the material expedient of equalising cable-lengths from servers to matching engines to neutralise any spatial advantage accruing to firms within the same location.[21] This speaks to the necessary material arrangement of spacings and timings which accompanies the contingent negotiations that affect the shape of the social structure of liquidity in particular and of markets in general.

But there remains a curious reluctance on the part of this materialism of markets, for all of its stress on space, history and agency, to accommodate a reflection on the systemic trends or logics that lend phenomena like HFT their intelligibility – in terms of the burgeoning role of this facet of finance capital at a considerable distance from productive investment, but also at the level of the dynamics of temporal acceleration and spatial relocation. The ban on the concept of capital – its sin that of totalisation – is critical here.

BUILDING SPACES FOR THE ANNIHILATION OF SPACE

It is not in my capacity to delineate the system dynamics that made it possible for market-making activities geared to rendering 'price discovery' more efficient to gain such prominence, once 'gaming the plumbing' – in Patterson's nice turn of phrase – became such a profitable concern.[22] Having said that, mainstream doubts that 'the welfare gains derived from HFT are minimal and perhaps even largely negative on a long-term investment horizon' indicate that super-profits made from the circulation of capital are indifferent or inimical to its production.[23] It is possible to push further the sociological suggestion that attention to the rise of HFT undermines the fables of a flat and frictionless capital. The vagaries of the emergence of HFT in different sites of finance capital, the institutional struggles over its particular shape, the elaborate contests that led to the 'fixing' of certain legal and technical parameters – all of

'The welfare gains derived from HFT are minimal, even largely negative, on a long-term investment horizon'

Capital by its nature drives beyond every spatial barrier

these are well served by a materialist micro-sociology of markets. But while opening up the regulatory, technical and material black boxes that much political economy ignores, this research programme risks black-boxing, erasing or bracketing out some broader tendencies and logics of capital accumulation – spatial ones in this case – generated by capitalist *imperatives*.[24] Against the 'sociologies of the social', MacKenzie et al. wish to argue that 'content may become context', that phenomena like HFT can't be contained by a prior understanding of the patterned historical dynamics of finance capital.[25] Only the most deliriously Laplacean of Marxists would argue that the particular arrangements of contemporary financial markets are 'inevitable' byproducts of a particular phase of accumulation. Yet the 'context' of capital itself can't be written out.

It is difficult not to be struck by the way in which the financial microcosmos of HFT exhibits some of the spatial logics and contradictions that have distinguished capital through its many conjunctural figures and historical transmutations. The revenge of matter and space, in an economic field whose drive to instantaneousness seems to obliterate spatial difference, corroborates, in the financial arena, a well-known observation from Marx's *Grundrisse*:

> The more production comes to rest on exchange value, hence on exchange, the more important do the physical conditions of exchange – the means of communication and transport – become for the costs of circulation. Capital by its nature drives beyond every spatial barrier. Thus the creation of the physical conditions of exchange – of the means of communication and transport – the annihilation of space by time – becomes an extraordinary necessity for it.[26]

For the costs of financial circulation 'physical conditions' are paramount – as manifested in the fierce competition over co-located server space, proximity to trading venues and access to data, and in related phenomena like the rush to acquire and develop real estate for data centres.

The monopolistic character of spatial competition, whereby 'relative locational advantage translates into excess profits', dictates that the annihilation of space by time 'accentuates rather than undermines the significance of space'; that the frictions and inertias of space 'can be overcome only through the production of space, of systems of communication and physical infrastructures embedded in the land'.[27] Spatial and social infrastructures are explicitly designed to minimise the turnover time of capital, or, in this case, the 'latency' of capital in circulation. David Harvey's gloss on the constitutively geographic character of the Marxian dialectic – 'space can be overcome only through the production of a fixed space' – is writ large in the architecture of data centres and the massive outlays for fibre-optic communications. The second part of his statement, however, according to which 'turnover time can be accelerated only by fixing a portion of the total capital in time', would instead require us to explore the way in which HFT firms which hold stock for as little as an average of 11 seconds, and liquidate their positions at the end of the day, relate to the necessary fixing in space and time of capital in other sectors of the economy.[28] Thinking of HFT through the prism of a historical-materialist geography, and vice versa, also puts a further kink in the dialectic. The oscillation between locationally and technologically driven strategies to accrue excess profits – 'the closer production approaches some spatial equilibrium condition (the equalisation of profit rates across locations, for example), the greater the competitive incentive for individual capitalists to disrupt the basis of that equilibrium through technological change'[29] – is here replaced by an apparent identity between spatial and technological competition (whether this is a dynamic that can be observed elsewhere in the economy is another matter).

Born in the midst of, and traversing rather unscathed, a period of financialisation and crisis, the algorithmic revolution embodied by high-frequency trading animates long-standing utopian and dystopian reflexes. The opacity of transactions happening fathoms beneath our perceptual threshold and far beyond our mathematical comprehension makes most 'representations' of this bleeding-edge of finance capital so many ciphers of our ignorance. The flash crash of 2010 nudged that ignorance into visions of impersonal, chaotic causalities – Skynet meets Y2K in a faceless data centre in New Jersey. Recent work in the sociology of markets provides an important corrective to fantasies and phobias of finance, by stressing the legal and institutional contingencies of HFT's emergence, but above all the manner in which attending to its operations dispels the equation of financialisation with immateriality and frictionlessness. A materialism that does not rest content with materiality but strains toward history and totality – a materialism of the really abstract – will need to articulate how the spatial dimensions of the algorithmic chase after excess profits in financial circulation can be routed back into the geographic strategies and aporias of productive capital in the long recession, spanning the unexperienceable speeds of algorithmic trading, the trend-lines of global capital and the lived time of our collective and political life.[30]

Alberto Toscano <sos01at@gold.ac.uk> teaches at Goldsmiths, University of London. He sits on the editorial board of the journal *Historical Materialism* and edits the Italian List for Seagull Books. He is the author of *Fanaticism: On the Uses of an Idea* (London: Verso, 2010), and is currently completing a book on the aesthetics of capital with Jeff Kinkle, *Cartographies of the Absolute* (forthcoming from Zero Books, blog at: http://cartographiesoftheabsolute.wordpress.com/)

FOOTNOTES

1 'Crashes and high frequency trading', http://www.bis.gov.uk/assets/foresight/docs/computer-trading/11-1226-dr7-crashes-and-high-frequency-trading.pdf

2 On the political valences of HFT's invisibility, an ironic byproduct of its claim to inject greater transparency into market-making, see Paul Jorion, *Le capitalisme à l'agonie*, Paris: Fayard, 2011, pp.136-61.

3 Alexis Madrigal, Market Data Firm Spots the Tracks of Bizarre Robot Traders,' http://www.theatlantic.com/technology/archive/2010/08/market-data-firm-spots-the-tracks-of-bizarre-robot-traders/60829/

4 Mirabeau, quoted in Susan Buck-Morss, 'Envisioning Capital', *Critical Inquiry*, 21.2, 1995, p.440.

5 See Will Wiles, 'Fluid Assets: The Economic Waterworks of the MONIAC', *Cabinet* 47, 2012, and Michael Stevenson, 'The Search for the Fountain of Prosperity' (http://www.dextersinister.org/MEDIA/PDF/TheSearchForTheFountainOfProsperity.pdf), for the enlightening vicissitudes of one such model, and its actual plumbing. Timothy Mitchell has argued for the constituent part played by such models in establishing the very idea of *the* economy. See 'Fixing the Economy', *Cultural Studies* 12.1 (1998), pp.82-101.

6 Donald MacKenzie, *An Engine Not a Camera: How Financial Models Shape Markets*, Cambridge, MA: The MIT Press, 2006.

7 Susan Buck-Morss, 'Envisioning Capital', op. cit., p.447.

8 Ibid., p.463.

9 See Michael Najjar's photobook *High Altitude*, Bielefeld: Kerber Verlag, 2012, and the catalogue essays by Kevin Slavin ('How Algorithms Changed the World') and Paul Wombell ('Subprime Sublime').

Najjar is the visual hook for Slavin's TED talk on HFT, where he also touches on the graph images of algorithms in operation, their shapes calling forth fanciful names: 'The Knife', etc. Available at: http://www.ted.com/talks/kevin_slavin_how_algorithms_shape_our_world.html. Najjar's work can be found at: http://www.michaelnajjar.com/ipad/gallery_high_altitude.html; the pieces *Volatile Smile (photographs)*, 2010, and *Volatile Smile (installation)*, 2011, can be found at Geissler/Sann's website, with texts by Frank Wagner and Brian Holmes, both of which dwell on the political, cognitive and aesthetic enigma of the dark screens and vacant rooms: http://geisslersann.com/

10 Scott Patterson, *Dark Pools: The rise of AI trading machines and the looming threat to Wall Street*, New York: Random House, 2012, pp.297-8. 'With electronic trading, a placeless, faceless, postmodern cybermarket in which computers communicated at warpspeeds, [the] physical sense of the market's flow had vanished. The market gained new eyes – electronic eyes. Computer programmers designed hunter-seeker algorithms that could detect, like radar, which way the market was going' (Patterson, p.7).

11 Ibid., pp.295-6.

12 MacKenzie traces the particular design of the Stop Logic Functionality that intervened to stop the 'flash crash' of 2010 in the Merc's experience of 1987's Black Friday. See Donald MacKenzie, 'Mechanizing the Merc: The Chicago Mercantile Exchange and the Rise of High-Frequency Trading', 2012, available at: http://www.sps.ed.ac.uk/__data/assets/pdf_file/0006/93867/Merc11.pdf

13 This *détournement* of Marxian terminology – to suggest that we think of the ratio between constant and variable capital within the domain of finance is intended as a provisional, experimental response to the problems about 'materiality' raised by recent sociological literature on finance. A sustained engagement would require a critique of the literal use of terms like 'fixed' (capital, which is for Marx but a part of constant capital), 'material', and so on, especially in order to avoid 'the confusion of the categories of fixed and circulating capital with the categories of constant and variable capital', a confusion leading to the kind of category mistake that prevents us from thinking how fixed capital can also be *mobile*. As Marx goes on to write, in a crucial passage: 'the formal characteristic that arises from the circulation of value is confused with a concrete [*dinglich*] property; as if things,

which are never capital at all in themselves, could already *in themselves* and by nature be capital in a definite form, fixed or circulating'. See *Capital, Volume 2*, (trans.) David Fernbach, London: Penguin, 1978, p.241. The formal (or abstract) characteristics of the capital-relation are precisely what a sociological concern with materiality risks occluding.

14 'The idea that life is essentially based on intellect, and that intellect is accepted in practical life as the most valuable of our mental energies goes hand in hand with the growth of a money economy'. Georg Simmel, *The Philosophy of Money*, London: Routledge, 2011, p.162.

15 Donald MacKenzie, Daniel Beunza, Yuval Millo and Juan Pablo Pardo-Guerra, 'Drilling Through the Allegheny Mountains: Liquidity, Materiality and High-Frequency Trading', *Journal of Cultural Economy* 5.3, 2012, p.280.

16 Ibid., p.281.

17 http://www.bbc.co.uk/news/business-15722530; see also Patterson, p.291.

18 *Dark Pools*, p.45.

19 See Alfred Sohn-Rethel, *Intellectual and Manual Labour: A Critique of Epistemology*, London: Macmillan, 1978, p.22. For more on Sohn-Rethel, see my 'The Open Secret of Real Abstraction', *Rethinking Marxism* 20.2, 2008, pp.273-287.

20 'In 2007, the NYSE has launched a $500 million initiative dubbed Project Alpha. The plan was to build a mammoth computer trading facility on the site of an old quarry in Mahwah, New Jersey. The length of several football fields, the 400,000-square-foot building would allow computer-driven trading firms to put their computer servers right next to the NYSE's matching engine – the computers that brought buyers and sellers together in the frictionless ether of cyberspace. Twenty-inch-wide pipes pumped in water to cool the computers. Twenty surge protectors, each the size of a tank, protected the site against power outages', *Dark Pools*, op. cit., pp.281-2; http://www.nytimes.com/2012/09/23/technology/data-centers-waste-vast-amounts-of-energy-belying-industry-image.html?pagewanted=all&_r=0

21 'Issues of fairness arise within HFT itself. Within a data centre, different firms' servers are inevitably going to be located at different distances from the matching engines, and such is the concern within HFT over even tiny time lags that this is an issue of some sensitivity. Trading venues have responded by imposing equal cable lengths so that time delays are equal. The resultant coils of fibre-optic cable (technically unnecessary, but needed for fairness) are a physical reminder that we are dealing here with "the creation and assemblages of Spacing(s)" and "Timing(s)", not simply with "a priori . . . space and time"'. 'Drilling Through the Allegheny Mountains', op. cit., p.289.

22 *Dark Pools*, op. cit., p.2.

23 'Crashes and high frequency trading', op. cit.

24 Some of the reasons behind these shortcomings of the ANT-inspired sociology of financial markets – among them the danger of producing a 'hagiography of knowledge' in which the world turns into 'a kind of *kampfplatz* of contesting performativities' – are compellingly laid out in Dick Bryan, Randy Martin, Johnna Montgomerie and Karel Williams, 'An important failure: knowledge limits and the financial crisis', *Economy and Society* 41.3, 2012, pp.299-315.

25 The formulation is from Bruno Latour, *Reassembling the Social: An Introduction to Actor-Network-Theory*, Oxford: Oxford University Press, 2005. I have criticised this formulation in 'Seeing it Whole: Staging Totality in Social Theory and Art', *Sociological Review* 60 (2012), Issue supplement S1: *Live Methods*, pp.64-83.

26 Karl Marx, *Grundrisse*, London: Penguin, 1973, p.536.

27 David Harvey, *The Limits to Capital*, London: Verso, 1999, p.389.

28 David Harvey, 'Money, Time, Space and the City', in *The Urban Experience*, Baltimore and London: The Johns Hopkins University Press, 1989, pp.190-2.

29 *Limits to Capital*, op. cit. p.393.

30 One of the conundrums such an inquiry would face can be allegorised by thinking through the relationship (which is hardly a linear one) between two of the Chicago locations photographed by Geissler/Sann: the already mentioned algorithmic trading offices of *Volatile Smile*, 2010, and the vacant foreclosed homes of *The Real Estate*, 2009.

DESTRUCTIVE DESTRUCTION? AN ECOLOGICAL STUDY OF HIGH FREQUENCY TRADING

How is High Frequency Trading's drive to efficiency affecting market dynamics as a whole? In their analysis of the financial arms race, **INIGO WILKINS** *and* **BOGDAN DRAGOS** *find that far from beating entropy, algorithmic trading simply redistributes it more unequally than ever*

What follows is an account of the concepts of information and noise as they apply to an analysis of high frequency trading according to 'heterodox economics'. This account will highlight the evolutionary path that has led to the present micro-structure of financial markets and allow for a diagnosis of the contemporary financial ecology. High Frequency Trading (HFT) is a subset of algorithmic trading which works at very low time horizons (100 milliseconds) and requires massive information processing capacities. Following recent developments such as flash crashes and various technical break-downs, it is crucial to unpack the black-box of algorithmic high-frequency trading in order to understand its potential impact on wider social and economic systems. This will entail the application of various scientific theories to the financial domain that extend classical models of reversible functions, and go beyond models based on efficiency and equilibrium, encompassing a much wider class of irreversible transformations.

According to heterodox economics, the development of thermodynamic theory brought an end to the dominance of classical physics in economic theory, in particular the dogma of efficient markets hypothesis, and reversal to equilibrium. It is this significant theoretical upheaval that allows Nicholas Georgescu-Roegen to say that the law of entropy is the basis of the economy of life at all levels.[1] Writing in the turbulent '70s, amidst the oil crisis, it became apparent to him that classical economic theory could no longer be an adequate model

in addressing the huge problems of third world underdevelopment, depletion of natural resources, increasing pollution, overpopulation, etc. In his attempt to deal with these issues, he recognised that the main barrier in repositioning economic theory on new grounds was its reliance on Newtonian mechanics. As the Midnight Notes Collective argue, Enlightenment thought was concomitant with a drive to extract absolute surplus value during the first wave of real subsumption in the industrial revolution.[2] Georgescu-Roegen advocated the replacement of this idealised paradigm with thermodynamics whose second law (that the entropy of an isolated system tends to a maximum) would offer a much more fruitful theoretical foundation for economics. It should be noted at this point that although economic theory is even now still dominated by reversible models based on the supposition of efficiency and equilibrium at the abstract level, in practical terms thermodynamics had already significantly altered the political economy through the 19th century preoccupation with exhaustion, leading to a 'science of work' that concretised in the Taylorisation of the work-force after WW1.

The true novelty of Georgescu-Roegen's formulation lies in his proposal for a fourth law of thermodynamics, in which it is not only energy that is subject to decreasing returns, but also matter; 'friction robs us of available matter'.[3] He thus identifies an ultimate supply limit of low entropy matter-energy; a 'source of absolute scarcity' consisting of a terrestrial stock and a solar flow.[4] This should not be understood as a reductionist account capable of explaining the causal structure of *everything*, but rather the identification of an abstract functional schematic whose explanatory coherence may be supplemented or extended by further theoretical devices. In particular, although thermodynamics can help to describe the conditions of class struggle and the divergence between market valuation mechanisms and the actual value of resources, it cannot account for the lived experiences of the former, and offers no substantial critique of the latter. However, it does allow for the reinsertion of the economic process into much wider physical, chemical and biological processes. For if the entropy law operates at all levels, then one can understand the economic process as a continual exchange between low and high entropy, just as dissipative systems maintain coherence through the reduction of energy gradients. An energy gradient is a differential, such as that between hot and cold, or between disparate prices, whose value can be tapped through the application of work. Although this is a naturalised view of finance, it must be clearly stated that such a naturalisation does not entail a valorisation of present economic conditions. Rather, the economy, like the environment, exhibits a high degree of structural and functional redundancy, such that a great number of contingent modes of organisation are possible. Let's be clear here, to say that something is natural is not to say that it is good; after all, a tumour is natural. It is just to argue that it is subject to a materialist analysis, without claiming to exhaustively describe all its aspects. Moreover, we must not conflate biological and economic ecologies, but rather treat them in their specificity.

It is useful, at this point, to clarify the distinction between low and high entropy. For the purpose of elaborating an ecological economics, Georgescu-Roegen understands the economy as a process that transforms available free energy into unavailable bound energy, that is to say it is the exploitation of a gradient. The former may be understood both as specific concentrations of material-energetic structures, such as oil or gold, and the potentiality for value extraction offered by living labour, while the latter is exemplified by waste, pollution, highly diffuse forms of matter-energy such as heat, and those forms of dead labour that no longer afford value extraction.

The economic process is the modulation by which a certain dissipative system maintains itself by continually 'inputting' free energy and 'outputting' bound energy. This entails a local growth of efficiency, or increase in the throughput of energy, that evolves according to the maximum entropy principle (MaxEnt), where the entropy of the microstates that do not correspond to the successful application of a function or technology are maximised such that the energetic cost is minimised for a given utility.[5] This local reduction of entropy is 'observer dependent', however it also necessarily results in an increase in 'observer independent' entropy according to the maximum entropy production principle (MEPP).[6] Effectively this means that biological, technical and economic evolution all lead inevitably towards an amplification of entropy at the environmental level. Nevertheless there is a high degree of contingency that determines the rate of throughput.

Within the field of evolutionary economics the notions of energy and information gradients become essential in understanding the dynamics of socio-economic change. In this sense, a certain abstract evolutionary matrix is common to all open systems, whether physical, chemical, biological or socio-economic.

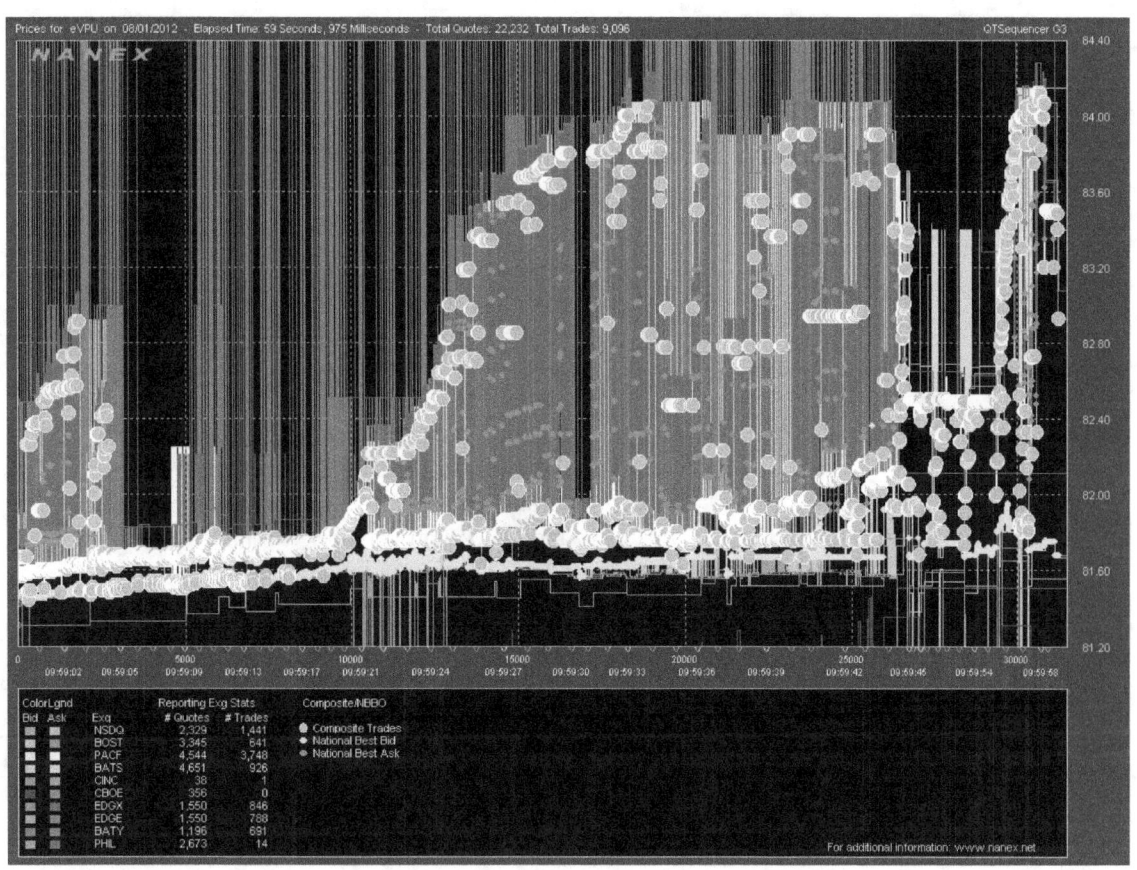

A Nanex chart from 08/01/12 showing the bid and the ask in one stock (a utilities ETF), and how at first the bid/ask are tight, but then just before 10:00 AM went totally wild

Markets may be defined as dissipative structures coping in an entropic/noisy environment by reducing both energetic and informatic gradients

If there is an energy gradient available, a simple dissipative structure will exploit it. Similarly, if there is an information/knowledge gradient available, a socio-economic structure will grow and develop around this continual process of reduction.[7]

Ever since Friedrich Hayek and Eugene Fama, information has become a crucial vector in understanding financial markets. For Hayek, markets are a way of collecting and aggregating available information. Fama understood efficient markets as reacting instantly to new information, thereby unproblematically reflecting all available information. While we certainly do not agree with the wider premises and conclusions of these liberal economists, it is important to understand economic systems as collective calculating devices that compute transient equilibriums.[8] Balancing economic, computational and thermodynamic perspectives, markets may be defined as dissipative structures coping in an entropic/ noisy environment by reducing both energetic and informatic gradients. This becomes particularly apparent in modern capitalist economies. The current swarm of financial actors, including human, non-human and hybrid systems, feed off the social production of knowledge and its informational friction. An evolutionary process of variation, coordination and selection leads to differential levels of fitness and to huge asymmetries in terms of collecting and processing information, and hence to the creation of increasingly complex structures with higher rates of change. Such systems are characterised by non-linear risk situations featuring high interconnectivity and super-spreaders that amplify contagion.

In this sense, the main activity of finance is the bearing of uncertainty, but more precisely the reduction of an energetic and informatic gradient, fuelled by the ever-growing heterogeneity of the market.[9] Financial actors are not only an intermediary between producers and users of information, but they also 'assume a hermeneutic function' of performative interpretation, and moreover occupy the point of overlap between an information network and a liquidity network.[10] Maintaining itself at that particular juncture allows the financial intermediary to access and reduce a very steep energy/information gradient. The investment bank therefore sits at the nexus of an informal information marketplace for price-relevant information.[11]

Our argument is that High Frequency Trades (HFTs) are complex socio-technical systems that thrive both through the production of noise and by the reduction of information gradients, operating at a high rate of throughput and offsetting noise/entropy to the wider financial ecology. In order to explain these claims it is necessary to briefly chart the evolution of computing within finance and the subsequent appearance of algorithmic trading. From carrier pigeons and the transatlantic telegraph cable to contemporary ICT, finance has always been a site for intensive technical innovation. This is no surprise, inasmuch as financial actors thrive by accessing and reducing information gradients and exploiting communication inefficiencies.

More recently, the shift from open-outcry face-to-face trading to automated electronic trading has represented a huge leap in efficiency and the reduction of transaction costs. However, even Milton Friedman was aware that there is an 'intrinsic paradox built into the assumption of efficient markets', since efficiency is maintained by detection of inefficiencies, the closer to absolute efficiency the less inefficiencies can be discovered; so the market

can never achieve absolute efficiency.[12] There is thus a complex dialectical interplay between drives to market efficiency and inefficiency. As the market approaches efficiency, there are less opportunities for arbitrage by informed traders (who gauge the discrepancy between the current price and the fundamental value of the underlying asset), and uninformed 'noise traders' progressively dominate the market.[13] This inevitably leads to the inflation of bubbles, with the subsequent collapse in fundamental values (when it is not brought on through market manipulation) occurring in an entirely unpredictable manner.

The market thus oscillates asymptotically around the attractor of zero information friction in an incomputably random orbit. While this movement receives its impetus from the dialectical, or apparently co-constitutive relation between efficiency and inefficiency, its trajectory and effects are far from reversible, resulting in the non-dialectical destruction of whole swathes of economic actors largely at the base of steep energy gradients.[14] Witness the wave of repossessions following the sub-prime mortgage crisis, or the asymmetric distribution of debt organised by the austerity regime. A point made by Evan Calder Williams following Amadeo Bordiga's description of capital as 'Murderer of the Dead.'[15]

Ever since the mid '80s, there has been an incredible growth in the adoption of ICT and algorithms in the marketplace. From the computer terminals that were simply assisting human traders to contemporary HFT software, we have seen the emergence of this new financial ecosystem, a highly complex computational matrix.[16] Algorithms are no longer tools, but they are active in analysing economic data, translating it into relevant information and producing trading orders.[17]

This transition represents a new phase of real subsumption affecting all economic actors and social conditions. That is, if labour relations were reorganised around mechanics in the industrial revolution, and then thermodynamics and cybernetics in the last two centuries, then the current phase of real subsumption may be understood according to contemporary scientific transformations. This is often called the 'nano-bio-info-cogno revolution', and is based on distributed networks and 'friction free' systems (i.e. superconductors, ubiquitous computing). However, the importance of Georgescu-Roegen is his assertion that no such friction-free economy is possible, since the drive to efficiency is limited by the absolute scarcity of low entropy resources and met with a corresponding increase of exhaustion or resistance issuing from labour power.

Neil Johnson et al. identify a 'robot phase transition' after 2006 where the sub-millisecond speed and massive quantity of robot-robot interactions exceeds the capacity of human-robot interactions. They argue that operating at such timescales is intrinsically unstable and 'characterized by frequent black swan events with ultrafast durations'.[18] While Nassim Taleb's black swan theory is contentious, the conceptual core may be subtracted from his wider project, and refers to high-impact real contingencies as opposed to the structured randomness that casinos and quantum physics display. Analogous to the well-known effect in systems engineering where small cracks in a fuselage build up to a breaking threshold, financial friction is so high that micro-fractures in the form of mini flash-crashes proliferate, threatening the whole ecology.[19] Moreover, through the logic of encapsulated coding they employ, algorithmic trading software platforms are intrinsically open to abusive practices, and

represent highly opaque and consequently 'unworkable interfaces'.[20]

In order to address the topic of HFT rigorously, we must not conflate the material specificities that define its heterogeneity; distinctions must be made between electronic, program and algorithmic trading, where HFT is a heterogeneous subset of all three.[21] 'The universe of computer algorithms is best understood as a complex ecology of highly specialized, highly diverse, and strongly interacting agents.'[22] Within this line of technical and financial innovations, we can see various types of trading strategies that employ an equally diverse population of market order types. Further, from an ecological perspective one can distinguish between various trading and execution algorithms, but also 'predatory' relationships. 'Strategies, markets and regulations co-evolve in competitive, symbiotic or predator-prey relationships as technology and the economy change in the background.'[23]

For example, pairs trading strategies (whose computational costs are so high they only took off after the '80s ICT revolution) unilaterally feed on the predictable price reversals engendered by portfolio balancing, just as short-term strategies prey on their long-term counterparts to the point of extinction.[24] Certain 'species' try to efficiently execute a trade, so as to achieve minimal market impact. They split large orders into smaller packs and execute them at certain time intervals. More evolved versions, like 'volume-weighted average price' (VWAP) algorithms, employ complex randomisation functions coupled with econometrics to optimise the size and execution times depending on overall trading volumes.[25] Moreover, new ecological niches have emerged in order to obfuscate the execution of large orders, known as 'dark pools'.[26] There are other types which try to profit from identifying and anticipating such trades, the algorithms sometimes referred to as 'predatory'.[27] Perhaps the best example of such a frequency-dependent evolutionary path, one that is well-known for its compulsive non-adaptive drive, is the proliferation of low-latency algorithms that profit from the transmission speed differentials inherent in the geography of the globally integrated financial system, and the material transformations these informatic relations entail.[28]

Such strategies of camouflage, mimesis and deception are endemic in predator-prey relationships, fuelling a run-away propagation of non-adaptive mutations according to the non-equilibrium dynamics of the 'Red Queen Effect', and are modelled in evolutionary game theory as crypsis.[29] In his discussion of the pathological tendencies of technological capitalism Ray Brassier cites Roger Callois' investigation of thanatropic mimicry, pointing out that such effects are irreducible to equilibrium models of dialectical resolution, and may often terminate in non-dialectical self-destruction.[30] 'In mimicking their own food,' Brassier writes, 'leaf insects such as the Phyllium frequently end up devouring each other'[31] He continues, some pages later:

> Enlightenment consummates mimetic reversibility by converting thinking into algorithmic compulsion: the inorganic miming of organic reason. Thus the artificialization of intelligence, the conversion of organic ends into technical means and vice versa, heralds the veritable realization of second nature [...] in the irremediable form wherein purposeless intelligence supplants all reasonable ends.[32]

Global finance can be seen as the staging ground for a continual redistribution of energy

Short-term strategies prey on their long-term counterparts to the point of extinction

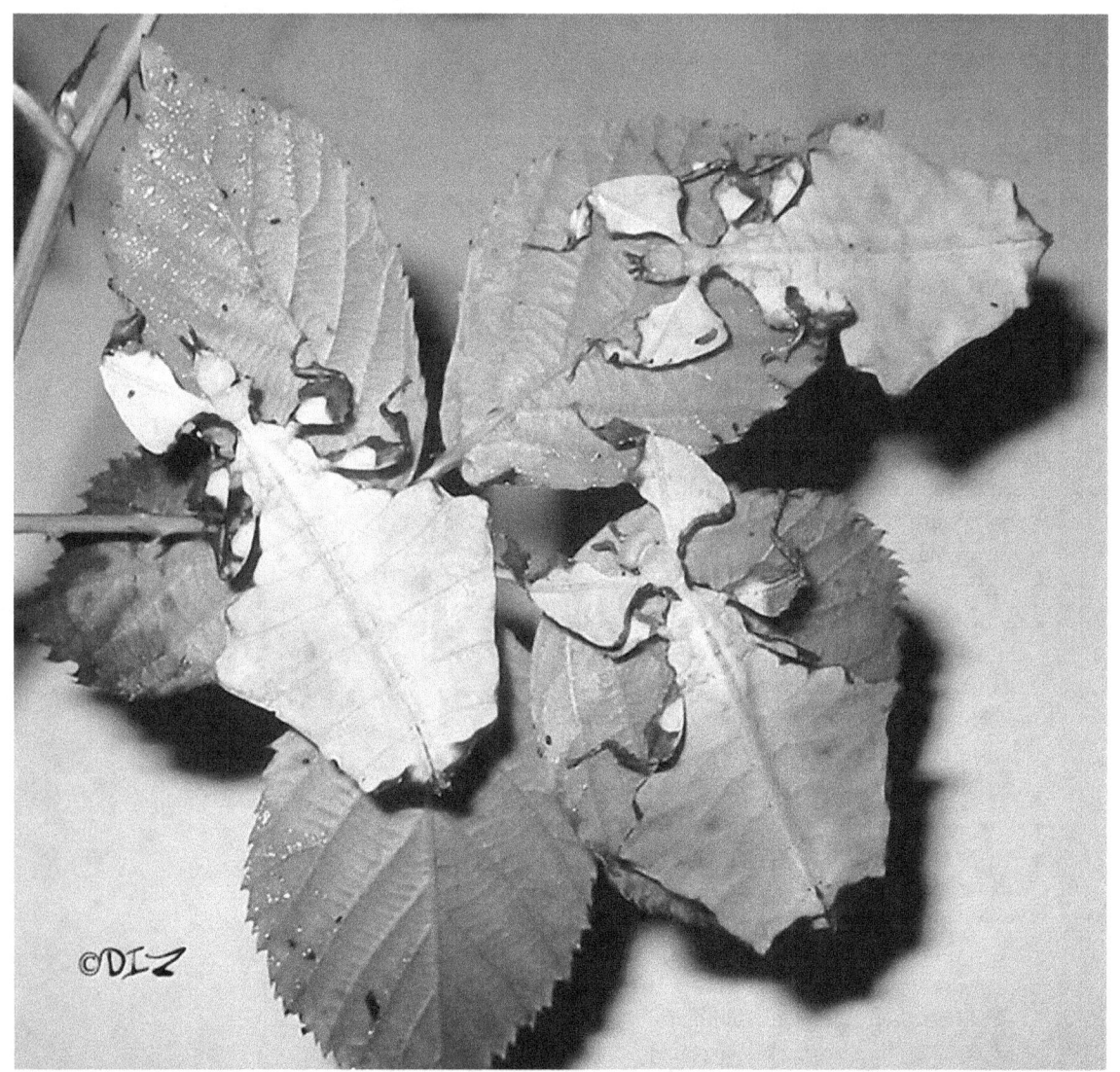

'Leaf insects such as the Phyllium frequently end up devouring each other'

and information gradients; HFT is a prime example of this kind of evolutionary landscape. At a high enough level of liquidity, information friction and disparity allow for the emergence of computationally intensive systems that can effectively reduce gradients and extract rents.[33] While it is true that HFT accounts for a large part of market transactions, the profits are not the most significant among market participants. In the end, all of the 'bigger' actors tolerate low-latency trading firms because they provide much needed liquidity. Nevertheless, HFT exists because at certain volumes of trading, they enjoy a systematic advantage, which is the result of a 'technicality' of trading that is opaque to outsiders.[34] They manage to 'survive' by exploiting information gradients that 'slower' market participants are unable to access.

> Nanex: On [...] Aug 5, 2011, we processed 1 trillion bytes of data [...] This is insane [...] It is noise, subterfuge, manipulation [...] HFT is sucking the life blood out of the markets [A]t the core, [HFT] is pure manipulation.[35]

Such reactions might seem dramatic, but they testify to the intense struggle going on in the computational matrix of finance every day. An ecological perspective emphasises the complex interdependencies between different financial 'species'. Every participant is constantly processing market noise in an attempt to reduce it as much as possible to relevant information. The subsequent decisions and market orders represent more noise for the other participants, that is to say, an irreversible output of high-entropy. As long as there is enough disparity and enough heterogeneity in the market, high-frequency traders can profit from the underlying friction and produce more noise. It is precisely this

persistent inefficiency of markets that informs heterodox economics.

Because of bounded rationality, financial traders can't do everything at once – they tend to specialise. These specialised traders interact with one another as they perform basic functions, such as getting liquidity, offsetting risks and making profits. A given activity can produce profits or losses for another activity. Inefficiencies play the role of food in biological systems, providing profit-making possibilities that support the ecology.[36]

The interaction of heterogeneous actors with different time horizons and a variety of strategies produces the inefficiencies that make up an information gradient. Ecological economics understands the market as a food web, which can be described in terms of a gain matrix defining the interdependencies between different species. At the bottom there are the basal species – slaves, serfs, proletarians, free labour, consumers, account holders, etc. These strata are preyed on by those further up the food chain – pension funds, insurance companies, mutual funds, retail banks; and they in turn feed larger financial institutions, such as hedge funds, brokers, investment banks, propriety trading, HFTs, etc. Each financial actor exploits the inefficiencies of the prey species and in the process produces new inefficiencies, further increasing the information gradient. Within this complex ecology there is a gradual stabilisation of predator-prey relationships, but, unlike an actual ecosystem, the financial system has a much higher rate of change, leading to more abrupt singular events like flash-crashes evolving according to an accelerated rate of punctuated equilibria, with multiple black swans and mass extinctions.[37]

During the 2010 flash crash, the main US stock index (which is a replica of the market as such) lost about 900 points in a few minutes, recovering most of that loss in the subsequent 15 minutes.[38] To put things into perspective, it represents the wipeout of about $1 trillion in a space of minutes.[39]

Following the media frenzy around this event, a variety of market actors have rushed to offer explanations for such a one-sided 'social' decision to sell. Part of the explanation lies in a lack of regulatory circuit breakers that would have automatically suspended the free-fall following the abnormally edgy HFT reaction to the discovery of a large 'iceberg' order. From black swans and fat fingers to possible market abuses like quote stuffing (the production of noise in order to obtain a good position in the order book queue), it seems that the causal structure of such events are so complex and opaque that there will never be a definitive explanation. However, we may state with confidence that such occurrences are the kind of irreversible outputs that characterise the hyper-diversity of contemporary socio-technical ecology. Both the SEC-CFTC (2010) report, and the more recent Foresight review have shown that the impetus of the flash crash cannot be traced back to any firm engaged in HFT. Nevertheless, HFT strategies are the present culmination of a tendency towards efficiency of information throughput that inevitably ends up offsetting huge volumes of noise to the wider financial ecology. The question is not so much the good or bad intentions of HFT, but its impact on the resilience and robustness of the overall system. Though speculative trading is often driven by 'fictitious capital', it has real effects in the world, such as food price spikes that may lead to rioting or starvation. As Andrew Kliman argues, against underconsumptionist explanations such as David Harvey's or Michael Hudson's, the current crises are not causally reducible to fictitious

finance, rather both are the effects of deeper contradictions within capitalism, indexed by the inexorable tendency of the rate of profit to fall.[40]

Following the sociology of information systems and risk, we could translate this as a result of exchanging high-frequency/low impact events for low-frequency/high impact ones or an exchange between low and high entropy.[41] In this sense, any increase in efficiency (throughput) of one part of the system ends up being dissipated to the rest of the system as noise.[42] If HFT has any part to play in the flash crash, it is because it can be said to represent a real push for efficiency, but one that nevertheless produces unintended consequences for the rest of the financial ecology. Inasmuch as it diminishes the risk of trading through higher matching speeds, HFT allows buyers and sellers to reduce their transaction costs considerably. But the reduction of risk is not actually a reduction as such, and must be understood as a redistribution, or a parametrisation of the fitness landscape of the financial ecology. The crucial point here is that, given the present regulatory framework, which is supported by collusion and corruption at the national and international level (i.e. Federal Reserve, IMF, ratings agencies), a local growth in throughput efficiency enabling the accelerated tapping of low entropy resources offsets the increased high entropy to those that are not able to bear it. While the occupants of prime positions on the energy matrix loll around in a rich bath of liquidity, an increasing number are forced to pay for this exuberance with their jobs, their homes, and ultimately their lives. Ray Kurzweil's overzealous enthusiasm for the coming 'singularity', when human 'intelligence' is eclipsed by machines, appears wilfully myopic when we witness the effects of the 'robot phase transition'. While algorithmic hordes of parasitic vampire squids and zombie capitalists compulsively gorge on blood and brains, their exhausted victims lie all around, twitching to the non-periodic outbursts of transient code – the singularity turns out to be just another accelerating extension of exploitation.

Phenomena such as flash crashes are the inevitable outputs of a financial ecology that tends towards the non-linear emergence of noise saturation peaks. At such critical points of friction, something is bound to break. This does not simply apply to market crashes.[43] The present financial ecology maintains an unsustainable rate of throughput and a thanatropic mode of crypsis in the proliferation of strategies for digital subterfuge. In order to address the critical situation of contemporary finance, several liberal beliefs must be overcome: trust in the efficacy of competitive market mechanisms for computing equilibriums, such as the valuation of natural resources and labour; confidence in the capacity of finance to self-regulate, or to be merely a question of discovering the regulatory mechanisms for stabilisation, as it is for Michael Hudson, etc.; and faith in the doctrine of sustainable development, which denies the fourth law of thermodynamics. Though finance tends towards efficiency and equity it can never achieve these states since it feeds off the noise created by information asymmetries and structural inequality, and aggressively maintains these disparities in order to extract value from the resulting ecological niches. The demand for transparency is not enough. We should not be placated by a little noise reduction. Friction must be turned around and fed back into the central mechanisms of the system, rather than being dissipated into the margins. As Reza Negarastani argues, we must find 'alternative ways of binding exteriority... remobilized forms of non-dialectical negativity'.[44]

Inigo Wilkins <inigowilkins@yahoo.com> is a PhD student at the Centre for Cultural Studies, Goldsmiths. His thesis title is 'Irreversible Noise'. He is also a research fellow working with *Mute* magazine and the Post-Media Lab at Lüneburg University on the question of the subsumption of sociality

Bogdan Dragos <bogodin@yahoo.com> is a PhD candidate at the Centre for Cultural Studies, Goldsmiths. His research interests comprise Philosophy of Technology, STS, Heterodox Economics and Sociology of Financial Markets. Currently, he is preparing a thesis on co-evolution of technology and financial markets as complex socio-technical systems

FOOTNOTES

1   Heterodox economics comprises thermo-economics, bio-economics, evolutionary economics and ecological economics; Nicholas Georgescu-Roegen, *The Entropy Law and the Economic Process*, Cambridge, Massachusetts: Harvard University Press, 1971, p.4.

2   Midnight Notes Collective (George Caffentzis, Monty Neill, Hans Widmer, John Willshire), 'The Work/ Energy Crisis and the Apocalypse', *Midnight Notes*, Vol. II, #1, 1980.

3   Nicholas Georgescu-Roegen, 'Energy Analysis and Economic Valuation', *Southern Economic Journal*,1979, 45, 4: p.1033.

4   Paul Burkett, *Marxism and Ecological Economics: Toward a Red and Green Political Economy*, Brill, 2006. p.145.

5   The maximum entropy principle is the prime doctrine of Bayesian probability theory, which states that 'the probability distribution which best represents the current state of knowledge is the one with largest information-theoretical entropy.' http://en.wikipedia.org/wiki/Principle_of_maximum_ entropy. In the evolutionary economics use of the term, it is thought as one with the 'maximum power principle', as formulated by Jaynes and Lotka, which describes the physics of evolutionary systems. H.T. Odum defines it thus: 'During self-organization, system designs develop and prevail that maximize power intake, energy transformation, and those uses that reinforce production and efficiency.' H.T. Odum 'Self-Organization and Maximum Empower', in *Maximum Power: The Ideas*

and Applications of H.T. Odum, C.A.S. Hall (ed.), Colorado: Colorado University Press, 1995, p.311.

6   Carsten Herrmann-Pillath, *Foundations of Evolutionary Economics*, Edward Elgar, forthcoming. Available at SSRN: http://ssrn.com/abstract=1781469

7   Stanley Metcalfe and John Foster, *Evolution and Economic Complexity*, Edward Elgar Publishing, 2007, and *Economic Emergence: an Evolutionary Economic Perspective*, Max Planck Institute of Economics Jena, Evolutionary Economics Group, #1112, 2011. This statement should not be taken dogmatically however, since as Elinor Ostrum demonstrates there are diverse ways in which collective self-organisation can govern common-pool resource problems that effectively reduce or stop gradients from being tapped at a rate that ends in a 'tragedy of the commons'. Elinor Ostrum, *Governing the Commons: The Evolution of Institutions of Collective Action*, Cambridge: Cambridge University Press, 2008.

8   Michel Callon and Fabian Muniesa,'Les marchés économiques comme dispositifs collectifs de calcul', *Réseaux* 21(122), 2003, pp.189-233.

9   Alan Morrison and William Wilhelm Jr, *Investment Banking: Institutions, Politics, and Law*, Oxford: Oxford University Press, 2nd Revised edition, 2008, p.4.

10 Laurence Gialdini and Marc Lenglet, *Financial Intermediaries in an Era of Disintermediation: European Brokerage Firms in a MiFID Context, 2010, p.23*. Available at SSRN: http://ssrn.com/abstract=1616022 or http://dx.doi.org/10.2139/ssrn.1616022

11 Alan Morrison et. al., op. cit., p.72.

12 J. Doyne Farmer and Spyros Skouras, 'An Ecological Perspective on the Future of Computer Trading', *The Future of Computer Trading in Financial Markets*, UK Foresight Driver Review – DR6, 2011, p.12.

13 Andrei Shleifer and Lawrence Summers, 'The Noise Trader Approach to Finance', *Journal of Economic Perspectives*, Volume 4, Number 2, 1990, pp.19-33.

14 Despite the dialectic of efficiency and inefficiency there is a general trend toward efficiency indexed by the fall in bid-ask spreads. James Angel, Lawrence Harris, and Chster S. Spatt, 'Equity Trading in the 21st Century', Marshall School of Business Working Paper No. FBE 09-10, 2010. Available at SSRN: http://ssrn.com/abstract=1584026 or http://dx.doi.org/10.2139/ssrn.1584026

15 Evan Calder Williams, *Combined and Uneven Apocalypse*, Zero Books, 2011, p.188. Amadeo Bordiga argues that capital functions not just through the 'creative destruction' that Shumpeter identifies, but also through a 'destructive destruction' necessitated by the build-up of dead labour. Amadeo Bordiga, 'Murder of the Dead', Battaglia Comunista, No. 24 1951; http://marxists.org/archive/bordiga/works/1951/murder.htm

16 Marc Lenglet, 'Conflicting Codes and Codings: How Algorithmic Trading is Reshaping Financial Regulation', *Theory, Culture & Society*, November 2011, 28: 44-66, p.2; Fabian Muniesa, *Des marchés comme algorithmes: sociologie de la cotation électronique à la Bourse de Paris*, Thèse de doctorat (PhD Thesis), Ecole des Mines de Paris, 2003.

17 Ibid., p.3

18 Neil Johnson, Guannan Zhao, Eric Hunsader, Jing Meng, Amith Ravindar, Spencer Carran and Brian Tivnan, 'Financial black swans driven by ultrafast machine ecology', *arXiv*, 7 February 2012.

19 Didier Sornette, *Why Stock Markets Crash*, Princeton University Press, 2003.

20 Michel Callon and Fabian Muniesa, 'Les marchés économiques comme dispositifs collectifs de calcul', *Réseaux 21*(122), 2003 or 'Economic Markets as Calculative Collective Devices', *Organization Studies*, 26(8), 2005, p.1236; Alexander R. Galloway, *The Interface Effect*, Polity, 2012. pp. 25-54.

21 Aldridge offers a broad description of different 'algorithmic' classes into electronic, algorithmic, systematic, high-frequency, low-latency, market making, etc. Irene Aldridge, *The Evolution of Algorithmic Classes*, 2010, p.4.

22 J. Doyne Farmer, Spyros Skouras, op. cit., p.6.

23 Ibid.

24 Ibid., p.16

25 Donald MacKenzie, Daniel Beunza, Yuval Millo, Juan Pablo Pardo-Guerra, *Drilling Through the Allegheny Mountains: Liquidity, Materiality and High-Frequency Trading* ,2012, p.9, http://www.sps.ed.ac.uk/staff/sociology/mackenzie_donald/?a=78186

26 James Angel, Lawrence Harris, Chester S. Spatt, *Equity Trading in the 21st Century*, Marshall School of Business Working Paper No. FBE 09-10, 2010, http://ssrn.com/abstract=1584026 or http://dx.doi.org/10.2139/ssrn.1584026

27 Themis Trading 2008, 2009

28 Donald MacKenzie, op. cit.

29 U. Dieckmanna, P. Marrow, R. Law, 'Evolutionary Cycling in Predator-Prey Interactions: Population

Dynamics and the Red Queen' *Journal of Theoretical Biology*, Volume 176, Issue 1, 7 September 1995, pp.91–102; G. D. Ruxton, T.N. Sherratt & M.P. Speed, 'Avoiding Attack: The Evolutionary Ecology of Crypsis, Warning Signals and Mimicry': Oxford University Press, 2004.

30 Ray Brassier, *Nihil Unbound: Enlightenment and Exctiction*, Basingstoke: Palgrave Macmillan, 2007, p.43.

31 Ibid.

32 Ibid., p.47.

33 Foresight: The Future of Computer Trading in Financial Markets (2012) Final Project Report. The Government Office for Science, London

34 Donald MacKenzie, op. cit., p.20.

35 Ibid., p.18.

36 J. Doyne Farmer, op. cit., p.6.

37 Stephen Jay Gould & Niles Eldredge, 'Punctuated Equilibria: the Tempo and Mode of Evolution Reconsidered', *Paleobiology* 3 (2), 115–151, 1977, p.145; Doyne Farmer, op. cit., p.14.

38 On May 6th 2010, the US stock market experienced one of the most severe price drops in its history; the Dow Jones Industrial Average (DJIA) index dropped almost 9% from the beginning of the day - the second largest point swing, 1,010.14 points, and the biggest one-day point decline, 998.5 points, on an intra-day basis in the history of the DJIA index. Anton Golub, John Keane, *Mini Flash Crashes*, 2011, p.1 and Anton Golub, John Keane, Ser-Huang Poon, *High Frequency Trading and Mini Flash Crashes*, HFT Review, 2012, http://arxiv.org/pdf/1211.6667v1.pdf

39 For a time, equity prices of some of the world's biggest companies were in freefall. They appeared to be in a race to zero. Peak to trough, Accenture shares fell by over 99 percent, from $40 to $0.01. At precisely the same time, shares in Sotheby's rose three thousand-fold, from $34 to $99,999.99. Andrew Haldane, 'The Race to Zero', International Economic Association Sixteenth World Congress, Beijing, China, 2011, p.1, http://www.bankofengland.co.uk/publications/Documents/speeches/2011/speech509.pdf

40 http://thecommune.co.uk/2012/04/29/interview-with-andrew-kliman/

41 Niklas Luhmann, *Risk: A Sociological Theory*, AldineTransaction, 2005; Jannis Kallinikos, *Governing Through Technology: Information Artefacts and Social Practice*, Basingstoke: Palgrave Macmillan, 2011. Claudio Ciborra and O. Hanseth, (eds.) *Risk, Complexity and ICT*, Cheltenham:

Edward Elgar Publishing, 2007. Elena Esposito, *The Future of Futures: The Time of Money in Financing and Society*, Cheltenham: Edward Elgar Publishing, 2011; Nicholas Georgescu-Roegen, *The Entropy Law and the Economic Process*, Cambridge (MA): Harvard University Press, Massachusetts, 1971.

42 Carsten Herrmann-Pillath, *Foundations of Evolutionary Economics*, Edward Elgar, forthcoming. Available at SSRN: http://ssrn.com/abstract=1781469

43 The year 2012 has seen the NASDAQ debacle on the Facebook IPO, the problems with BATS' own IPO and the recent collapse of Knight Capital Group. All of them have been attributed to software problems.

44 Reza Negarastani 'Drafting the Inhuman: Conjectures on Capitalism and Organic Necrocracy' in L.R. Bryant, N. Srnicek, G. Harman (eds.), *The Speculative Turn – Continental Materialism and Realism*, Melbourne: re.press, 2011, p.199.

FELLOWSHIP OF THE WRONG

In a land where the warp-speed pursuit of profits is turning the very tools of trade against the terms of value, a land not dissimilar to our own, a battle between Orcish bots and market-fearing hobbit coders rages. But can the Fellowship of the Wonk pull off its algo-flash-mob attack on the fulcrum of the brown-out? What would be unleashed by such a feat? A code-splitting tale run by BENEDICT SEYMOUR, with illustrations by RONA TUNNADINE

\document class: {saga}
\begin {document}
\begin {algorithm}

PART 1 – AN UNEXPECTED JOURNEY INTO HIGH FREQUENCY TRADING

A plague of Orcs is haunting Middle-Class. The people of Wall Shire are scared. Hard working finance hobbits and their families are being put out of business. All the powers of Market have entered into a 6-part franchise to exercise this spectrum of High Frequency Trading.

The Orcs are as ubiquitous as they are obscure. Most human folk do not even know that they exist, yet they dominate the financial markets, in particular Equities – the trading of stocks and shares. Their brother goblins, known to us as 'bots', are rife throughout the Great Net and have infested all the lands of Middle-Class from Amon Zon (Elvish for shopping), to Númenor (personal loans), and across the whole domain of Fangbook and Twii-dûr (social networking).

The human words for 'Orc' derive from the mathematical term, 'algorithm' – so the feral horde are known to finance folk as algos, algobots, or bots. In the eyes of science they are no more than algorithmic programs that run on computers and carry out repetitive lists of instructions. The Orcish bot is simply a complex equation expressed in lines of code, a set of commands by which the bots can get at the price of traded assets, buying and selling them on the market servers of the NYSE and NASDAQ. But because the Orc bots are so swift in their computing, they can find profits where no human trader could. The Orcs exists within a different temporal and spatial dimension, using speed to create and make money out of the smallest imaginable differentials in price. They produce the conditions which they then exploit, churning up the price of everything to wring out incrementally accruing returns. The bots are pound wise because, not in spite, of their penny-mania. Accumulating fractions of a cent over the course of a day as they zoom in and out of short term positions, they squeeze a fortune out of a 'long tail' of microscopic trades.

Consider the contrast with human trade, in which the trader invests in the shares of productive companies, seeking to make a profit by the rise or fall of firms and their products. In the process, the goodly go-betweens create jobs and useful commodities for all. Not so the Orcish bots – they move too fast to think about the final ends of trade. They hold positions for mere seconds or milliseconds, rushing in and out of shares and bonds, not caring if the human business on which they feed survives or fails. Some say they are a boon, bringing price discovery and liquidity to the parched markets, making trading cheaper, faster, more open to the humble hobbit. But while they help establish the prices of and market for stocks, providing a permanent supply of avid buyers and sellers,

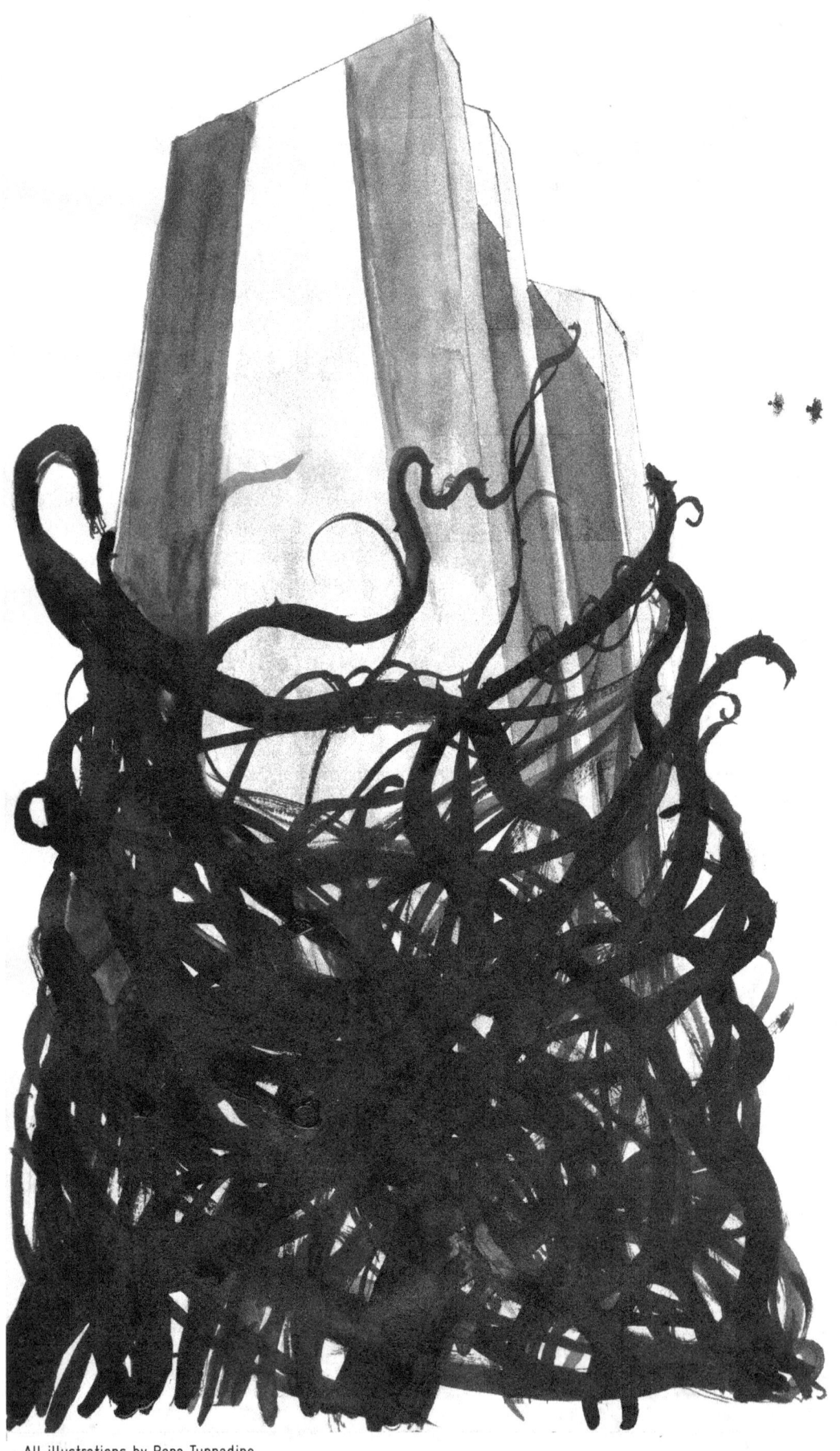

All illustrations by Rona Tunnadine

their speed conceals as much as it reveals. Their price revelations cause values to fluctuate with ever greater volatility. For the bots are febrile creatures, they feed on the difference between prices, exploiting sudden changes in the status of companies and the shifting behaviour of the market itself. Bots feed on bots in a spiral of feedback. They can make a market or ravage a company like a plague of locusts descending all at once on a single field. They make trading happen by providing a flock of potential buyers and sellers, but when the bots disperse, taking liquidity with them, they leave the market dry as a desert. No wonder human traders are petrified.

The invasion began around the time of the Great Crisis. As volatility increased in markets primed with fear and sovereign debt, the Orc bots stormed the citadel. Imperceptible at first, they battened on the trade in stocks and bonds, pestering and pummelling the markets' honest burghers. They demanded prices, prices, prices – but then would fail to buy, or buy then sell again, over and over. At once ruthlessly focused and hopelessly dim, they'd all rush in one direction, then turn around and rush back, rampaging through the market like a mob of zombies. Rapt in a recursive loop, the Orc bots would spend hours at a time soliciting quotes from a single company, reacting to shifts in market perception they themselves created. Feral window shoppers entranced by their own reflection. City hobgoblins.

Algorithms accelerate the process of assessment, indeed they teeter on the brink of suspending it entirely. As the Orcs swarmed into the domain of human judgement they risked its annihilation. They defile the realm of abstraction, shake the frame of equivalence to pieces and throw it back together, ever so slightly out. Human traders were confused,

alternately concerned and contemptuous, as if industrial workers had suddenly stormed the trading pit, the pure realm of speculation, knocking through the division of head and hand. The bots extend the dull propulsion of the machine to the highest spheres of financial reason. But many humans were only too eager to trade with them, if only because they seemed to reanimate the market. The Orcs created a simulacrum of activity to fill the post-crunch void, an imitation of a thriving economy for a world facing the chronic contraction of wealth. Some say it was the exotic financial instruments – derivatives, CDS and CDOs – that came before them, the toxic SIVs, swart swaps, and other spawn of VAR, that battered down the Chinese walls of finance and blazed a trail for the Orcish rout. It was these dastardly meta-contracts, models and money-like claims, still primitive and analogue in many ways, that cracked open the Vale of Exchange and made a way for Orcish ruin. The darkling bots were just the latest in a train of raiders, wonky equivalents and crooked complexities by means of which the rich and corrupt elders of Middle-Class hoped to go on cheating their destiny, deferring the disaster they themselves had unleashed. But could these human masters really command their new 'helpers'? Were they not instead become the plaything of the Orcs – or some darker purpose of which the bots were but the front end?

Thousands of times a second the bots would make their enquiries, buy, sell, or simply move on to their next mark. The automated traders could beat any human merchant to the quote, transacting in the blink of an eye. Soon, professional human merchants, with no ambition but to husband the modest fortunes in their care, were losing out to the Orcish onslaught. Honest dealers had to admit defeat, outdone by a spectral competitor, broken by a

Something there is within the very market that threatens to overwhelm its reason, or its reason to be

mere machine. Some grew angry and cried out for Ned Ludd to come and dole out justice to these robot interlopers. Former fund managers, who knew only the simple toil of productive investment, with narry a speculative bubble nor asset stripping operation to their name, found themselves suddenly obsolete, flung on the heap by a plague of anonymous bots.

Within a few frantic months the Orcs had grown to outnumber humans in the electronic pits. Soon they swarmed so thick and fast the very market seized. The first crash was so fast it was almost subliminal, but for a few tense moments billions were wiped from the value of shares, vast corporations teetered on the brink. Who knew what would happen next? – the riotous bots were out of control, human capitalists felt a shiver of fear.

The people of Wall Shire had not worried much when the bots first appeared. Many credulous and avaricious hobbits adopted them to execute their trades and sought to gain by the Orcish algos' speed. But when the Flash Crash came the good people of Middle-Class began to pay attention. The citizens of Wall Shire discussed and debated the Orc invasion, wondering if and when the markets would go down again. But others said the bots were plague enough in any case, and must be reined in or run out of town. The bots ate up the time and space of trade like a plague of locusts. Infesting and devouring the exchanges where they thrived, some said they were slowly driving out good trades with false and bad, like a flood of spam drowning an inbox. Just hosting these voracious hordes was costing the yeoman data farmers ever more of their hard earned loot.

And now the algos' dominion is expanding, ever-bigger servers must be constructed to accommodate the teeming, quote seeking plague. Vast towers, tunnels, and complexes are built to host these unproductive bots. And all because their human masters (but are they masters, or merely puppets?) claim they make it easier and quicker to do business.

The Orcish bots, or so the Tylers of Durden claim, are little more than an occupying army. They colonise the servers and make the markets do the work of Sour Ron – the Dark Lord of Code. If the Legend be true, Sour Ron is a disgruntled über-geek gone over to the side of darkness. Sour Ron sees everything with a single eye the size of Fangbook and Twii-dûr combined. His black agents, faster than thought seethe within the very substance of the Value Crystal – the true source of the physical world, or so the Old Songs tell.

The whisper goes about that Sour Ron means to return, and when all the human fund managers are gone, picked off by his murderous, microsecond legions of code, he will take over the market. The first great convulsion – the Flash Crash of 2.45 – was just a warning of what is to come. The Orcish bots go on bombarding the exchanges with millions of quote requests a day, yet the volume of actual transactions remains the same, even falls. For nanoseconds the bot assault slows down the network, causing a 'brown out' of the market, and they steal by this momentary stasis an advantage over their ugly brother bots. Using speed to bring sclerosis to the very frame of trade, they gouge a profit from the form of Exchange itself. They shake it to a halt, spamming honest burghers till the market's quote-stuffed maw coughs up an instant's leverage. They smash and grab, loot then riot on.

Each trading day as the market stops to draw a shattered breath, the Orc bots disperse, rushing back into the shadows leaving nought but a trail of phosphorescent square and saw-tooth trading graphs behind them – the only clue as to their brutal logic. The Knights of Nanex – a group of noble men skilled in the ways of data but sworn to defend human trading – set nets to catch the bots then scry their lurid entrails. Using the tools of their craft the Knights plot and parse the algo code, teasing out the method in their madness. They sift the static of these headless raiders, throw their shapes onto the screen, pinning up the ultra-fast and invisible like butterflies, luminous hoodlums. But all they can do is infer the hidden hand of human coders behind the algorithmic rages, guess at the mortal greed and strategy that makes humans turn the market's tools against the terms of trade itself. Peering into the darkness they fear to glimpse the bigger picture – the more than human madness here – but they sense it, that 'something' more vast and abstract, more sublime and more unspeakable, than the bots themselves. Something there is within the very market that threatens to overwhelm its reason, or its reason to be.

No one knows whom the Orc bots really serve, as their human – some say semi-human – 'controllers', the High Frequency men, lurk at the bottom of Dark Pools and never see the light of day. Spurning the honest guilds and lavish websites of market-fearing folk, they hide behind single page portals and conduct their dealings with the Orcs furtively. Their trades are secret, coded and recoded by The Internalisers, creatures of the interstices who turn every transaction into a Black Box, hidden from the sight of God. The bots surge on, server space is no sooner expanded than the bots guzzle it up again, glutting on the margins then disgorging themselves at the close of trade. Visible to none but Sour Ron with his all-seeing-eye, the bots grow ever quicker, racing toward lightspeed like an errant neutrino – perhaps beyond. Rumour expands to fill the void of knowledge. Sour Ron, they whisper, intends to break the laws of physics or bend them to his will - or so it is written in the blogs - to breach the rule of space-time itself. The dark One is biding his time, just waiting till the day when, busted open by the algo rout, the market stalls but cannot close. Battered into stasis by the Orcs' siege engine, jammed like the aperture of a broken camera, this endless moment is the strait gate through which Sour Ron will enter, rise up and seize control of the social synthesis all by - and for - himself. The supersonic prattle of the bots will stop, their incessant, empty trades will cease - and who can say what happens then?

Others laugh nervously, mutter that Sour Ron is just a fable, the figment of some stoned coders' overactive brain. Nonetheless, all Wall Shire agree that the Orc bots' frantic machinations could soon put production of the Value Crystal itself at risk... Someone must do something about these feral equations, this pernicious mob of math. But what?

PART 2 – THE QUEST BEGINS

The Fellowship of the Wonk, a bunch of hairy legged hobbit Quals & elven Quants, come together. They are resolved to free the land from the Orc bots' pestilential proliferation. Lead by their spiritual guide, McGandalf, and after barely 15 months of intensive discussion, the Fellows set out on their Quest.

To beat the bots, the Fellowship believe, they must first wrest a quotation for the true value of derivatives on Canadian peameal bacon from the evil Quote-Dragon, Smug. Smug is said to live atop the Tower of Algos in the heart of Manhattan. Once they have his quote they will - or so the Legend says - be able to lead him to pasture at an allotment on the edge of Riverside

Drive. There they plan to slay him through a humane and controlled deleveraging.

The population of Middle-Class are sceptical. What the fuck are algobots anyway?

Undiscouraged, the band of hobbits, elves and ex-particle physicists ride on until they reach the foot of Smug's tower.

PART 3: THE DESPERATION OF SMUG

The Tower is an enormous skyscraper full of algobot-infested servers. It is located at the edge of Manhattan's Midtown, convenient to all major global information networks. The Orcish algos need the servers to thrive. They suck directly on high capitalism's deepest bong pipe - a sub-Atlantic cable known in the trade as the Great Pipe. Their human masters (or are they merely their hosts, even their Slaves?) are busily constructing more such mega-structures on which the bots may feed. Selling out their own kind for a mess of transactional revenue, the Tower's traitors make a nice living while the bots gnaw away at Hard Working Investors' and Fund Managers' daily bread.

In order to gain entry to the Tower, the Fellowship must first work out the hopelessly overencrypted runic formulae left behind by chronic show-off and coder manqué, Sour Ron. Before his fall Sour Ron was known as the Sorcerer of Source Code and is responsible for making the IT infrastructure of most of the Fortune 500 indicipherable to any other programmer.

YE SIDEBAR

In the quest of a job for life, or so it is fabled, Sour Ron wrote himself into the data structure of the top finance houses of the USA. Others talk of a magic ring with which he can control the NASDAQ, and hint at a connection to Bernie

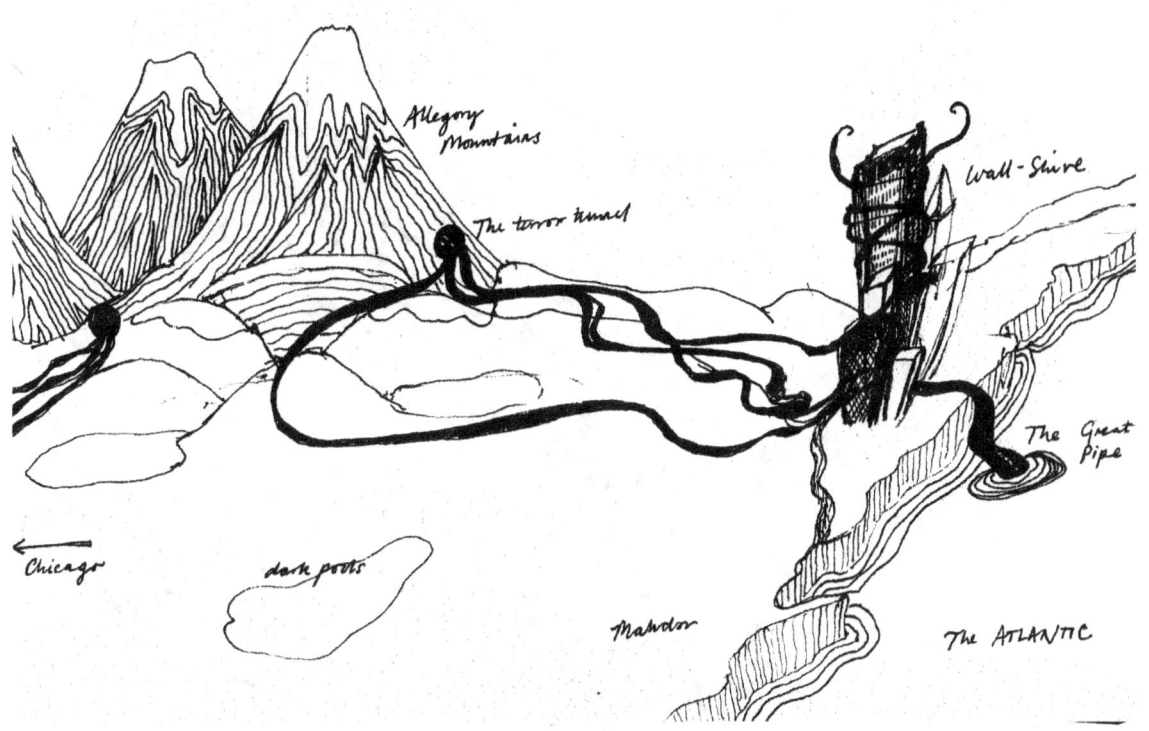

Madoff, the fallen Ponzi elf – once a prime mover in the world of automated trading before his magic formula failed. But such speculation boots (nor reboots) us naught, and we must resume our tale.[1]

HERE ENDS YE SIDEBAR

With the help of the good wizard ('Dave') Mandrel, the Fellows are able to parse Sour Ron's horribly overgrown code and gain access to the Tower. Once inside, our heroes slowly scale the vertiginous mountain of server cable and rather boring looking black boxes. They stave off chronic tedium by imagining and doing battle with various goblins, gremlins, and glitches along the way. When all else fails they pause to rewatch *Lord of the Rings* box sets until the sweet release of sleep steals upon them (generally in just a few shakes of an algo's quote).

At the top of the Tower they confront the dragon Smug only to discover that he's just a giant animatronic papier-mâché mock up operated from a curtained booth by pop sociologist, Kraven Savlon. 'Ignore the bespectacled geek behind the curtain and listen to me, the mighty Smug!', he cries before admitting his deception.

The Fellows force Savlon – who only wanted to be popular and is not really All Bad – to put together a TED talk calling for the world's Orc-meisters to reprogramme their monstrous hordes. The Senior Elven Council

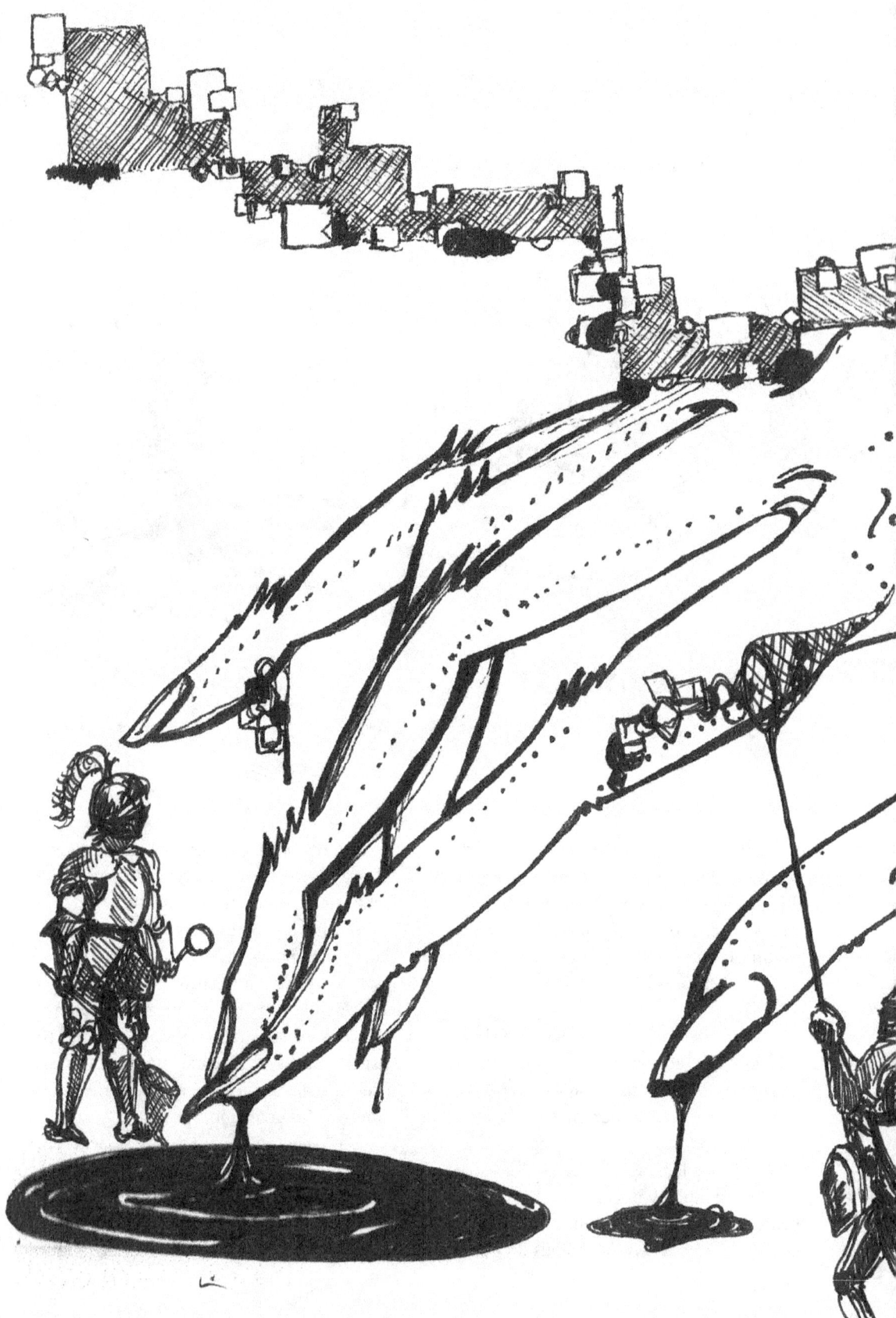

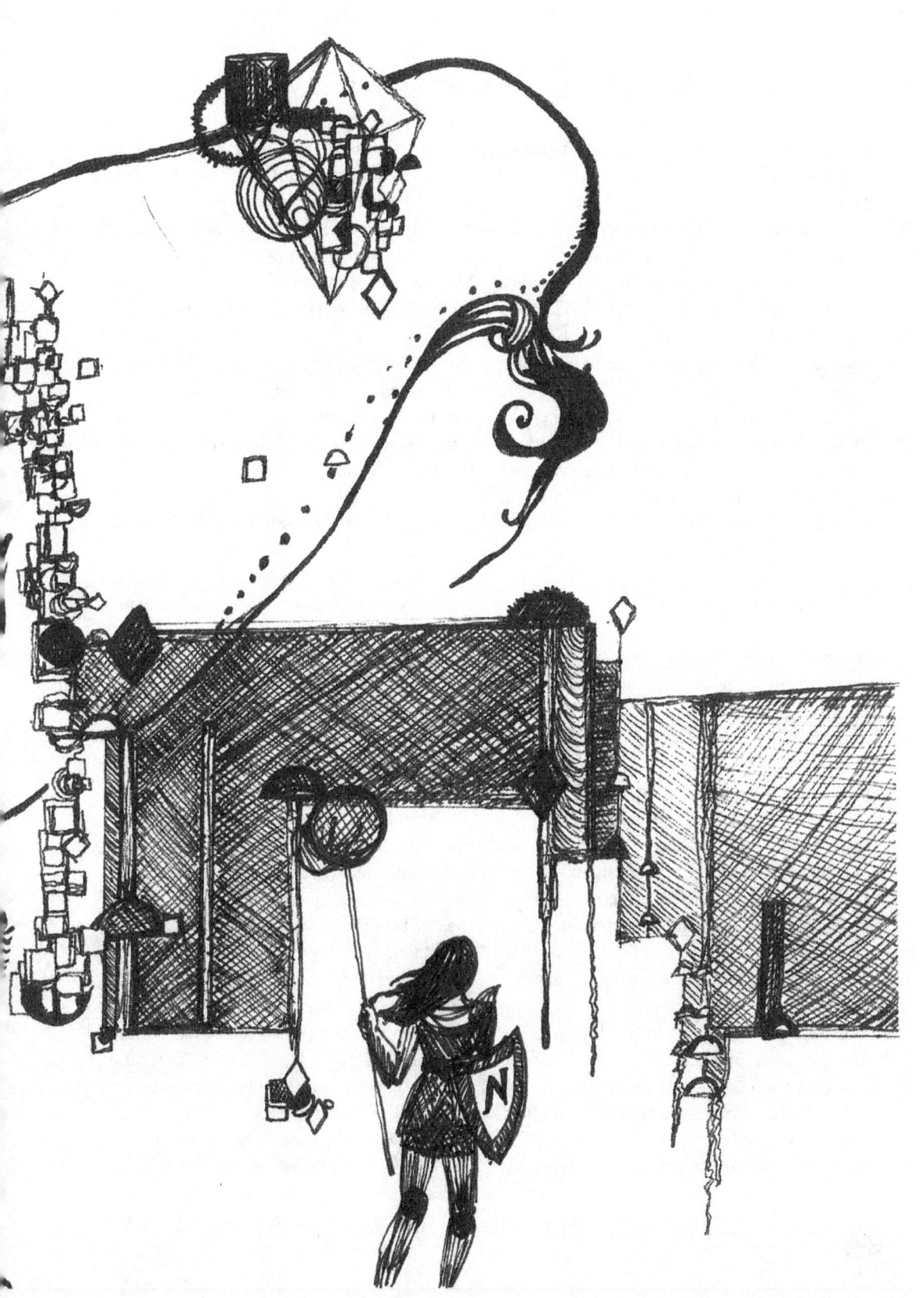

takes Savlon's broadcast to heart and introduces global regulations to ensure the market-fearing conduct of bots going forward. From now on all bots must hang onto the quotes they solicit from the traders of stocks and bonds for at least a nanosecond before getting second helpings. Mandrel is promoted to Fiscal Elf and draws up a charter of decent coding to which all the programmers in Wall Shire have to subscribe, and they all live happily ever after...

Until the next day that is, when the entire financial system collapses and a mysterious group known only as The Bane mass a vast and irascible rabble in the county of Manhattan, but a league from Wall Shire. They demand a solution to stuff, like now.

PART 4: MAHDOR, MYSTERY AND SUSPENSE

While The Bane's shadowy leadership council pause at the edge of Wall Shire, caught in an intense internal debate about the precise interpretation of one of the equations in Marx's Mathematical Notebooks, the Fellowship reconvene for an emergency meeting.

A long Powerpoint presentation by the anthrohobbit Daisy Graybeard argues that the only answer to the open social crisis and the Orc assault lies deeper within the crystal system itself – further south east, to be precise, in the land of Mahdor. The Fellowship can heal the wider malaise, restore production and appease the mob, but only once this more fundamental structural problem is properly addressed. The Algo Tower was not the real source of the Orc bots, declares Graybeard, rather they must turn their attention to Sour Ron's vast Mahdor complex, an Orc bot ridden data hub of which the Tower was just a subordinate node. The Orcs all depend on Mahdor far more than they did the Tower, and in any case, the only way to

stop the victory of time over space is to go to where the rot starts and pluck out the spores. Although the Orc bots have no particular home or source, they do seem to pour out of the earth in Mahdor. So striking them as they appear is as good as tearing up their roots.

The other Fellows are very impressed by Graybeard's oration. Hear hear – we pretended ourselves into this mess, we can pretend ourselves out of it! A small fat comment hobbit called Hamfist Harveybuck chimes in to support Graybeard: We must be radical, stop the source code at source, maybe even introduce a Tolkien Tax.

At this point McGandalf chooses finally to speak up. To take out Sour Ron's naughty bots would require much greater firepower than we can muster. And even a Tolkien tax won't stop the blasted Orcs – they'll just adjust to the new terms and conditions and renew their assault. No, instead the answer is to turn the markets themselves against the Orc offensive.

At this the Speculative Realelf, Eyli Ayweiwei, pipes up – 'There's no such thing as Black-Scholes! In the brownout of philosophy all bots get browned off!'

After a moment of stunned, blank silence, and while the rest of the Fellowship are trying to work out what the fuck Ayweiwei is on about, Gandalf resumes his argument. To get free of the Orc bots the Fellowship must make it look like Mahdor just isn't working properly – then they'll be able to get the regulatory powers to fix it. Once this is accomplished, and little by little, they can restore a less abstract form of exchange, placing control back in the hands of elves, hobbits and the other market-fearing anthrofolk of Middle-Class.

The Fellowship once more cheer in approval and Gandalf continues. The only way to zap Mahdor without attracting attention from Hobbiton Security is to traverse the Terror

Tunnel through the Allegory Mountains, to Chicago. There they will block up the light pipes and bombard the Mahdor servers with a bolt of superintense data of less than a picosecond in duration. The Fellowship can then release a press release declaring that the Chicago exchange is

There's no such thing as Black-Scholes! In the brownout of philosophy all bots get browned off!

just too much for Mahdor to handle and that Mahdor itself must be shut down. It'll be so fast no one will ever know the data blurt was caused by elves not bots. Some of the Fellows are unsettled – isn't it terrorism? What if they blow up the Terror Tunnel by mistake? But Graybeard backs up Gandalf – it's not terror, it's just a form of illegible propaganda by the deed. A deed so fast no one can even read it, sending a message only we can interpret. And besides, we should act as if we're free already. This will be far more efficient and sustainable than just smashing up Mahdor – and isn't that exactly what the Orc bots were doing already, in a way? Their assault made nature itself indecipherable, a rioting no one could read. We must use the same methods if we are to stop their loathsome scrawl for good. Once the light pipes no longer function there will be no need for property destruction nor legislation, and everyone can return to hearty, hobbit-friendly forms of barter – a middle earthly paradise.

At this the Fellowship cheer and toss their copies of Graybeard's blockbuster (*5000 Years of Doh*) in the air, declaring their commitment

to personal exploitation and capitalism with a hobbit face.

With little time to lose the Fellowship set off (after a brief ritual farewell lasting no more than 500 million thousand terrabillion nanoseconds) and are soon in the foothills of Allegory. They have various scrapes and adventures along the way however, and some very long and boring discussions with giant trees on the subject of recycling.

Once inside the mountain in the pitchy blackness of the Terror Tunnel, Froideur, the coolest of the hobbits, has a decisive encounter with a bitter and creepy geek called Colum. Colum lives in total darkness and subsists on a diet of code and coca cola.

At this point we need a brief flashback –

HERE BEGINS FROIDEUR'S FLASHBACK:

Froideur is the only one who can decipher the social runes and discern the political-historical content of supposedly neutral technologies. While hiding from the evil enchanter, Wagedlabour, he spent a decade in the open source Elven library in Rivendell and learned to read the runic incunabula of the dead white wizard, Luxenmarx.

Froideur subsequently lead Ye Dept. of Degeneration thru Culture at the Clevershop of Goldensmiths in the Shire of Operaish. He also set up the Elventhink Lab and was beginning to explore the spatio-conceptual limits of neoliberal Hobbiton when the Orcbot assault began. Only massive funding cuts and his sudden and total pauperisation forced Froideur back into fighting tights and into the Fellowship of the Wonk.

HERE ENDS FROIDEUR'S FLASHBACK

Having got lost and fallen into the clutches of the bitter geek, Colum, Froideur gets to spend quality time with the unsavoury coding quant and is treated to a litany of self-aggrandising monologues.

Colum speaks a purely recursive and self-referential prattle directed to himself in the third person: 'we hates it nasty shivery lightspeed fibreoptic pipes, we'll brown them out with algoglut and overcodes, won't we, my precioussssss...'.

While holding Froideur captive Colum boastingly reveals that he has a special algorithm that can fuck up all the others: 'One rune to rule them all, one rune to find them, one rune to bring them all and in the brown out bind them!', he intones.

Eventually the ingenious Froideur is able to wriggle free of his bonds and, realising 'rune' is just New Age bollocks for 'code', he locates the equation which can reverse the algo assault for good. It is locked away in Colum's laptop in a folder cunningly labelled 'Non-preciousssss stuff'.

Armed with the algorithm, Froideur catches up with and rejoins the Fellowship in the heart of the Allegory mountains. He is just in time to stop them blasting Mahdor with superfluous data. Instead they upload Colum's code to the system which, attacking the value form in its totality, causes all trading everywhere to cease all at once, very fast.[2]

PARTS 5, 6 AND N: COMMUNISM IS REAL HUMAN FELLOWSHIP

Just as The Bane and their multitudinous mob are about to (finally!) storm Wall Shire, they are apprised of the news, and instead set about drafting a short transitional programme that redeploys the existing technological resources of the planet in a socially useful and environmentally sustainable way.

Within days they have refunctioned the Terror Tunnel and the global matrix of algos and cable into a supercomputer. A few hours later it has worked out the formula for non-carbon based energy and an 18 point plan for converting the existing infrastructure such that it functions on a 'from each according to her ability to each according to her needs' model.

Sour Ron returns from his secret underground ranch in Arizona and offers to decipher all the stuff he has snarfed up with flowery code, and is soon busy beating the financial-military-post-industrial complex into

---

Reapplying the loan value calculation equations for the payday loan site Wonga he reverses the effects of global warming

---

figurative ploughshares. Reapplying the loan value calculation equations for the payday loan site Wonga he also reverses the effects of global warming – the interim solution proposed by the liberated algos being, incidentally, to float giant nodding ducks in the world's oceans. This has the accidental side benefit of preventing it from raining in the former United Kingdom ever again. When the population have finished venting unassuaged historical stores of hatred on the maimed and eyeless bodies of ConDem MPs and ATOS managers, many people even choose to remain in the ex-UK, though it is for the most part soon rezoned as the Middle-Class Museum of Commodities Money Fictitious Capital and Money-like Financial Instruments (M-C-M – C-M-M-M), a popular amusement park themed around the ~~value form~~.

Soon the newly housed and centrally heated hobbits, humanoids and ex-sub-humans of the world are living peacefully side by side, work is abolished and the Bane – who got a little uppity toward the end of the transition – are put in charge of allocating socially useful labour tasks to the remaining population of barely-necessary workers until they can get with their own (non) programme. The latter contingent comprises precisely 3 former SERCO managers and one self-made man (independent) whose job it is to automate the remaining unautomated bits of social reproduction that nobody doesn't want automating, without asking any one else for help.

They are still working on it as our story closes, the camera pulling back slowly to reveal an epic vista of self-constructing, all-sided housing and Roomba factories, melted yuppydromes, hollow skyscrapers, and capacious infinity pools requidified out of the material residue of the value form like some sublated and denoumenalised grey goo. Hobbit, elf and the other figments frolic together, drunk on lemonade zoomed from the ocean via a million tiny filaments, up from the Great Pipe, down into the Tower, right through the Allegory Mountains, and all the way, fresh, into the sparkling pool.

YE ENDE

P.S. – No Orcs were used in the writing of this Legend. Any resemblance between hobbits, elves or social theorists depicted in this saga and actually existing life forms is purely contingent. Anything is possible, although some things are more unnecessary than others.[3]

YE VERY ENDE

PPS – IF puzzled GOTO beginning. Re-read. IF still puzzled GOTO:

Alberto Toscano's 'Gaming the Plumbing: High-Frequency Trading and the Spaces of Capital', pp.74-85, and Inigo Wilkins and Bogdan Dragos, 'Destructive Destruction? An Ecological Study of High Frequency Trading', pp.86-99.

Endwhile
\end {algorithm}
\end {document}
\end {saga}

Benedict Seymour ‹ben@kein.org› is a contributing editor to *Mute*, teaches on the MFA Fine Art at Goldsmiths College and is completing a PhD on film and financialisation at University of Wolverhampton

YE ENDEN NOTES

1   That is it does not boot us, not that it does not not reboot us – that were a pleonasm or negation of the negation, even. We are not self-valorising value already.

2   Faster than an algobot in fact. N.B. algobots can conduct a trade in less time than it takes you to blink. In the time it takes you to read this sentence, for example, the vast accumulation of commodities that comprises capital could be sold and sold back to its original owners 11 billion times. In fact it has been. Some claim that this is the refutation of Benjamin's invocation of Kafka's riff about the coming world being exactly the same 'just a little different', but for each of these claims there are now 11 billion others to the contrary suggesting everything will change totally but wind up much the same.

3   Quentin Meillassoux, *After After Finitude*, Forthcoming, Rivendell: Finally Got the News Press.

THE GUEST

A short story by **MIRA MATTAR** exploring the annihilating
power of luxury

Initials have been sewn into the white gloves. CL. Barely visible. Off-white on white. On laundry day C.L. can identify them. She won't let the other girls borrow her sewing kit. They can mix and match for all she cares. Limey bitches.

C.L. wears the gloves to unpack the guest's belongings. She mustn't allow any naturally occurring oils to travel from her fingertips to the guest's things even though, in this case, neither the guest nor her belongings are of much value. Still though, C.L. likes to know who she's dealing with. She concludes she's dealing with an inefficient person. When she talks to her she will play up her accent, let in a few jibes at the boss' expense. She likes to make people feel comfortable that way.

Regarding colour and shape, the guest had packed aiming to minimise impact. One of the placement consultants at the agency said the mothers always look through your things. Traces of criminality or deviance had been left well behind, locked in a drawer, in a desk, in a room, in a house. But though she had located her smartest most casual smart-casual clothes, the guest still somehow got it wrong. The child she is there to teach cringes and asks if she is really going out like that. (At least her English is improving. Conditionals are notorious.)

Stupid. All her things have betrayed and humiliated her. Twice used razor gross with stubble. Tubes squeezed haphazardly. Vulgar yellow toothbrush. Half peeled-off price labels. Off-brand pound shop crap. These are not protective amulets.

Here the soap is changed daily. All the toiletries onboard are by a well-known London perfumier and clothes designer whose name adorns every product. Once the name has

rubbed off the soap – which happens after only a use or two – it is replaced by an identical one and the guest is reminded. What happens to all those barely used and now anonymous soaps, she wonders.

At dinner everyone reeks of lime and grapefruit. It comes off them in waves. The hosts nod at the guest and smile. Neither can speak the other's language. Nothing else passes between them until a common word like 'iPhone' or 'tiramisu' seals the gap.

C.L. laid and decorated this table. She imagined it first and then made it match. She got these tiny magenta coloured feathers and stayed up late threading silver beads onto their stems. Her bunkmate kept asking her to turn out the light but she ignored her. Seeing the light reflect off the beads was more than worth the next day's petty shunning. There is a reason C.L. is the head stewardess.

The boss has a new bride who is keen to make her presence felt. She likes to eat from the communal platter with her fork. Territory. She loves the feeling it gives her. Despite all that is on offer the child refuses to eat anything but plain spaghetti for lunch and dinner. The boss doesn't like this.

When the guest returns to her cabin she finds everything exactly as it was when she first arrived. She has left no traces. She finds this oddly comforting and no longer feels the need to reach for her phone to look at photographs of loved ones. Even the tiny spot of blood she scratched out of a mosquito bite onto the bedcover has disappeared.

In the morning she is greeted as if for the first time. It seems they wake up every day with no memory. At breakfast she is overwhelmed. She can choose from all possible assemblages

*Everything matches everything,
new logics of colour. Minor storms.
Barracudas. Linen*

of hot and cold breakfast foods and drinks. Decisions are made through a combination of habit, preference and novelty. What is a Russian pancake? (She reaches out to try one.) The guest is unburdened, no longer having to tell a lover how she takes her morning tea, she is free of all – even the most minor of – commitments, promises and laws of self-governance. Finally weightless.

In the afternoon, a lesson:
Write your name.
No.
C'mon, we learned how to do it yesterday.
The guest hates herself for saying 'we'. The child refuses.
OK. Any word.
No.
Any letter then.
A look of glee travels across the child's face: she draws a giant X.
Good. How about another?
She draws a giant X.
I mean another letter, a different one.
She draws a giant X.
I like R. It's fun don't you think?
She draws a giant X. We switch to numbers. X becomes zero.

Meals. Sunsets. Flaps of toilet roll folded origami style into impossible points, Mojitos. Norwegian bottled water. High calibre ports spawning each other until there is no difference. Yachts with names like Waveduster and The Pulveriser. Everything matches everything, new logics of colour. Minor storms. Barracudas. Linen.

That night C.L. had laid the guest's pyjamas out on her bed for her. Washed and ironed. The guest stands at the foot of the bed looking at the flat shapes. The legs are splayed so that the material is flat and smooth against the bed. The long sleeves of the top are neatly pressed down, a little away from the body. The meditative pose of the empty clothes looks too peaceful to disturb. The guest takes off her clothes and climbs into bed beside the empty form, careful so as not to wrinkle or rumple it. She looks at it for a moment then goes to sleep curled in a ball with a pillow between her knees.

Mira Mattar ‹miramattar@gmail.com› ‹twitter.com/miramattar› is a sometime governess, freelance writer and contributing editor to *Mute* and *3:AM*. She blogs at http://hermouth.blogspot.com/

THE GARDEN OF EARTHLY DELIGHTS

Establishing a temporary experimental research station within spitting distance of East London's Olympic Park, The Crystal World proposed to decrystalise digital dystopia and recrystalise unlikely contingent cultures. MATTHEW FULLER *wades through the muck*

For several decades the most formally inventive exhibition in London has been the Minerals Gallery in the Natural History Museum. With a meteorite at its apex making a suitably off-world fulcrum, the tens of oak display cases ranked across the long light hall present hundreds of prime specimens of minerals in all their shockingly varied capacities of growth.

Whereas most of the other galleries in the museum are punitively but sparely interactive, or set out like walkthrough text books made with surfaces ready to be hosed down after each group of snot and grime exuding schoolchildren have been rammed through at the speed of their presumed attention spans, the minerals gallery offers you nothing except the capacity to encounter the utterly fecund world of basic matter. Each specimen is chosen to represent the idiotypical colouration, growth patterns and texture of certain chemicals and their mixes, and the world of minerals is, we learn, voluptuously and finely creative, and it becomes abundantly obvious, with the expressive capacities of elements as they mix under different conditions, that the universe is amazing. It is also rather disconcertingly neat.

Something of the universe's unruliness, its filthy playful accident, is rather more manifest in The Crystal World exhibition by Martin Howse, Ryan Jordan and Jonathan Kemp recently on at the Space White Building. Titled after J.G. Ballard's novel of encroaching strangeness, here the earth is transformed into a gigantic grunge chemistry set. The chemist Dmitri Mendeleev famously found the final proportions of the periodic table in a dream after much intense work of experiment and calculation, and something similar is going on here. The exhibition proposes intense links between matter, abstraction and the fantastic; the combination of computation, accident and intuition. In the periodic table, matter proceeds along two axes with a gradually changing set of qualities arranged by atomic weight and atomic number (a quality added later following work by Henry Moseley), changing in terms of conductivity, malleability, the ability to react with or combine with other materials and so on. The whole table, with each change arising from the accretion of one electron at a time, formulates, at a certain scale of analysis, all of the abundant expressivity of matter arising from what Mendeleev called the invisible world of chemical atoms.

The Crystal World project is an attempt to break that expressivity free from the constraints imposed on it by what can be called the norm-forms, normative formations, that run through contemporary culture. Set across the canal from and partly funded by the 'legacy' of the Olympic Park, one of the great excrescences of such, The White Building, seems a prime location in which to do so. But the particular focus of the show is on the way in which the fruits of the periodic table are yielded to us in computing and electronics.

Computing is a particularly interesting place to track such things because it can be both highly abstract and very concrete at multiple scales, from those of logic, to interface, to hardware and its interpolation with aesthetics and the social. Equally, due to the high degree of abstraction involved in computing, coupled with its fundamental qualities of generality – that it is capable of making possible, simulating and improving upon numerous kinds of machine – computing is a site where norm-forms are particularly potent and also highly contestable. What this exhibition proposes is that we go back to some of the fundamentals of computing, its 'primitives' in a sense, and to some basic chemistry, to see how they intermesh, but instead of routing them through the standard objects through which it is normally accessed – laptops, phones, synthesisers, software, and so on – we do so by working with what looks suspiciously like Hackney, or the debris of the glorious information age.

In the centre of the room, water from the neighbouring Grand Union Canal cycles through a tangled network of clear plastic tubes. Tinged with a spot of sulphuric acid it is pumped upwards to spatter down through a clump of assorted stones suspended from the ceiling on a steel grid and from there over a heap of broken motherboards on another grid, this one of a finer gauge and visibly sagging and corroding. From there it cascades into two large tubs made from sliced-open plastic water tanks set off from the floor on shipping pallets. Over the period of the show the canal water has yielded a good crop of white slime clinging to the wires and the tubes, undulating in trails as the drops run in.

From those two tanks, the enriched liquid is fed to six smaller ones fixed out of split polythene jerry cans sat in the upper quarter-part of one of the larger water tanks. In each of these a different set of ingredients stirs: heat sinks broken out of computing boxes, with a chunk of iron pyrites on top under a slow drizzle of acidulated canal; a tray of wood shavings thick with clumps of mycelium yielding a particularly toothsome ivory toned fungus; two trays of acid with assorted copper parts slowly oozing into luridly green, yellow or sky-blue tinctures and scums; two trays of silver nitrate, one with a black matt of congealed metal pinched by electrodes, another, some ancient gravy pierced by crocodile clipped pencils functioning as

---

This exhibition proposes is that we go back to some of the fundamentals of computing, its 'primitives'

electrodes. Leachate and contamination from one bowl to another, stirrings of electrons and molecules in the wrong places, this is the nightmare that the European Electronic Waste Directive was supposed to protect us against. Whilst I am there, a pipe flops out of its fixing and dumps a pint or so of best onto the floor which, judging from the grey traces of splashings, has seen a certain amount of disgorgement amidst the general miasma.

A miasma of course is a means of describing a state of matter that is disturbing, yet has not yet been analytically described, one that may be morally compromising. There's a romantic proposition here: matter is active, making its own state, analysis is superfluous by comparison with experiment with prurient oxides, chemical curds, and signals processing something. All of the separate parts of this system have their own microclimate, their own special set of currents, purities and congealments, but they all take part in a general economy of oozings based on drainage, cycling, dissolution and the light frazzle of electrically active acids and devices and substances sensitive to them.

To one corner of the larger mass sits a tiny delicate clutter. Rudimentarily modelled on the axon hillock structure that transfers and triggers electrical activity in the nervous system, thin angular copper wires connect in

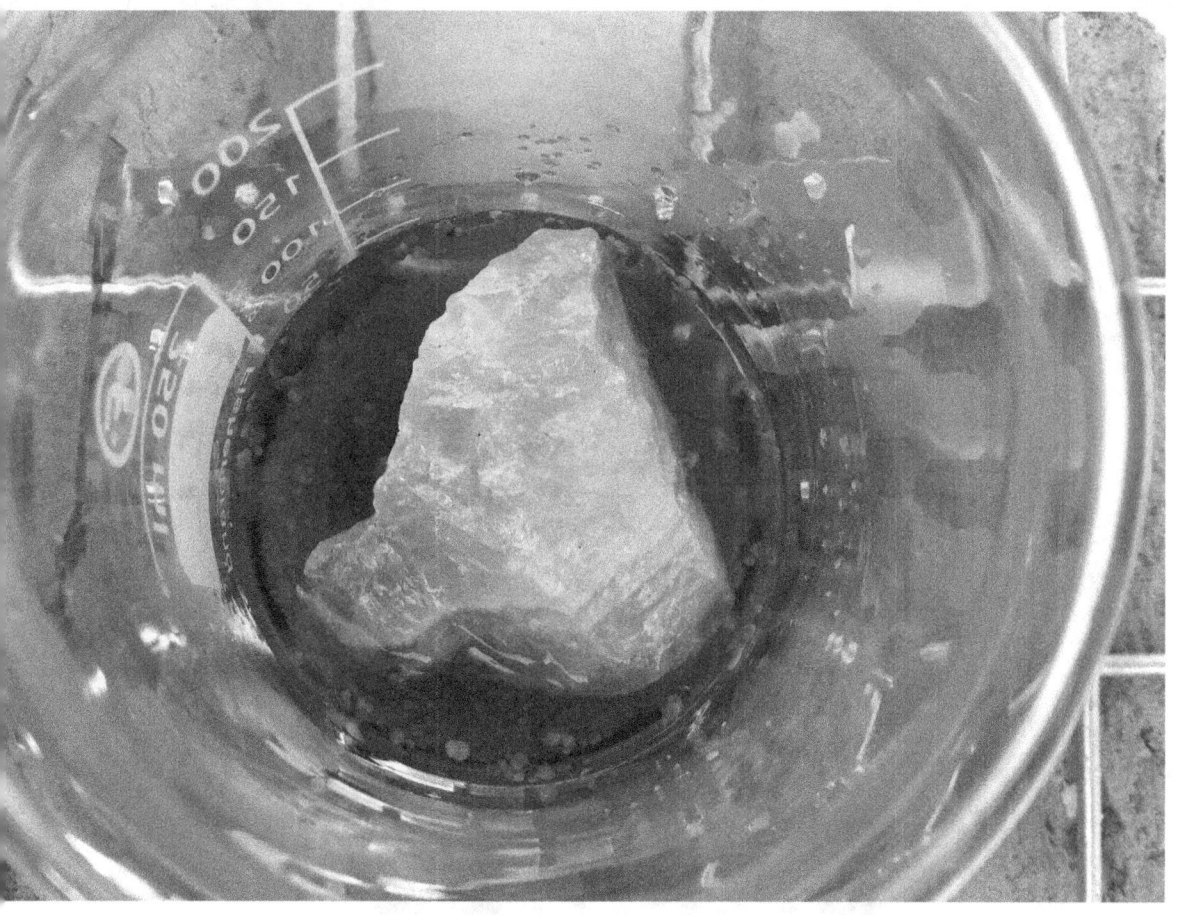

All images: Martin Howse, Ryan Jordan and Jonathan Kemp, *The Crystal World,* The White Building, London, 2012

groups of three to small chunks of chalcopyrites. The wires in turn are connected to a further set of tubes containing some fluid and a build-up of sodium crystals. Wired, these are plugged into an amp, feeding into a clutch of stray-looking speakers, magnets down, on the floor. Over the course of the month, this structure has gone from emitting a stream of clicks and crackles over a baseline of white noise, turning to occasional bleeps and pulsings, to silence. Something came loose, implying no particular dividing line between the broken and the rest.

Around the four corners of the room are various tables used for a five day open lab run as part of the show.[1] They are arrayed with the debris of chemistry labs and kitchens, fish bowls with electrodes and crystalline build up, silts and salts; books of minerology, alchemy and history next to a row of impressively molding pots of yogurt made of milk taken from cows. On another bench, fragments of computers are laid out with various crystalline

growths upon them. Hard drives soused in acid covered in white fuzz. Pickle jars full of Rochelle Salt crystals; clumps of quartz; fans wired to switches wired to speakers wired to magnets; a salad of circuit board fragments liberally dosed with short strips of copper wire to encourage impromptu networking, a small bone covered with glistening crystals laid out on a dark tray of untreated hardwood; powders, rusts, limonite, dried up daises, numerous nameless residues biding their time. From one of the four pillars, a pair of cassettes dangle, disgorging their tape, a yield of tiny white crystals on its surface.

A Ziploc bag of sulphur remains on one of the tables from a sizeable batch that was burned with a high voltage connection over on the floor. A clutter of vaguely scorched sticks and bricks remain from its handling. By the time you have examined all this material, the background buzz has gnawed its way into the forefront of your consciousness. The grey slag of the burned sulphur lies like a mini-Pompeii on the concrete.

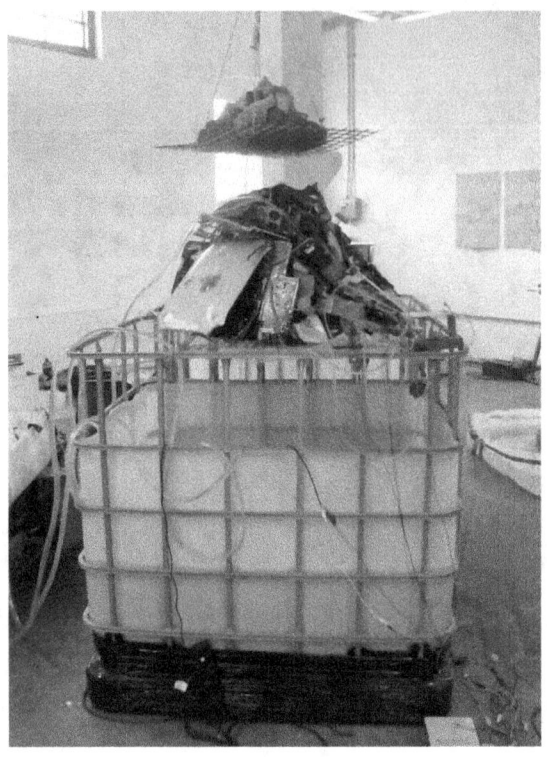

On another bench, a microwave oven sits atop another, jammed full of ceramic wool. Giving it this extra element turns the oven into a furnace capable of reaching over a thousand degrees centigrade, used to refine iron from haematite at over 1200°C. One of the bricks on the bench had both crushed haematite and melted iron still in its recesses. Many of the chemicals used in this show have been burned, siphoned, distilled and rescued from their accrual in circuit boards and devices. The remains of computing becomes chemical, a source for reconstitution. A wiki accompanying The Crystal World project gives extensive documentation on the techniques used to suck the gold out of circuits or drain the metals from ores. A library of materials used as sources can be downloaded as a reader.[2] A general principle of the work here being a gathering and proliferation of unexpected connections, through bodies of knowledge, through disjoint components and amongst elements, compounds and what they congeal.

Along the last wall, on top of some thick polythene sheet, lies the Earth Computer. Two thick lengths of copper lead into a tray set into a bed of mud, the tray containing lumps of scavenged copper and zinc in a solution of silver nitrate. What comes in and what goes out of this computer depends upon the stirrings of its components and what the earth might happen to send through it – lightning perhaps: the contraption is due to be buried nearby after the closure of the show. Like all of the constructions here, each concentration of work is not strictly delimited for contemplation. Residues of its making, sheets of notes, buckets, bottles, scraps of stained paper, cracked panes of glass, highly skirtable puddles, all lie around. Some large sheets of paper are pinned to the wall incidentally bearing traces of spillage, a crop of small mustard coloured crystals surrounded by an aura of blue leavings.

To one side, two cracked cases of once desirably sleek and pokey high-end Macs support the polythene-wrapped carcass of another computer. Filled with motherboards, wood shaving and acids and prepared with spores, it forms the ground for another crop of pale fungus. The ground beneath is white with the puddles of crystals drained out from the little patch of paradise that it forms. Lying on the floor next to it, a PC case full of broken circuit boards funnelled full of haematite and aluminium powder, lit for a while and then promptly doused, sits scorched and faintly aromatic. Five lightly carbonised brick parts lie around as some kind of witness to a process.

The other top cut from one of the larger tanks sits on the floor full of fluid, its bowing sides held up by a haulier's strap. At its centre is a section of a clay pipe a forearm's length across. Inside is a clump of more sandy earth and within this a chunk of silicon and three small clay flowerpots holding various solutions, with two electrodes trailing in. The silicon was melted from powder into tiny 'chips', achieved by getting the microwave to work at over 1410°C. Silicon powder itself was made in the lab with ordinary sand and magnesium with heat and hydrochloric acid added – a move towards a dirty silicon chip.

The surface of the liquid is a dull brown that, gathered into an archipelago of salts, has grown into a kind of skin, as puckered and glistening as something in aspic. There is rust around one of the electrodes. A car battery opened, a Leiden jar devolved into a near Neolithic technology growing a new culture of scums and delicate membranes into a pond full of bitter consommé, a pit from a leather works that in turn grows its own epidermis. The landscape of The Crystal World, one of spillage, broken components, leachate and electrical bleeds suffused with a tang of corrosion sits across from the imagined universe of trickle-down and high performance flesh, the two cosmologies insulated by the Grand Union. The expressive variety of the table mapped by Mendeleev inevitably outpaces the power of accidental computing – as understood in terms of mere input and output – simply on the basis of sheer likelihood, its combinatorial capacity magnificently abundant here. But, as electrons circulate amongst and between the compounds, this exhibition also shows how close they are and how much their inter-relations proliferate.

Matthew Fuller's <m.fuller@gold.ac.uk> recent books are *Elephant & Castle,* Autonomedia 2012 and, with Andrew Goffey, *Evil Media*, MIT Press, 2012, http://www.spc.org/fuller/

INFO

The Crystal World Exhibition by Martin Howse, Ryan Jordan and Jonathan Kemp took place at The White Building, 28 August to 1 September 2012. The Crystal World Open Workshop took place at the White Building 17 July to 21 July 2012.

FOOTNOTES

1   For information on participants see: http://crystal.xxn.org.uk/wiki/doku.php?id=the_crystal_world:space:opening
2   The Crystal World documentation wiki is at http://crystal.xxn.org.uk/wiki/doku.php

AT THE LIMIT: SELF-ORGANISATION IN GREECE

In Greece a resurgence of self-organising under crisis conditions is drawing on an established repertoire of existing alternatives. ANNA O'LORY – member of the group and journal Blaumachen – describes these initiatives' central features and exposes their integral limits

Anja Kirschner and David Panos' recent film, *Ultimate Substance*, influenced by Alfred Sohn-Rethel's work, links money as the universal equivalent to forms of thought and social organisation: the quantification of activity through an abstract equivalent corresponds to abstraction in thought and scientific quantification. For us, the important consequence of this is that not only exploitation, but the imposition of accounting on social life is itself denaturalised. In the film money is not critiqued for not corresponding to value in a precise enough way. It is critiqued precisely for being what it is: a universal equivalent that mediates exchange and, simultaneously, a form of value.

In Greece, today, as the state withdraws from the reproduction of labour power in the form of welfare, replacing it with workfare and policing, while capital, small and large, is forced to withdraw from investment and production, throwing a large section of the population out of the labour contract and into informal or precarious labour and unemployment, there is a resurgence of self-organising activity as well as of interest in it, notably on the part of the state. This self-organising activity is a direct response to the removal of previous sources of reproduction (wages, pensions, welfare), presenting itself as a *necessity*. Not only is this self-organisation symptomatic of the crisis, but it is itself pervaded by it. The aim here is to lay out some thoughts about these activities, not from the perspective of whether these activities are right or wrong, or whether people should be doing something else, but in terms of the kinds of limits or contradictions they face. Money,

commodity exchange, value and abstract labour will be of central relevance to this discussion.

Commodity exchange is precisely what constitutes alternative economy initiatives for alternative currency networks or 'time banks', whose numbers are rapidly increasing in the crisis.[1] The idea behind these schemes is, on one hand, to create economic activity where there is little and, on the other, to create communities and relations of solidarity among residents of a local area. A localised currency, whether time-based or not, restricts options, and protects its members from external competition. It could be said to be a form of micro-protectionism. In addition, it strives to form a community among its members. These two aspects of these initiatives are closely interlinked and their contradictions prefigure future tensions within this interrelation.

Simple exchange relations among members mean that we are talking of home-based production, dependent on the wider economy outside it, being penetrated by the crisis. On the other hand, a community based on simple exchange, both in past modes of production and today, forms necessary ties of interdependence around local property, rather than voluntary relations among individuals. It is an open question as to whether the recreation of such interdependent communities today could lead also to the creation of communities of struggle, that would not hinge on the issue of local identity and local property, coming into conflict with those outside it.

In these micro-markets we already have a general equivalent that measures exchange value, whether it be alternative money or time,

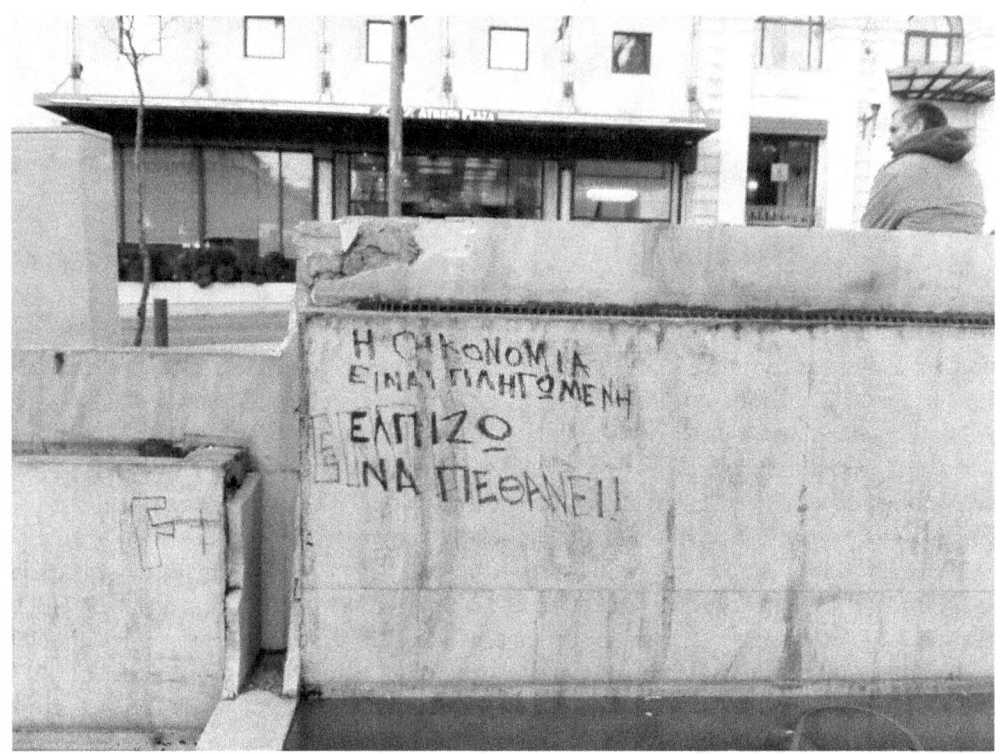

'The economy is injured, I hope it dies.' Graffiti, Athens c.2012.

as well as production *for the market*, which means the commodity labour is already equalised through exchange, thus abstracted from its concrete, specific qualities. Time banks, however, motivated by a notion of equality, use concrete labour time as a measure of wealth, ignoring variations in productivity, intensity and complexity of labour. The coexistence of these variations, however, will need to be negotiated for this principle of equality to be valid. Equalisation of different labours in the market needs its adequate form. This negotiation can either lead to the time-currency becoming actual money, i.e. not pegged to *concrete* labour time, or the need for strict and constant controls on the qualities and types of labour exchanged that would prevent

the expansion of the micro-market. The time bank cannot expand without introducing the form of money, and it cannot avoid introducing money without shrinking. If it does expand, its difference from the mainstream economy would tend to disappear.

The perspective that sees alternative economies as something more than attempts at survival in the crisis and seeks moments of resistance *in what they are and not in their self-overcoming*, views money as mere domination, or as a mere symbol, instead of what it is: an abstract equivalent, a function, the most sufficient medium of exchange. Commodity exchange *necessitates* money, it is not 'dominated' by it. Exchange, abstract labour, the division of labour, are all preconditions of the production of value, in other words, capitalism. They are not 'genuine' relations that then come to be appropriated by capitalists. Capitalist social relations are not less capitalist when money is replaced with something else. And the abolition of money as a mediator of the relations of production cannot take place without the abolition of all the other mediations that support and are supported by money, through the whole of society and not just locally.

Social projects that enact free giving are having to face such limits in their attempt to provide social services that the state has withdrawn. These projects are both a symptom of, and equally essential for, survival in the crisis. They range from kitchens that hand out food to the homeless, to clothes exchanges, to 'social grocery stores' (stores selling cheaply basic commodities that have been donated), to nurseries and free lessons for children, being organised both by political groups as well as more spontaneously. Healthcare is a case in point, as there are a few self-organised medical centres in cities around the country. These centres are run by health workers who offer their services for free, and all space, equipment and medicine is donated.[2] They are part of health workers' struggles and of the fight for universal free healthcare, attempting its decommodification in practice. Their contradiction, however, becomes most evident when the demand for autonomy (with self-management in the imagined horizon) also emerges within these projects. Solidarity health centres are expensive, and the time comes when comrades' donations are not enough. Then, the problem of autonomy is clear: either accept funding from corporations, NGOs or the state, or it is impossible to continue. Meanwhile, the dismantling of the public health service may make a refusal seem insensitive.

Commodity exchange necessitates money, it is not 'dominated' by it

Despite these widely acknowledged problems, what participants see as hopeful in their attempts is building a 'subjectivity of solidarity' which they directly link to workers' self-management. The limit, here, though, is not in the subject but in the possibility of the practice itself. The meaning of their action does not depend on the act itself, and it is not a matter of subjectivity, but everything depends on the context. Direct, selfless giving, however necessary, cannot stop healthcare being systematically mediated by money. Meanwhile, the coexistence of unpaid health workers alongside private clinics and a shrinking public health service means the exploitation of these workers at a general social level. Perhaps in a different, broader situation of rupture encompassing the whole of society, in an all out conflict against the capitalist class and the state, where the mediations of money and exchange would be thrown into question, such organisations could acquire a different significance or dynamic. There again, new limits would emerge - for example the question of the power relations between doctor and patient and the division of labour, which both presuppose capitalist social relations.

The generalisation and convergence of such ruptures is not the same thing as the spreading of autonomous spaces, or the multiplication and enlargement of what is often called 'the commons', however. *The reason for this is that the form of autonomous organisation is always a community whose members have common interests and a common property.* Property is not abolished but rather belongs to a community. What is inside it is always defined by its outside and its boundaries. On one hand, an autonomous community faces all the risks of localism, even nationalism; on the other, its boundaries 'against capitalism' are anything but foolproof.

Capitalism is not only not actively opposed or ruptured by communities of sharing, but it is a condition of the existence of such autonomous communities, which inevitably depend on capitalist commodity production and exchange for their survival (except if they are primitivist communes). Sharing has no intrinsic meaning independently of what is being shared and under what conditions it is being shared. It could evade money at an individual level, but is not intrinsically *against* it - it can equally be an outcome of friendship or an ingredient of capitalist production.

These contradictions of community and property are most evident in projects that aim to 'liberate' public space, particularly in Athens. If a lovingly planted occupied park, intended to be a haven of collective solidarity activity in the middle of the urban jungle, is as much a public space as any other in the city, it will inevitably be a locus of the same social contradictions. It follows that there are few options to maintain what such a park's organisers see as its integrity, beyond actually policing the space. Indeed, some of those who wish to defend such spaces do in fact police access to them by junkies and drug dealers - usually immigrants - and street clashes between those defending the space and those seeking to 'misuse' it are not uncommon.

The discourse of autonomy that underlies many of these initiatives views the self-management of production as its ultimate goal. While current attempts at self-management are not that many, they are increasing, again - and importantly - as a symptom of the crisis and efforts to avoid unemployment.[3] These projects are, again, more dependent on the vicissitudes of the market than on their members' decisions. To remain competitive, workers very often voluntarily work longer and harder, unpaid, viewing themselves as

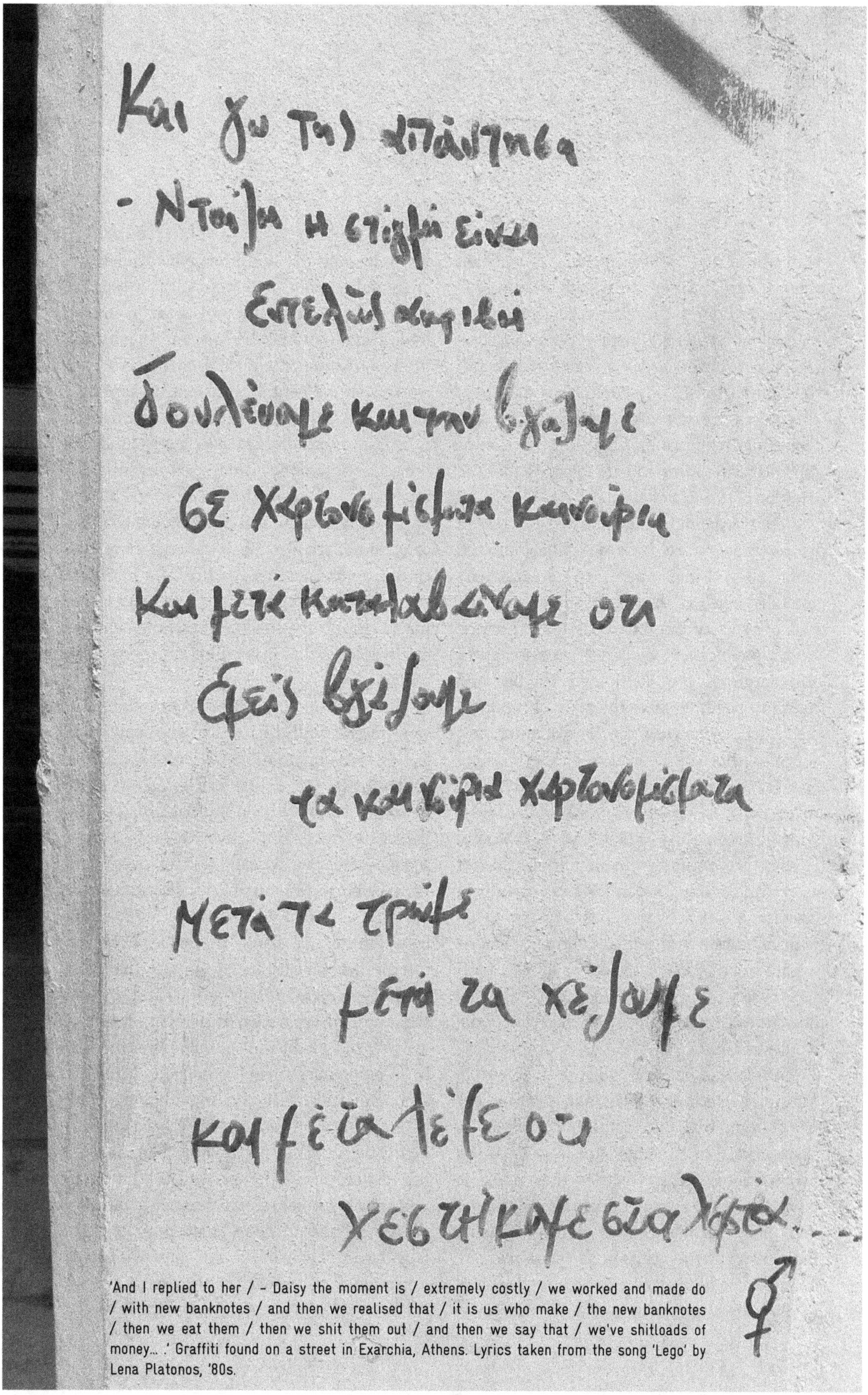

Και γω την απάντησα
– Νταίζυ η στιγμή είναι
        Εντελώς ακριβή
δουλέυαμε και την βγάλαμε
    σε χαρτονομίσματα καινούρια
Και μετά καταλαβαίναμε ότι
    Εμείς βγάζαμε
        τα καινούρια χαρτονομίσματα

Μετά τα τρώμε
        μετά τα χέζουμε
και μετά λέμε ότι
        χεστήκαμε στα λεφτά...

'And I replied to her / – Daisy the moment is / extremely costly / we worked and made do / with new banknotes / and then we realised that / it is us who make / the new banknotes / then we eat them / then we shit them out / and then we say that / we've shitloads of money... .' Graffiti found on a street in Exarchia, Athens. Lyrics taken from the song 'Lego' by Lena Platonos, '80s.

both worker and business owner, while, when there is surplus, they reinvest it in new self-managed ventures. The relation between labour and capital is still here, just not personalised as capitalist and worker, but still existing within the same subjects. So, despite the fact that these enterprises are not *subjectively* driven by the motive of accumulation, they still function as capitalist enterprises and are forced to face the question of self-exploitation.

The viewpoint of such practice, the reason its participants see it as a political project, while often being careful to recognise its 'imperfections', is that it looks towards the ideal of a society of autonomous, self-organised worker-producers, where commodities and surpluses are distributed equally and collective planning takes the place of capitalist competition. This view, the view of autonomy, supposes that the definition of the working class is not in relation to capital but is inherent to it; that the society of workers can exist without reproducing capitalist social relations, or that the continued production of value, of accounting, of imposing an abstract quantifying equalisation of activities, has nothing to do with capitalism. It essentially formalises what we are in our present society as a basis for a new society, which is to be constructed as the liberation of what we are – the liberation of the worker as a *worker*.

We cannot consider self-management in a historical vacuum. Today, self management is not a triumph but a last resort, seen as a solution to unemployment. Grassroots organisations, today, whether they organise on the basis of workers' identity, or that of democracy and autonomy, or all three, face the limit posed by the status of the class relation. They cannot be part of a class unity, because of the class fragmentation that is made even worse by precarity and unemployment in the crisis and economic restructuring. We see that the very capacity of the proletariat to find in its relation to capital the basis for constituting itself as an autonomous class and in a powerful workers' movement has all but disappeared. This is precisely why self-management today is a last resort, rather than a revolutionary project. Autonomy and self-organisation represented a historical moment of the history of the class struggle and not formal modalities of action. Their decline is not the retreat of class struggles, but the decline of a historical stage of class struggles. Today, the struggle is not fought on the basis of class unity, but the class contradiction plays itself out *within* social struggles.

The battle *against self-organisation itself* can emerge within battles in the name of a 'better' self-organisation, and find its limits, contradicting itself. The battle against state or corporate co-optation and legalisation, the defence by more combative elements against squats becoming 'social co-operatives', and the rebellion against managerial control in co-operatives, all boil down to the contradiction between, on one hand, the subjectivity and inter-individuality put forward as the most 'positive moment' of self-organisation, and, on the other, the separation of labour as a distinct activity, the production of value, the division between production and reproduction, and the autonomisation of the conditions of production as economy. In such battles, should they be generalised, the perspective of revolution could begin to move away from class self-affirmation and towards a self-recognition as a category of the capitalist mode of production. And this is a dynamic of rupture and not one of the continuity and growth of the self-organised sphere. It prefigures the self-supersession of the subject that previously found in its situation the capacity to self-organise.

This rupture and its generalisation, however, does not happen without organisation, without an upfront collision against the capitalist class and the state on a wider scale. It takes organisation when proletarians take on various tasks necessary for the development of their struggle: blocking roads, laying siege to police stations, blocking supplies to the forces of order, seizing essential commodities, and so on. The question here is not one of spontaneity versus organisation, but of expropriation versus the appropriation and management of what exists in the construction of a new economy. Organisation can be something other than the formalisation of a preceding subject, of what proletarians are in existing society, as the basis for a new society and economy. And such organisation would emerge not as a voluntary decision but out of the necessities of the struggle against the opponent class, through which the situation of proletarians can become not something to organise, to defend and liberate, but something to abolish.

Anna O'Lory is a member of Blaumachen, http://www.blaumachen.gr, a communist group based mainly in Thessaloniki, Greece, who produce a journal of the same name and contribute to *SIC – International Journal for Communisation*, http://sic.communisation. net/en/start

INFO

This text was written with contributions by other members of Blaumachen and presented at the event Money in the State of Crisis: the Example of Greece, a discussion organised as part of the closing of the exhibition, *Ultimate Substance*, by Anja Kirschner and David Panos, at Neue Berliner Kunstverein, 27 January 2013

FOOTNOTES

1   There could be up to 40 such networks around Greece today.

2   The necessity for these centres arose as increasing numbers of people are losing access to healthcare as they lose their jobs or work informally, while most immigrants never had access. These centres are usually openly politicised and part of doctors' struggles against the dismantling of public healthcare, which is progressing at very high speed. Specialist services are closing around the country, while lack of staff, equipment and supplies is endemic. Most disturbingly, childbirth in a public hospital now costs over c. €500, going up to €1,000 for a Caesarean even for those with access to the health service, while the amount doubles for those who do not. Health workers are also owed wages, as has become increasingly common for workers across most sectors in the past three years.

3   Initiatives are usually started by unemployed friends or ex-colleagues who decide to begin a new self-managed venture in their area of skill. The most successful and well known co-operatives right now are cafés and restaurants, i.e. high labour and low capital intensive businesses. Another well known project is that by the ex-employees of *Eleftherotypia* newspaper, who split away from the company when the original management co-opted the self-management initiative of the workers. The most ambitious is an ongoing attempt by the ex-employees of VioMe, a metal constructions company, to restart its activity by putting together their unemployment benefits as capital.

WHOSE REBEL CITY?

In **Rebel Cities**, David Harvey exhaustively tracks capitalism's turn to real estate speculation and rent extraction, while imagining a reciprocal and reinvigorated urban politics. But his neglect of autonomous urban struggles in '70s Italy and concentration on rights suggest an adherence to older political forms inadequate to the attack of the social factory – writes NEIL GRAY

David Harvey's *Rebel Cities: From the Right to the City to the Urban Revolution* (2012) draws together some of his key texts on urbanisation, providing an opportunity to make a critical assessment of his work on urbanism, not least his application of 'the right to the city' concept first formulated by Henri Lefebvre in 1967; a concept that has long held potential for urban praxis, but which Harvey acknowledges often remains a mere 'chimera'.[1]

Harvey's argument is strongest when invigorating Lefebvre's late 1960s 'urbanisation of capital' thesis in developed capitalist economies, suggesting a necessary corollary for current modes of organisation arising therefrom:

If the capitalist form of urbanisation is so completely embedded in and foundational for the reproduction of capitalism, then it also follows that alternative forms of urbanization must necessarily become central to any pursuit of a capitalist alternative.[2]

Implying an enhanced role for social reproductive struggles, this immanent dialectical critique challenges the privileging of the workplace as the exemplary site of revolutionary change. But while Harvey provides empirical weight and a systemic basis for an urban politics, he neglects some of the more interesting forms of radical urban praxis in the recent era: the urban struggles in 1970s Italy, characterised here by Lotta Continua's 'Take over the City' slogan, feminist debates around social

reproduction, and Sergio Bologna's description of 'territorial community activism'.[3]

Rebel Cities does, however, suggest the potential for a productive dialogue, via Lefebvre, between the area of autonomy and critical urban theory through an immanent critique of capitalist relations.

THE RENT DEVOURS ALL

One uses space just as one uses machines.[4]

At a time when post-war Marxist analysis saw urban questions as largely derivative and superstructural, Lefebvre countered that industrialisation was increasingly being supplanted by urbanisation. Indeed, the 'crisis of the Left' in the early 1970s, he argued, was in part related to a reduction of everyday urban life to 'a repressive and banal urbanism' subject to 'the limitations of national development programs'.[5] The fundamental question Lefebvre posed in *The Survival of Capitalism* (1973) remains central today: how does capitalism survive and continue to produce new capitalist spaces? His answer:

we cannot calculate at what price, but we do know the means: *by occupying space, by producing a space.*[6]

The control of space was no longer just about the control of objects in space; space itself produced, and was now bought and sold as an 'ultimate object of exchange':

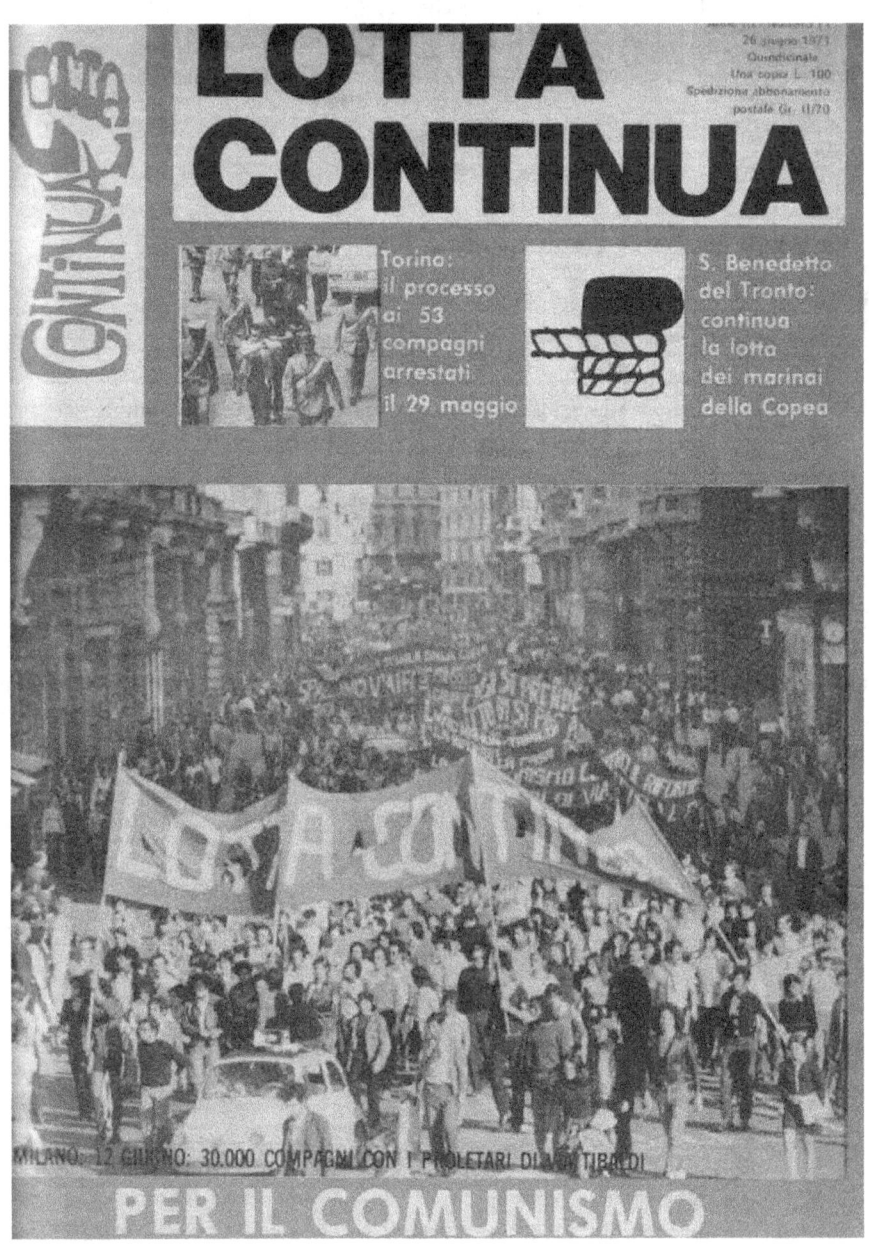

Lotta Continua, 26 June 1971

Space is no longer only an indifferent medium,
the sum of places where surplus value is created,
realized and distributed. It becomes the product of
social labour, the very general object of production,
and consequently of the formation of surplus
value.[7]

Evaluating space in this way risks underestimating all the other means by which surplus value is generated, but Lefebvre's total critique of the 'fragmentary sciences' was exemplary, and his thesis that capitalism, running out of profitable, productive means of accumulation, found new territory for accumulation in the conquest of space is now writ large in global cities worldwide.[8] For Lefebvre, the production of space was intimately bound up with capitalist *crisis*. Real estate speculation functioned, he argued, as a supplementary and complementary territory for exploitation in times of industrial slowdown:

As the percentage of overall surplus value formed
and realized by industry begins to decline, the
percentage created and realized by real-estate
speculation and construction increases. The second
circuit supplants the first, becomes essential.[9]

Harvey has done much to expand Lefebvre's urbanisation thesis via theories of space-time compression, accumulation by dispossession, monopoly rent, and creative destruction of the land. All resurface here, but his theory of the absorption of capital and labour surpluses through urbanisation is given a particularly extended workout.[10] Large-scale urban infrastructural processes, he argues, provide a stabilising 'spatial fix' for the surplus capital problem, and attendant surplus labour problem, especially in times of over-accumulation and economic and political crisis. When Baron von Haussmann took charge of Paris' public works in 1853 after the crisis of 1848, Harvey notes, he understood his mission clearly: creative destruction of the land, and a resolution of the surplus capital and unemployment problem by way of urbanisation.[11] To initiate these changes, Haussmann needed new financial institutions and debt instruments: a proto-Keynesian system of debt-financed infrastructural urban improvements. The 'fury for building' that Louis-Auguste Blanqui witnessed, had predictable inflationary results: 'The rent devours all, and they go without meat', noted a commentator of the time.[12]

This strategy, Harvey argues, was echoed in the US in the 1940s post-depression era, where the urban planner Robert Moses found a solution to the capital and labour surplus problem through fixed capital production, absorbing huge amounts of capital and potentially politically volatile labour through debt-financed highways, major infrastructural transformations, and large-scale suburbanisation, all lubricated through a transformation of financial and administrative structures and a turn to debt-financing.[13] As Harvey notes, however, the crisis of 1848 was only deferred by Haussman, giving rise to the events of the Paris Commune in 1870. Meanwhile Moses' suburbanisation plan hollowed out the fiscal capacity of US inner cities generating the urban crisis of the 1960s, defined politically by 'white flight' and the urban revolt of ethnic minorities. As Harvey argues, long-term investments in the built environment are, 'a kind of last-ditch hope for finding productive uses for rapidly accumulating capital'.[14] Yet 'capital switching' from productive capital to real estate has long been seen as an indication of crisis in economic orthodoxy, providing only a temporary solution to the production centred

'Capital switching' from productive capital to real estate has long been seen as an indication of crisis

over-accumulation crisis, and becoming instead a crisis of asset values with strong links to property.[15]

Given the speculative scale of urban development globally, Harvey suggests a deferral of crisis of staggering proportions. Depending on the particular capital and state conjuncture, these urban developments present uneven scenarios geographically, but Harvey argues they are in principle similar to that of Hausmannisation, with the added caveat that the financialisation/urbanisation nexus has since exploded exponentially.[16] 'The China Story' he relates is apposite. In 2011, fixed asset investment (a broad measure of building activity) had risen 25 percent in one year, and real estate investment 37 percent. Urban investments equalled nearly 70 percent of the nation's GDP, and real estate spending surpassed foreign trade as the biggest contributor to China's economy, with 'growth' fundamentally tied to inflationary spending on real estate and government investment in urban infrastructure.[17] After general housing privatisation in 1998, housing prices had reportedly risen by as much as 800 percent in cities such as Beijing and Shanghai in the preceding five years.[18] In second-tier cities, a typical home was reportedly 25 times the average income of residents. Much of this debt-financed urban speculation is fictitious, what Harvey describes as 'an infinite regression of fictions built upon fictions', representing claims to property rights or income based on a projected realisation of future revenue that is never guaranteed.[19] A wave of defaults and the possibility of economic collapse remains 'very real', while vast processes of primitive accumulation and the extraction of absolute surplus value from labour mean that social contradictions and class struggle are rife.[20]

As Harvey noted long ago in *The Limits*

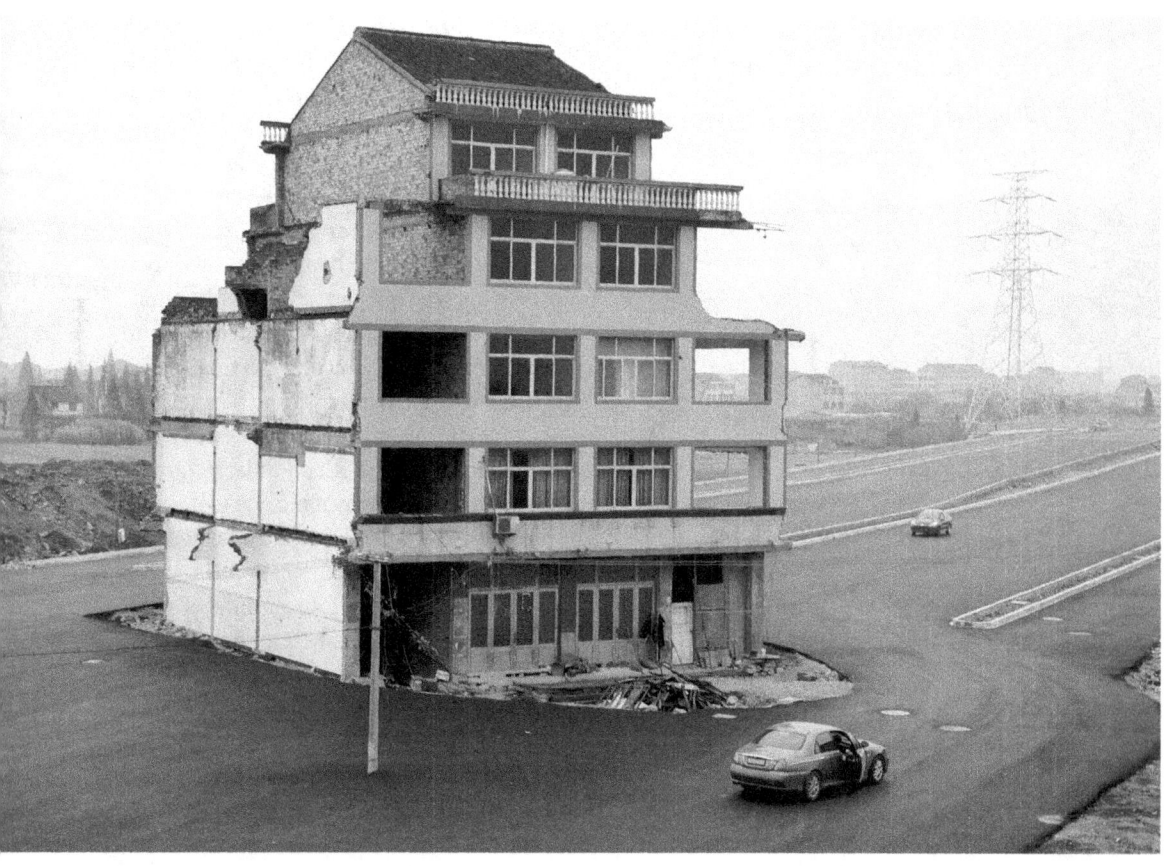

A 'nail house' whose owner would not permit demolition, Wenling, China 2012

*Rental incomes are an
unproductive 'free lunch' stolen
from the economy at large*

to *Capital* (1982), class power is increasingly articulated through rental payments, and his work here helps us understand the material basis of the 'rentier economy'. Economic rent, as Michael Hudson emphasises, can take the form of licensing fees, interest on savings, dividends from stock, or capital gain from selling a property or land, but is primarily drawn from housing and property. This is the profit one earns simply by owning something; an 'unearned increment', which, to the financier or capitalist, is 'earned in their sleep'.[21] As Hudson argues, rental incomes are an unproductive 'free lunch' stolen from the economy at large, forcing an ever-higher proportion of income to be spent on rent and basic social subsistence. Writing presciently of the US in 2006, Hudson saw a 'new road to serfdom' in an empire of debt: 'In the odd logic of the real estate bubble, debt has come to equal wealth'.[22] Just as the rich, he says, require an abundant supply of the poor, so does the rentier class require an abundant supply of debtors. But this dynamic is fictitious, and inherently unstable, in the sense that the parasitic financial system destroys the host's ability to pay the debt.

Despite the all too obvious impact of capitalist urbanisation, the organisational forms adequate to challenge this expropriation have yet to fully develop as an expression of common interests.

FOR A POLITICS OF SPACE

I repeat that there is a politics of space, because space is political.[23]

The Paris Commune of 1871 was an exemplary urban revolt for Lefebvre, and Harvey here argues it was founded on both a labour question (the abolition of night-work in bakeries) and

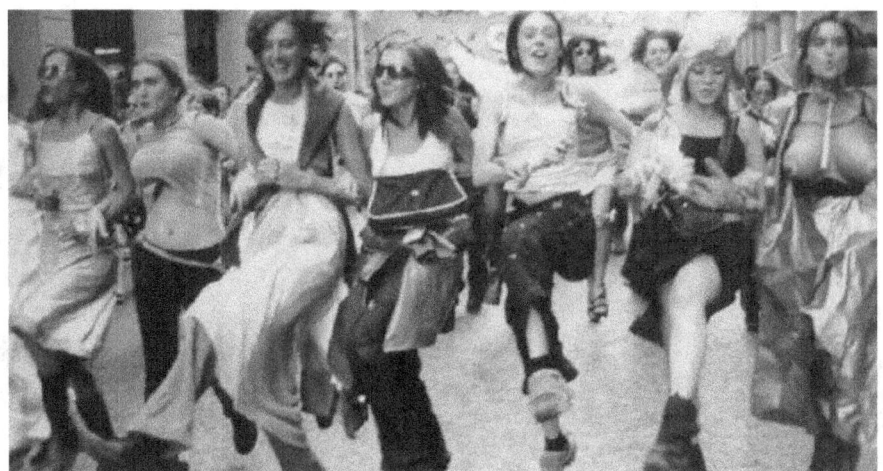

Lotta Femminista, Italy, early '70s, photo by Tano D'Amico

an urban question (a moratorium on rents): production *and* social reproduction. For the traditional Left, social reproduction has often been considered as ancillary, but where 'conventional workplaces are disappearing in many parts of the so-called advanced capitalist world', he argues, the dynamic of class exploitation is now felt increasingly in living space and not in the factory, while wage concessions, if won at all, are routinely stolen back at the level of consumption through inflation and property speculation.[24] The externalisation of the costs of basic social reproduction and environmental degradation, then, necessitate an urgent political response on urban terrain.

This moves us usefully beyond reified conceptions of 'the working class', and sectional interests within and between organised trade unions. Harvey uses numerous examples of urban organisation, from the Paris Commune, 'Red Vienna' and the 'Houses of the People' in Italy, to Occupy Wall Street (OWS). Yet, the emphasis on social reproduction, composition, and community organising that Harvey sees in

his description of El Alto in Bolivia, his major example of urban organising in *Rebel Cities*, or in his treatment of the 'Hollywood Ten' film, *Salt of the Earth* (1954), only serves to highlight the elisions as much as the inclusions in his analysis.[25]

Lefebvre, yes, but no Situationist International? No *dérive*, no psychogeography? Harvey suggests there are no examples of how one might organise a city (presumably at government level), 'because there is no systematic historical record of evolving political practices on which to base any generalisations'.[26] But surely there are outliers? The reformulation of the concepts of work and class that Harvey extols, for instance, were widely developed through the concept of the 'social factory' and class composition within autonomous Marxist currents in 1960s and 1970s Italy. Major struggles against the recuperation of wages in the reproductive sphere were widespread in the 'self-reduction' movement, Wages for and *against* Housework campaigns, and the rent strikes, squats and occupations around housing that set off a series of struggles in the areas of

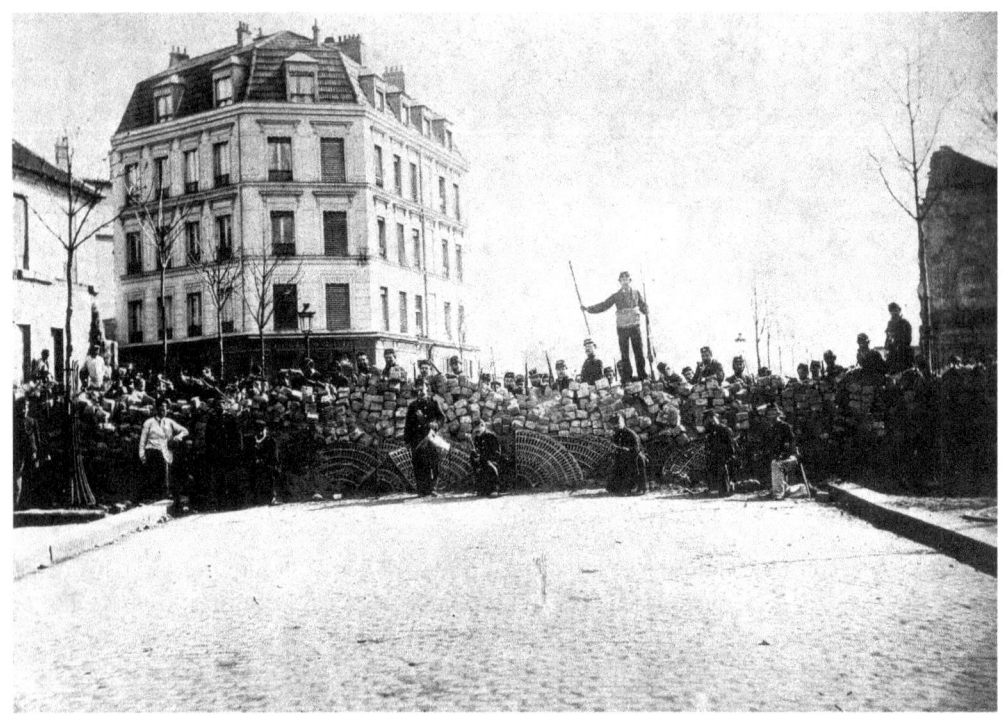

A barricade in Paris, 1871

social reproduction including transportation, health and prices.[27]

This aporia, moreover, undermines Harvey's attempt to accurately describe the relation between the workplace and the social reproductive sphere. Arguing, for instance, that 'Red Bologna' in 1970s Italy serves as a model for contemporary urban struggles disavows the reformist nature of the controlling Italian Communist Party (PCI), and the brutal state power that underpinned it.[28] As 'Bifo' Berardi has noted, Bologna was the city of 'capitalist-communist power', where the productivist PCI pitted regular workers *against* 'irregular, unemployed, precarious, underpaid young proletarians', conservatively retrenching the classical worker rather than recomposing class struggle in ways adequate to contemporary conditions.[29] 'The Historic Compromise' of 1973, between the PCI and the conservative Christian Democrats, saw the PCI and unions committed to sacrificing the workers on the pyramids of accumulation, explicitly assuming the task of forcing the working class to accept a policy of 'sacrifice' and 'austerity' after the economic crisis of 1973, in the name of 'national unity'.[30]

Autonomy, in this context, represented forms of organisation which, 'no longer accepted the union as mediating agent, no longer accepted the line of the PCI and its strategy of compromise and acquiescence'.[31] The Italian autonomous currents of the 1970s are the elephant in the sitting room of Harvey's discussion.[32] The caricatured account of 'autonomy' he offers – flattening out important differences between anarchism, autonomism, *autogestion* (self-management), worker co-operatives, moral and solidarity economies and community collectives – only serves to undermine his often valid critiques of horizontalist organisational fetishism, state *disavowal*, and small-scale 'alternative' production that remains under capitalist relations.[33] 'Autonomy', however, might be seen more productively as an attempt to abandon idealised transhistorical theoretical frameworks in order to find a theoretical apparatus adequate to the contemporary situation.[34] Crucially, this has entailed struggles *within* struggles on the Left, something which Harvey's rather programmatic analysis and calls for 'organizational coherence' tend to neglect. As Selma James put it in her seminal *Sex, Race and Class* (1973), 'nothing unified and revolutionary will ever be formed until each section of the exploited will have made its own autonomous power felt'.[35] The limits of a 'unity' proposed by the 'white male blinkered Left' are still the limits autonomous movements face today.

If, as Harvey argues, history needs to be rewritten to include urban struggles over social reproduction, and crucially gender composition, then 'Laboratory Italy' deserves closer attention, particularly as the response of autonomous Marxist currents to de-industrialisation and class decomposition was more critical and sustained than other European countries.[36] As industry was restructured in the 1970s, on the back of fiscal crisis and an all too familiar austerity program, struggles rapidly moved on from the factory desert to the wider community. The feminist movement, largely excluded from the workplace, provided a major, if often under-acknowledged, inspiration. With the home reconfigured as the centre of social subversion, new perspectives for organisation were opened

'Nothing unified and revolutionary will ever be formed until each section of the exploited will have made its own autonomous power felt'

up. When feminists raised the question of housework, the trade unions were forced to acknowledge that as organisations they dealt:

(a) only with the factory; (b) only with a measured and 'paid' work day; (c) only with that side of wages which is given to us and not with the side of wages which is taken back, that is inflation.[37]

While unions fought to retain a sense of working class identity in the factory desert, as the feminist group *Acqua in Gabbia* ('Water in Cage') noted, these were increasingly regressive and conservative solutions to the problems facing the working class as a whole – a defensive solution to a disappearing reality.[38] With de-industrialisation, political re-composition was no longer occurring through the base of the unified mass worker, but across the whole social terrain. In *Take Over the City – Community Struggle in Italy* (1973), Lotta Continua documented multiple forms of struggle beyond the factory walls including rent strikes, mass occupations and mass squatting in 'a direct response to the tyranny of rent'.[39] Rent strikes and occupations were combined, and a discourse of rights was directly linked to *appropriation* as in the popular slogans: 'The only fair rent is no rent!', and, 'Housing is a right. Why pay rent!'[40] Class conflict was extended directly over the entirety of social consumption and was understood as, 'a struggle for the re-appropriation of social wealth produced by the working class but unpaid by capital'.[41]

Describing the 'new social subjects' of 1977, Sergio Bologna argued that groups like Lotta Continua were reacting to city planning as a space of intervention in class dynamics.[42] As he noted, there was a specific relation between the property market and the monetary crisis: with declining profits from industry, speculation in property and land took up an increasingly important role in investment. In this context, the dominant forms of struggle for these subjects became a project of 'conquering and managing' their own spaces in a process of 'territorial community activism'.[43] Bologna's understanding of shifts from industrialisation to urbanisation foreshadow Michael Hudson's by thirty years, but Bologna analyses the subjective, political side of class composition, not just its technical side (capital's plans). Caught between a workerist analysis of the factory-based 'mass worker' and post-autonomous readings of 'immaterial' or 'affective' labour, autonomous urban struggles in Italy have often been neglected, even within the autonomist milieu. However, beyond the Jeffersonian moral abstractions that Harvey offers in his concluding analysis of OWS – where 'the people of the United States' are proud of 'their democracy', and where another revolution might be based on 'social justice, equality' – the Italian example offers a deeply material analysis based on autonomous class behavior and a sharp attention to the changing nature and potentialities of class composition.

FROM THE RIGHT TO THE CITY TO TAKE OVER THE CITY?

Beyond an abstract rights claim, what radical utility does the concept of the 'right to the city' have for the present era, and how might it become, as Harvey suggests it could, 'both working slogan and political ideal' for a new urban politics? Harvey is well aware of the problem with 'rights' discourse in a context where private property rights and the profit rate trump all other notions of rights. He also well understands the role of violence in enforcing private property, often citing Marx's critical injunction on rights discourse: 'between equal rights force decides'.[44]

What he suggests is the right to the city concept as a focused collective right, a political class-based demand filled with 'immanent but not transcendent possibilities' - not a right to what already exists, but a right to rebuild and re-create the city in a totally different image.[45] However, the very idea of rights tends to emphasise distribution rather than production - the potential of a 'fair' distribution of the products of labour through 'equal rights' - thereby disavowing the exploitative mode of production itself and falling prey to the separation of political and economic spheres.

As Silvia Federici argued in *Wages Against Housework*, it is one thing to organise communally and then demand that the state pay for it, and another to ask the state to organise communal production: 'In one case we regain some control over our lives, in the other we extend the State's control over us.'[46] The reality is that reformist struggles over rights will continue to constitute part of the field of struggle, and Harvey is right to suggest they may open up the possibility for more radical conceptions. However more radical praxis, providing a genuine threat to stability, has to be generated in the first place. With social reproduction becoming at once the site and the content of struggle, 'take over the city' suggests a politics that places the direct appropriation of social resources on the immediate horizon without waiting for permission from a state that would dispense this as a 'right'.

Neil Gray <neilgray00@hotmail.com> is a writer, and occasional film-maker based in Glasgow. He is currently doing a PhD on the urbanisation of capital, class composition and the politics of space.

FOOTNOTES

1 David Harvey, *Rebel Cities*, London: Verso, 2012, p.xvi.

2 Ibid, p.65.

3 See Sergio Bologna's seminal class composition analysis. Sergio Bolgona, 'The Tribe of Moles', 1977, in Sylvère Lotringer and Christian Marazzi (eds), *Autonomia: Post-Political Politics*, Los Angeles: Semiotext(e), 2007. Available at: http://libcom.org/library/tribe-of-moles-sergio-bologna

4 'Social Product and Use Value', in Brenner and Elden (eds.), *Henri Lefebvre: State, Space, World - selected essays*, Minneapolis: University of Minnesota Press, 2009, p.188.

5 *The Urban Revolution*, op. cit., p.148. This thesis is suggestive of the Situationist International's critique of urbanism of course, and less obviously, the Italian autonomist conception of the 'social factory', where production was seen to extend beyond the factory walls.

6 Henri Lefebvre, *The Survival of Capitalism: Reproduction of the Relations of Production*, London: Allison and Busby Limited, 1976, p.21. Lefebvre's emphasis.

7 *The Urban Revolution*, op. cit., pp.154-155.

8 His understanding was rooted in a critique of the capitalist division of labour, as was his critique of political economy and the state - a fact disavowed in many interpretations of Lefebvre's avowedly *communist* perspective. 'If we define communism not as a being or a "state" (the pun is intentional) but as movement, and in movement, towards a possible future, established as such, then I lay claim to being an excellent communist'. See, *Henri Lefebvre: Key Writings*, Elden, Lebas, Kofman, (eds.), London: Continuum, 2003, p.234.

9 *The Urban Revolution*, op cit., p.160.

10 The thesis of surplus absorption reappears in several of Harvey's latest articles and books, including *Rebel Cities*. A condensed online version can be found in 'The Right to the City', *New Left Review*, 53, September-October, 2008, http://newleftreview.org/II/53/david-harvey-the-right-to-the-city

11 *Rebel Cities*, op cit., p.7.

12 The 'Haussmannization' section in Walter Benjamin's *The Arcades Project*, provides some characteristically telling and entertaining observations of this period, pp.120-149.

13 This strategy helped pacify indebted workers,

prioritise private home ownership, stimulate the commodity-economy, and entrench gender roles in the productive and reproductive spheres. Reforms in housing mortgage finance were central to suburbanisation plans. The establishment of Fannie Mae (Federal National Mortgage Association) in 1938, the GI Bill, and the Veterans Mortgage Guarantee Programs, were key instruments in establishing private home-ownership as a pillar of the American Dream. See also, Maya Gonzalez, 'Notes on the New Housing Question', *Endnotes* II, 2010, http://endnotes.org.uk/articles/1

14 For those with access, cited in Brett Christophers, 'Revisiting the Urbanization of Capital', *Annals of the Association of American* Geographers, 101:6, 1347-1364, p.1349.

15 For 'capital switching' see ibid. The creation of the built environment can act as a form of crisis displacement, but it also constitutes 'the limits to capital', as it tends to freeze productive forces into a fixed spatial form.

16 Chapter 2 of *Rebel Cities*, 'The Urban Roots of Financial Crisis', details this nexus extensively, pp.27-66.

17 As much as the new southern industrial areas have developed, the old northern areas have been gutted. China's industrial growth is based on intensified absolute and relative surplus value extraction (increasing the length and intensity of the working day and increasing productivity via technical means) rather than job creation. As *Endnotes* report, *China did not create any new jobs in manufacturing between 1993 and 2006*, which suggests, as Harvey argues, that urban investment in China is a response to a deeper crisis in production. *Endnotes* ii, 'Misery and Debt', 2010, p.48, http://endnotes.org.uk/articles/1

18 Just as neoliberalism in the UK was given a major boost by public housing devaluation and privatisation (through 'right-to-buy' subsidies), so China's 'economic miracle' was accelerated through the devaluation and bargain basement sell-off of State Owned Enterprises (SOEs).

19 *Rebel Cities*, op.cit., p.40. And not just in China, as numerous 'ghost estates' from Africa to Ireland testify. See for instance, Louise Redvers, 'Angola's Chinese-built ghost town', BBC, July 2012, http://www.bbc.co.uk/news/world-africa-18646243

20 See China Labour Bulletin research report, 2012 for an analysis of the growing workers' movement between 2000-2010: http://www.clb.org.hk/en/node/110024. See also, *Aufheben*, 'Class Conflicts

in China', http://libcom.org/library/class-conflicts-transformation-china

21 Michael Hudson, 'From Marx to Goldman Sachs: The Fictions of Fictitious Capital', *Critique: Journal of Socialist Theory*, Volume 38, Issue 3, 2010, pp.419-444, http://michael-hudson.com/2010/07/from-marx-to-goldman-sachs-the-fictions-of-fictitious-capital1/

22 Michael Hudson, 'The New Road to Serfdom: An Illustrated Guide to the Coming Real Estate Collapse', *Harper's*, May 2006, http://harpers.org/archive/2006/05/the-new-road-to-serfdom/

23 Henri Lefebvre, 'Reflections on the Politics of Space', *Antipode,* Volume 8, Issue 2, 1976, http://onlinelibrary.wiley.com/doi/10.1111/j.1467-8330.1976.tb00636.x/abstract

24 *Rebel Cities*, op cit., p.57, p.129.

25 Herbert.J.Biberman (dir), *Salt of the Earth*, 1954, http://www.youtube.com/watch?v=aXTcDUxu22A

26 *Rebel Cities*, op cit., p.140.

27 Silvia Federici's text, 'Wages *Against* Housework', sets up a potentially explosive dialectic between a struggle for recognition of unpaid exploitative labour while at the same time rejecting the 'role' of the houseworker – a problem sometimes associated with Wages *for* Housework campaigns. Federici's position is linked inextricably to the wider autonomous position on the refusal of work: http://caringlabor.files.wordpress.com/2010/11/federici-wages-against-housework.pdf. For more on these urban forms of struggle around reproduction see: Lotta Continua, 'Take Over the City – Community struggle in Italy, 1973': http://libcom.org/library/take-over-city-italy-1972-lotta-continua

28 See Max Jaggi, Roger Muller and Sil Schmid, *Red Bologna*, Writers and Readers Publishing Cooperative, 1977. The book, cited by Harvey as a key description of municipal socialism, is essentially a eulogy to the PCI. For an indication of the PCI's political policing with regards to the movement of Autonomia, see Tiqqun, *This is Not a Program*, New York: Semiotext(e), 2011, pp.32-35. Bologna's Mayor Renato Zangheri of the PCI in 1975: 'Reformism makes reforms and, of course, these reforms take place within capitalism. It makes improvements on the margin, improves capitalism', ibid, p.200. For a comprehensive analysis see, *Autonomia: Post-Political Politics*, Lotringer and Marazzi (eds.), 2007.

29 Franco 'Bifo' Berardi, 'First Bifurcation: 77 the year of premonition', in *Precarious Rhapsody*, p.22.

30 Franco 'Bifo' Berardi, 'Anatomy of Autonomy': http://

strickdistro.org/wp-content/uploads/2012/05/
AnatomyofAutonomy.pdf

31 Ibid.

32 This blind spot may be political and ideological.
Both the Italian (PCI) and French (PCF) Communist
Parties were advocates of Eurocommunism.
These strategies were supported by key figures
in Structuralist and Regulationist approaches
(Althusser and Poulantzas respectively), who have
had a significant impact on Marxist geographers,
including Harvey. For instance, Harvey cites the
regulation approach as a key theoretical influence
for *The Condition of Postmodernity*, Oxford:
Blackwell Publishing, 1990, pp.173-179.

33 A critique well delivered in Marx's *Critique of the
Gotha Program*, 1875. A key text for Lefebvre, and
one often cited by Harvey, http://www.marxists.org/
archive/marx/works/1875/gotha/index.htm

34 An excellent exposition of this tendency, following
in Marx's footsteps, can be found in *Excursus 1*,
in Hardt and Negri's *Multitude,* London: Penguin,
2006, p.140. One doesn't have to accept that the
'immaterial labourer' is the new paradigmatic
figure of labour to accept the overall point that
social theory must confront contemporary reality as
it is, not as it once was, or how we'd like it to be.

35 Selma James, 'Sex, Race and Class', 1974, http://
caringlabor.files.wordpress.com/2010/11/james-
sexraceclass-read.pdf

36 The Situationist Internationale in France have a
claim here, but while 'May 68' lasted only a few
months, the practices of the extra-parliamentary
Left in Italy extended over a decade.

37 *The Power of Women and the Subversion of
Community*, Dalla Costa and James, Berlin: Falling
Wall Press, 1972, http://caringlabor.wordpress.
com/2010/07/28/mariarosa-dalla-costa-women-
and-the-subversion-of-the-community

38 In Robert Lumley, *States of Emergency: Cultures of
Revolt in Italy from 1968 to 1978*, London: Verso,
1990, p.328.

39 Formed in 1969, from the worker-student
movement, and disbanded in 1976, Lotta Continua
(Permanent Struggle) were the largest extra-
parliamentary group of the radical left in Italy. In
1971, the group launched its 'Take Over the City'
programme. See the 'Episodes in Big Flame History:
No.6' for a short overview: http://bigflameuk.
wordpress.com/2009/05/30/lotta-continua/; Lotta
Continua, 'Take Over the City - Community struggle
in Italy, 1973': http://libcom.org/library/take-over-
city-italy-1972-lotta-continua

40 Ernest Dowson, 'The Italian Background', *Radical
America*, Vol.7 no.2, March-April 1973. Available,
along with other texts on Italian working class
struggles in the 1970s, http://libcom.org/library/
radical-america-working-class-struggles-italy.

41 See, Bruno Ramirez, 'The Working Class Struggle
Against the Crisis: Self-Reduction of Prices in Italy',
1975, http://www.prole.info/texts/self-reductionitaly.
html

42 'The Tribe of Moles', op. cit.

43 Ibid.

44 See, Karl Marx, The Working Day, *Capital*, Volume 1,
London: Penguin, 1990, p.344.

45 *Rebel Cities*, op cit., p.136-138.

46 Silvia Federici, 'Wages Against Housework', 1975:
http://caringlabor.wordpress.com/2010/09/15/
silvia-federici-wages-against-housework

PROUD TO BE FLESH:

A MUTE MAGAZINE ANTHOLOGY OF CULTURAL POLITICS AFTER THE NET

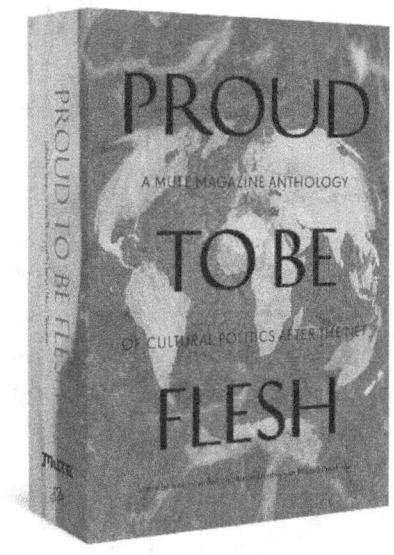

Edited by Josephine Berry Slater and Pauline van Mourik Broekman with Michael Corris, Anthony Iles, Benedict Seymour, and Simon Worthington

Compiling 15 years of *Mute* content, *Proud to be Flesh* offers 624 pages of some of the magazine's best writing, including interviews, essays, polemics and more. Divided into nine chronologically arranged chapters treating key themes associated with the 'digital revolution', *Proud to be Flesh* provides a unique history of a turbulent era and an excellent teaching tool.

Hardcover **£44.99** Softcover **£24.99**
Now available on Kindle **£7.81**

Proud to be Flesh can be purchased at all good bookshops, or previewed and ordered online at **metamute.org/proudtobeflesh**

For further enquiries, contact Howard Slater <**howard@metamute.org**>

Published by Mute Publishing in association with Autonomedia

Softcover ISBN 978-1-906496-28-9
Hardcover ISBN 978-1-906496-27-2
Kindle ASIN - B0085WV7WU

'This collection of articles from the many incarnations of the *Mute* project is a great read, and a summation of that remarkable period of recent British history running from 1994 to 2009.'
-James Heartfield,
Spiked Review of Books

'Essential reading for anyone interested in the ways in which evolving technology and business practices transform our culture - and how we might oppose such influences.'
-David Barrett, Art Monthly

'At a time when recent advances in digital technologies are still considered innovative yet remain an unexplored field for many of us, *Mute* can already claim scholarship in this area. I think *Proud to be Flesh* is an invaluable reference tool for researchers and it should be on the desks of all digital media curators and educationalists.'
-Nayia Yiakoumaki, Archive Curator, Whitechapel Gallery

 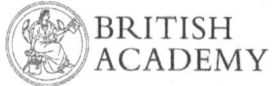

Supported by Arts Council England and The British Academy

BACK CATALOGUE:
OPENMUTE PRESS AND MUTE BOOKS

Since 2005, OpenMute Press has been helping artists, writers and other independent producers bring their book ideas to fruition using Print On Demand, Short Run Press (which is also used to make our magazine) and, more recently, eBooks. Our back-catalogue also includes the first titles from Mute Books and Mute Publishing's anthology, *Proud To Be Flesh*. In addition to all the usual online retailers, these diverse publications are made available through **Metamute.org/services**

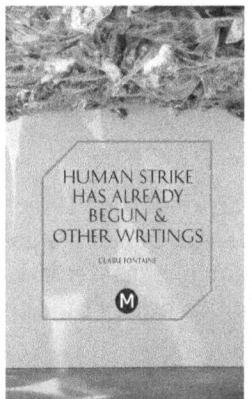

Claire Fontaine
Human Strike Has Already Begun & Other Writing
(Spring 2013)

The term 'human strike' was forged to name a revolt against what is reactionary even – and above all – inside the revolt. It defines a type of strike that involves the whole of life and not only its professional side, that acknowledges exploitation in all the domains and not only at work. The human strike is a movement that could potentially contaminate anyone and that attacks the foundations of life in common; its subject isn't the proletarian or the factory worker but the 'whatever singularity' that everyone is. Part of the PML Books series, a collaboration between Mute & the Post-Media Lab.

ISBN - 978-1-906496-88-3 / £5
eBook ISBN - 978-1-906496-89-0 / £2.89

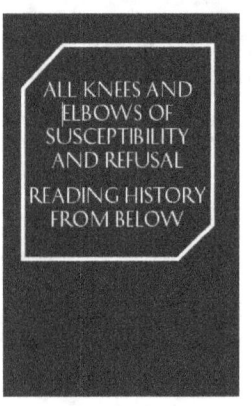

Anthony Iles & Tom Roberts
All Knees and Elbows of Susceptibility and Refusal – Reading History From Below
(Dec 2012)

All Knees and Elbows surveys the work of a number of British and international left historians and groups, assembling a critical and necessarily partial picture of the practice of 'history from below': historiographical tendencies which sought to uncover the agency of 'ordinary people' in challenging capitalism and developing different forms of social organisation. Artwork by Rachel Baker. Co-published with Transmission Gallery and The Strickland Distribution.

ISBN - 978-0-9565201-3-5 / £8.99

eBook ISBN - 978-0- 9565201-4-2 / £8.99

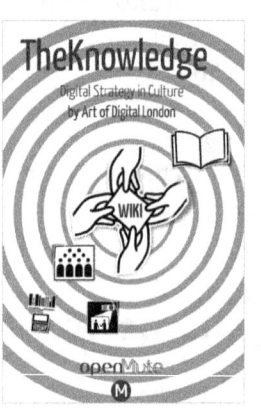

OpenMute
TheKnowledge - peer learning for digital strategy in culture
(Apr 2012)

The Art of Digital London (AoDL) is a digital strategy network for cultural organisations. its programme encompasses digital salons and surgeries, online resources and monthly meetups.

Alongside a series of specially commissioned articles, TheKnowledge compiles and synthesises all the information and experiences generated by AoDL and offers key digital strategies and guides for the creative and organisational dimensions of all cultural production.

ISBN - 978-1-906496-68-5 / £4.49

Kindle ASIN - 978-1-906496-69-2 / £2.56

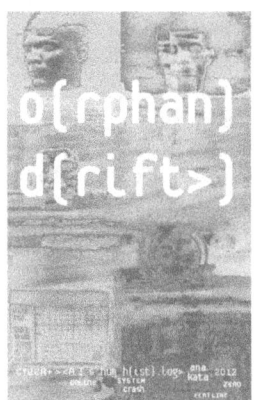

Various
O(rphan) D(rift>)
(Apr 2012 - 2nd edition)

Second edition published by Cabinet Editions / OpenMute London. Originally Published in 1995 by o(rphan)d(rift>) / Cabinet Editions 1st edition 978-1-9064968-07.

Drift. Adrift. Not simply leaving a shore, but diverting a course, a fluidity. where it goes, we are not planning to go... the shore of the ocean, displaces itself along with it.

ISBN - 978-1-906496-80-7 / £9.99

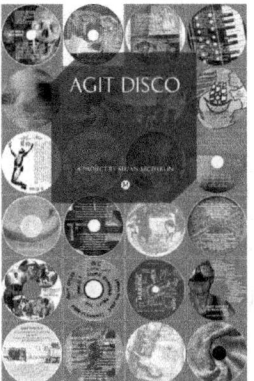

Sniff, Scrape, Crawl...
{on privacy, surveillance and our shadowy data-double}

Renée Turner
Sniff, Scrape, Crawl... {on Privacy, Surveillance and Our Shadowy Data-double}
(May 2012)

Crawling and scraping, the ambient social network creates a portrait of who we are, and maps our demographic character. Where once surveillance technologies were associated with the government and military, the web has fostered a participatory and less optically driven means of monitoring and monetizing our lived experiences. This book explores current debates on privacy and surveillance in the digital age.

ISBN – 978-1-906496-81-4 / £10.00

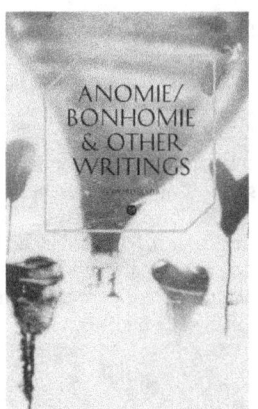

Stefan Szczelkun and Anthony Iles (Eds.)
Agit Disco
(Jan 2012)

Agit Disco collects the playlists of its 23 writers to tell the story of how music has influenced and inspired them politically. The book provides a multi-genre survey of political musics from a wide range of viewpoints, that goes beyond protest songs into the darker hinterlands of musical meaning. Each playlist is annotated and illustrated. The collection grew organically with an exchange of homemade CDs and images. These images, with their DIY graphics, are used to give the playlists a visual materiality.

ISBN – 978-1-906496-51-7 / £11.99

Howard Slater
Anomie/Bonhomie & Other Writings
(Jan 2012)

In this collection of writings, Howard Slater improvises around what Walter Benjamin could have meant by the phrase 'affective classes'. This 'messianic shard' and its possible implications leads Slater to develop a therapeutic micro-politics by way of a mourning for the Workers' Movement and a grappling with the 'becomings of capital'.

ISBN - 978-1-906496-72-2 / £9.99

Now available for Kindle, ASIN - B007KO5NP6 / £6.99

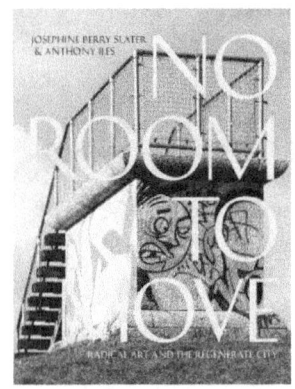

Josephine Berry Slater and Anthony Iles (Eds.)

No Room to Move: Radical Art and the Regenerate City

(Sep 2010)

As the Creative City model for urban regeneration founders, Anthony Iles and Josephine Berry Slater take stock of an era of highly instrumentalised public art making. Focusing on artists and consultants who have engaged critically with the exclusionary politics of urban regeneration, their analysis locates such practice within a schematic history of urban development's neoliberal mode. Featuring projects and interviews with Alberto Duman, Freee, Nils Norman, Laura Oldfield Ford and Roman Vasseur.

ISBN – 9781906496425 / £14.95

Now available on Kindle, AISN - B0085WV9AK / £6.41

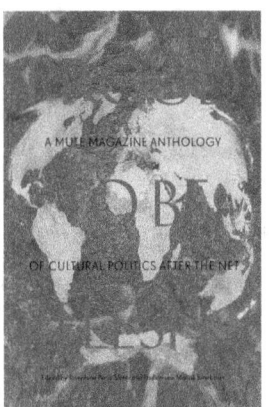

Josephine Berry Slater and Pauline van Mourik Broekman (Eds.) with Michael Corris, Anthony Iles, Benedict Seymour and Simon Worthington

Proud to be Flesh: A Mute Magazine Anthology of Cultural Politics After the Net

(Nov 2009)

Proud To Be Flesh offers an expansive collection of some of *Mute*'s finest articles and is thematically organised around key contemporary issues: Direct Democracy and its Demons; Net Art to Conceptual Art and Back; I, Cyborg; Reinventing the Human; Of Commoners and Criminals; Organising Horizontally; Art and/against Business; Under the Net - the City and the Camp; Class and Immaterial Labour; The Open Work.

Softback, ISBN – 9781906496289 / £24.95

Hardback, ISBN – 9781906496272 / £44.99

Now available on Kindle, ASIN - B0085WV7WU Price - £7.81

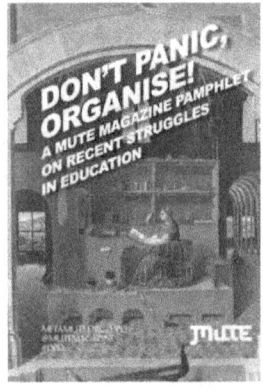

Don't Panic, Organise! A Mute Magazine Pamphlet on Recent Struggles in Education

(Dec 2010)

From the introduction: 'They should be understood as part of the more gradual process of what George Caffentzis, in his analysis of the international situation, calls the "breakdown of the edu-deal"; the inability for capital, and therefore the state, to pay for the costs of producing a well educated workforce or to guarantee that investment in education will result in a more vigorous economy and increased living standards for those with qualifications.'

ISBN – 9781906496548 / £2.99

eBook ISBN – 9781906496555 / Free

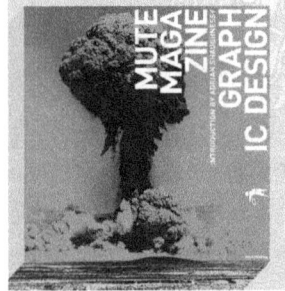

Damian Jaques, Pauline van Mourik Broekman, Adrian Shaughnessy and Simon Worthington (Eds.)

Mute Magazine Graphic Design

(May 2008)

In the early 1990s, long before the Internet became an integral part of life, a handful of pioneering magazines took it upon themselves to imagine the Internet into existence using fiction, interviews, speculative theory and experimental graphic design. Founded by artists Simon Worthington and Pauline van Mourik Broekman, London based *Mute* occupied a central position. *Mute Magazine Graphic Design* presents and contextualises its graphic output. [Published by Eight Books]

ISBN – 9780955432224 / £19.95

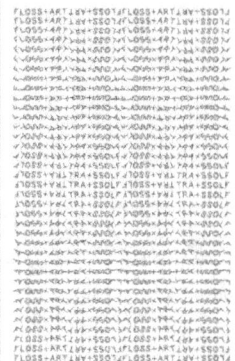

Aymeric Mansoux and Marloes de Valk (Eds.)

FLOSS + Art

(Aug 2008)

FLOSS+Art reflects critically on the growing relationship between Free Software ideology, open content and digital art. It provides a view onto the social, political and economic myths and realities linked to this phenomenon. Contributors: Fabianne Balvedi, Florian Cramer, Sher Doruff, Nancy Mauro Flude, Olga Goriunova, Dave Griffiths, Ross Harley, Martin Howse, Shahee Ilyas, Ricardo Lafuente, Ivan Monroy Lopez, Thor Magnusson, Alex McLean, Rob Myers, Alejandra Maria Perez Nuñez, Eleonora Oreggia, oRx-qX, Julien Ottavi, Michael van Schaik, Femke Snelting, Pedro Soler, Hans Christoph Steiner, Prodromos Tsiavos, Simon Yuill.

ISBN – 9781906496180 / £18.50

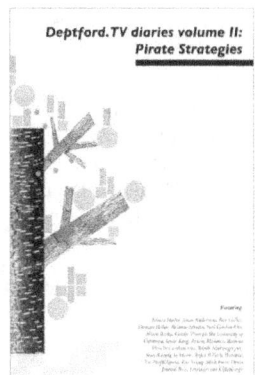

Deptford.TV

Deptford.tv Diaries II – Pirate Strategies

(Apr 2008)

This reader problematises the notion of 'tactical media' – calling for a more strategic approach. Contributors: Adnan Hadzi, Jonas Andersson, Ben Gidley, Duncan Reekie, Brianne Selman, Neil Gordon-Orr, Alison Rooke, Gesche Wuerfel, the University of Openness, Jamie King, Armin Medosch, Rasmus Fleischer, andrea rota, Bitnik Mediengruppe, Sven Koenig Jo Walsh, Rufus Pollock, Platoniq, The People Speak, Zoe Young, Mick Fuzz, Denis Jaromil Rojo, Lennaart van Oldenborgh'.

ISBN – 9781906496111 / £5

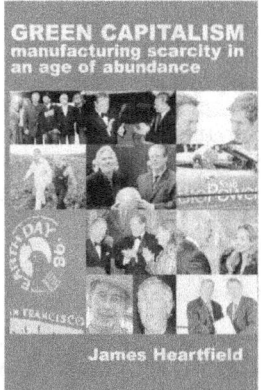

James Heartfield

Green Capitalism: Manufacturing Scarcity in an Age of Abundance

(Feb 2008)

A polemic against 'Green Capitalism' which James Heartfield accuses of profiteering from climate change and other environmental scares. Green capitalists like Zac Goldsmith and Al Gore are manufacturing scarcity to boost prices. The technological revolution has removed scarcity from most of our lives, but the green capitalists are trying to re-invent it.

ISBN – 9781906496104 / £7.50

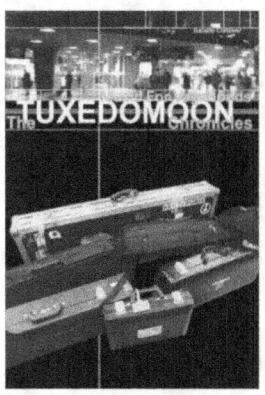

Isabelle Corbisier

Music for Vagabonds: the Tuxedomoon Chronicles

(Jan 2008)

Tuxedomoon is a group of musicians and performers that was formed in San Francisco in 1977. Their identity is as elusive as their geographical location. Tuxedomoon have attracted followers and gained cult status, never ceasing their quest for a permanently elusive and lost 'home' – some other America or the quaint Europe of their fantasies. From 2001 onwards, the author of this book found herself sucked into Tuxedomoon's spiral of vagrancy and travelled the world to meet the actors in this ongoing 30-year-old story.

ISBN – 9781906496081 / £19

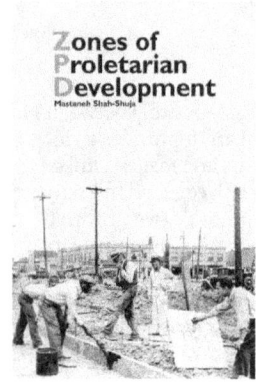

Mastaneh Shah-Shuja

Zones of Proletarian Development

(Jan 2008)

Zones of Proletarian Development is an attempt to theorise the anti-capitalist movement from a neo-Vygotskian perspective. Using Marx, Vygotsky, Bakhtin and Activity Theory, it analyses a series of proletarian activities including incendary May Day celebrations in London, carnivalesque football riots in Iran, the anti-poll-tax rebellion and the anti-war movement. It concludes by looking at past and current proletarian organisations and makes a number of proposals for future modes of organising conducive to radical consciousness and autonomous activity.

ISBN – 9781906496067 / £15

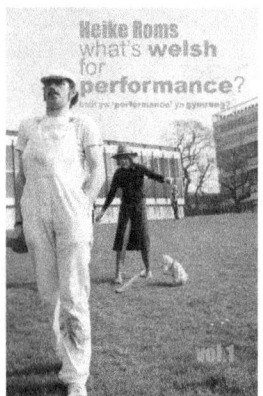

Heike Roms

What's Welsh for Performance?

(Dec 2007)

For more than forty years artists have been creating performances, happenings and other time-based art in Wales, yet their work remains largely confined to half-remembered anecdotes, rumours and hearsay. *What's Welsh for Performance?* tries to uncover Wales' hidden history of performance in conversations with key artists who have shaped this history since 1968. With: Shirley Cameron, Ivor Davies, Anthony Howell, John Chris Jones, Timothy Emlyn Jones, Andrew Knight, Roland Miller. Dr. Heike Roms is lecturer in Performance Studies at Aberystwyth University, Wales.

ISBN – 9780955392726 / £10

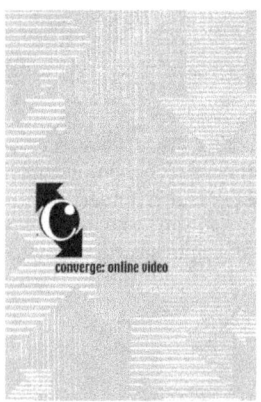

Converge – Online Video

(Oct 2007)

Using media as a means of working with, and empowering marginalised people in their communities is a practice that has emerged strongly in recent years, nurtured by the extraordinary growth of digital media and the Web. These developments have enabled a participatory culture – particularly online – in which young people are now more able to represent themselves and their concerns. This book offers first hand accounts of work across and beyond Inclusion Through Media, alongside critical analysis of many of the processes involved, and the policy issues it raises. The book includes an accompanying DVD.

ISBN – 9781906496005 / £9.99

E. Karaba (Ed.)

Feedback 4: Ideas that Inform, Construct and Concern the Production of Exhibitions and Events

(Sep 2007)

FeedBack 4 focuses on participatory art events and examines them from the point of view of the artist, the curator and the participant. It brings together contributions from many authors interested in curatorial debates.

ISBN – 9780955479687 / £6.50

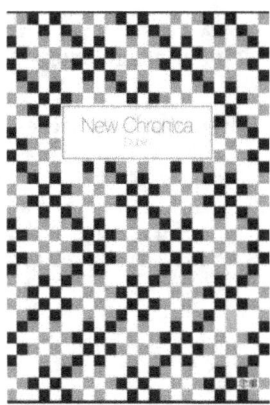

Steven Dickie

New Chronica Dublin

(Jul 2007)

New Chronica Dublin is a graphic novel and musical album download, based on a collection of contemporary folklore from the Irish capital. The dilution of identity and the inevitable displacement of population which the rebranding of economic and social areas brings, may result in this being the last opportunity to witness the community's galvanised common identity as it negotiates a position within the new Dublin.

ISBN – 9780955479663 / £10

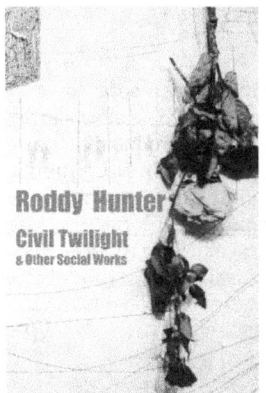

Roddy Hunter

Civil Twilight & Other Social Works

(Feb 2007)

Civil Twilight & Other Social Works explores the performance artwork of provocative Scots artist Roddy Hunter. Through the artist's own texts and archival documentation, Hunter introduces us to his methodology of research into the idea of urban civic centres as places where collective identity is formed.

ISBN – 9780955392719 / £10

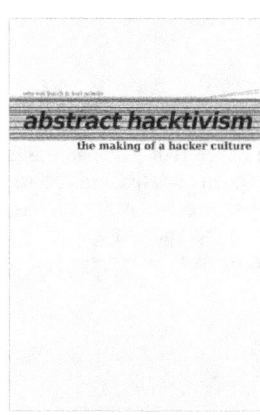

Otto von Busch & Karl Palmås

Abstract Hacktivism: The Making of a Hacker Culture

(Dec 2006)

In recent years, designers, activists and business people have started to navigate their social worlds on the basis of concepts derived from the world of computers and new media technologies. According to Otto von Busch and Karl Palmås, this represents a fundamental cultural shift. In the 19th century, the motor replaced the clockwork as the universal model of knowledge; new media technologies are currently replacing the motor as the dominant 'conceptual technology' of contemporary social thought.

ISBN – 0955479622 / £5

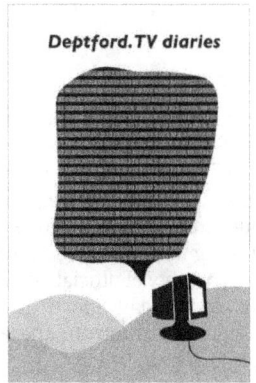

Deptford TV

Deptford.tv Diaries

(Dec 2006)

Deptford.TV is an audio-visual documentation of the regeneration process of Deptford (south-east London) in collaboration with SPC.org media lab, Bitnik.org, Boundless.coop, Liquid Culture and Goldsmiths College. Contributors: Adnan Hadzi, Maria X, Heidi Seetzen, James Stevens, Erol Ziya, Bitnik media collective, Andrea Pozzi, Andrea Rota and Jonas Andersson, alongside selected public license texts from Hakim Bey, Jaromil and Guy Debord.

ISBN – 0955479606 / £5

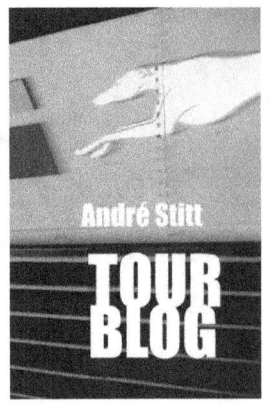

André Stitt

Tour Blog 2006: On Tour with Panacea Society USA

(Sep 2006)

No Sex, No Drugs, No Rock 'n' Roll. Just freak-beat, psyche-garage, prog-techno and artyness. Who do they think they are, these performance artists who want to be the new Golden Gods of Art-Rock? Find out as you join The Panacea Society on their 2006 North American tour. When asked by one of his students what he would be doing during the Easter break, performance artist André Stitt decided to write a tour diary.

ISBN – 0955392705 / £10

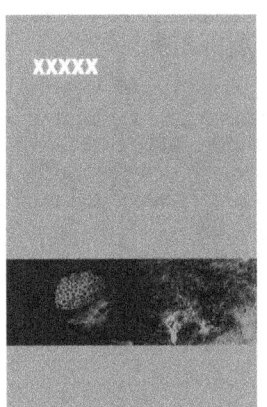

xxxxx

(Sep 2006)

[The] xxxxx [reader] proposes a radical, new space for artistic exploration, with essential contributions from a diverse range of artists, theorists, and scientists. Combining intense background material, code listings, screenshots, new translations, [the] xxxxx [reader] functions as both guide and manifesto for a thought movement which is radically opposed to entropic contemporary economies. xxxxx traces a clear line across eccentric and wide ranging texts under the rubric of life coding which can well be contrasted with the death drive of cynical economy with roots in rationalism and enlightenment thought.

ISBN – 0955066441 / £15

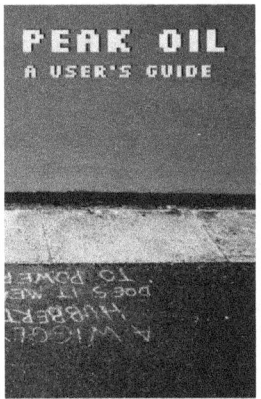

Popex

Peak Oil: A User's Guide

(July 2006)

This book is composed of two parts. The first part is the manual for the Peak Oil Olympics, a happening which took place on the 1st and 2nd July 2006 in Bristol, UK. This has been updated with documentation from the event, and expanded by the second part which is a look at Peak Oil from a more critical angle incorporating texts by George Caffentzis and Iain Boal which provide a more systematic analysis of what Peak Oil might mean.

ISBN – 0955066468 / £4

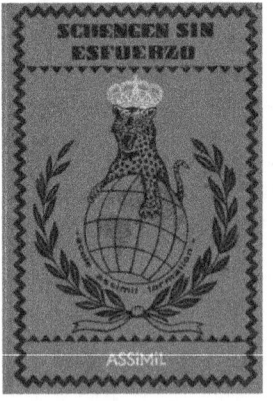

Vahida Ramujkic

Schengen with Ease

(Feb 2007)

'Extra-comunitarios', or citizens of non-European countries, have the 'extra' bureaucratic task of changing their status, to one that will allow them to move and work 'freely' within the European Union. The length and complexity of this process can vary depending on the type of 'extra-comunitario' in question. Almost everyone agrees that bureaucracy is the most boring thing in the world. *Schengen with Ease* is a compilation of material from a variety of official and non-official sources, brought together to explain how daily practices are affected by the application of the EU Foreign Legislation and the Schengen Agreement in the territory of the European Union.

ISBN – 0955066484 / £8.29

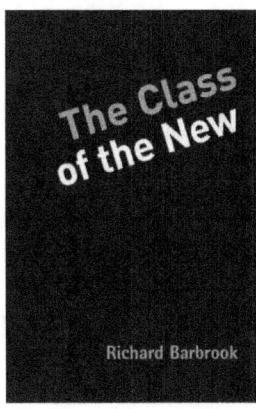

Richard Barbrook
Class of the New
(May 2006)

Netizens, elancers, cognitarians, swarm-capitalists, hackers, produsumers, knowledge workers, pro-ams... these are just a few of the monikers that have been applied to the new social class emerging from the networked workplace. In this short book, Richard Barbrook presents a collection of quotations from authors who in different ways attempt to identify an innovative element within society - 'the class of the new'. Announcing a new economic and social paradigm, this class constitutes a 'social prophecy' of the shape of work to come.

ISBN –0955066476 / £4

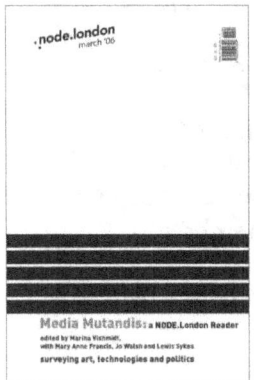

NODE.London
A NODE.London Reader - A Survey of Media Arts, Technologies and Politics
(Feb 2006)

The NODE.London reader, *Media Mutandis*, projects a critical context around the Season of Media Arts in London March 2006 and provides another discursive dimension to the events of October 2005's Open Season. It engages debates in FLOSS (Free/Libre and Open Source Software), media arts and activism, collaborative practices and the political economy of cultural production in the present day. Contributions from Sabeth Buchmann, Toni Prug, Armin Medosch, Simon Yuill, Chad McCail, Critical Art Ensemble, Jo Walsh, Richard Barbrook, Michael Corris, Harwood, Kate Rich, Agnese Trocchi, Matthew Fuller, Rasmus Fleischer and Palle Torsson, Brett Neilson and Ned Rossiter, Matteo Pasquinelli and Francis McKee.

ISBN – 0955243505 / £5

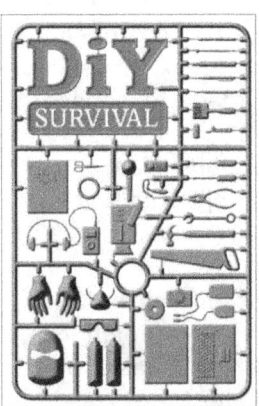

C6
DiY Survival
(Oct 2005)

DiY Survival - There is no subculture, only subversion. DiY or do-it-yourself survival is a collection of essays, tips and case studies collated from an online call for participation by the maverick art group C6. The eclectic mix presented within these pages shows the breadth and diversity of art/activism practice today. Whether that is creating wireless networks, pissing on national monuments or building cardboard friends, it is certain that these submissions show that practitioners are taking their work to new spaces and audiences, redefining, through the engagement with the community, what we have considered to be 'art'.

ISBN –0955066492 / £4.99

WWW.METAMUTE.ORG/SHOP

Please get in touch with us on **mute@metamute.org** with any queries about producing your book through OpenMute.

Further information and pricing is also available at **www.openmute.org**

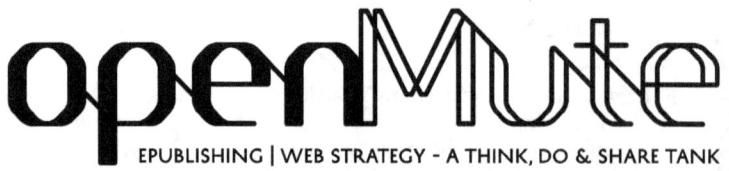

EPUBLISHING | WEB STRATEGY - A THINK, DO & SHARE TANK

METAMUTE.ORG/SERVICES

EPUBLISHING

POD BOOK PRINTING

We provide a service to consult, set-up and then manage a book title or library into digital print-on-demand book printing, from mass produced paperbacks to bespoke handmade artists books

EBOOKS/ KINDLE AND IPHONE BOOKS

OpenMute can create a variety of eReader book formats and place them into the relevant distribution and sales platforms, providing you with reports, user stats and sales payments

BOOK DESIGN, PRODUCTION AND EDITORIAL

The OpenMute team have years of experience in book design and layout, as well as production management and editorial work, proofing, style guides, indexing etc.

EBOOK CONVERSION, PUBLISHING AND DISTRIBUTION

Starting from £80

GUIDE PRICES
- £1 per 1,000 characters (including spaces), 0-80,000 characters charged at £80
- £1 per image
- £0.50 per footnote, £0.10 per automatic footnote

Finished eBook delivered as ePub and Kindle, proofing and distribution included (distribution opt out available). Client can edit book after signed off completed proof. Clean Word (docx) and HTML 5 files also provided with service.

Distribution options available, Kindle only, all major retailer and self distribution.

File types accepted - Indesign and word processing files preferred. PDF and all other file types carry a per 1,000 character fee of £0.5 in addition to normal fee.

CONTACT:OPENMUTE
EMAIL: SIMON@METAMUTE.ORG
SKYPE: MUTE.LONDON
TEL: +44 (0)20 3287 9005
WWW.METAMUTE.ORG/SERVICES

MUTE BOOKS

NEW TITLE

HUMAN STRIKE HAS ALREADY BEGUN & OTHER WRITINGS

CLAIRE FONTAINE

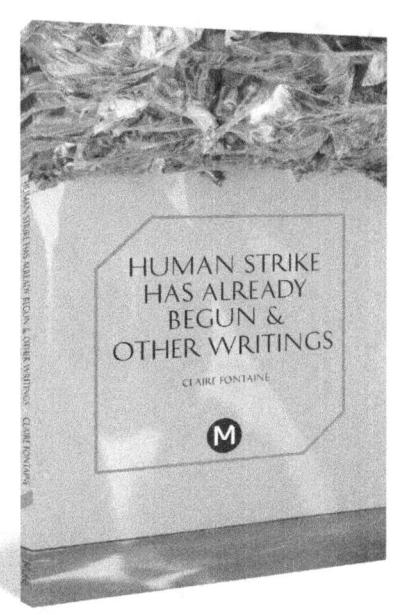

The term 'human strike' was forged to name a revolt against what is reactionary even – and above all – inside the revolt. It defines a type of strike that involves the whole of life and not only its professional side, that acknowledges exploitation in all domains and not only at work. The human strike is a movement that could potentially contaminate anyone and that attacks the foundations of life in common; its subject isn't the proletarian or the factory worker but the 'whatever singularity' that everyone is. This movement isn't there to reveal the exceptionality or the superiority of one group or another, but to unmask the *whateverness* of everybody as the open secret that social classes hide.

Part of the PML Books series, a collaboration between Mute & the Post-Media Lab

Publication: Spring 2013

Print ISBN: 978-1-906496-88-3
Price €5 £5 $5

eBook ISBN: 978-1-906496-89-0
Price €2.89 £2.89 $2.89

Free online

Sales & distribution enquiries, contact Howard Slater on <howard@metamute.org>

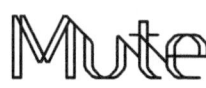 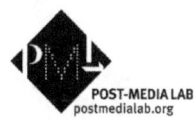

postmedialab.org/human-strike

www.ingramcontent.com/pod-product-compliance
Lightning Source LLC
Chambersburg PA
CBHW081559220526
45468CB00010B/2696